SACRAMENTO PUBLIC LIBRARY

3 3029 05568 5549

D0516543

S   ARY

4/2005

TRUE WITNESS

TRUE WITNESS

Cops, Courts, Science, and the Battle Against Misidentification

JAMES M. DOYLE

palgrave
macmillan

TRUE WITNESS

Copyright © James M. Doyle, 2005.

All rights reserved. No part of this book may be used or reproduced in any manner whatsoever without written permission except in the case of brief quotations embodied in critical articles or reviews.

First published 2005 by
PALGRAVE MACMILLAN™
175 Fifth Avenue, New York, N.Y. 10010 and
Houndmills, Basingstoke, Hampshire, England RG21 6XS.
Companies and representatives throughout the world.

PALGRAVE MACMILLAN is the global academic imprint of the Palgrave Macmillan division of St. Martin's Press, LLC and of Palgrave Macmillan Ltd. Macmillan® is a registered trademark in the United States, United Kingdom and other countries. Palgrave is a registered trademark in the European Union and other countries.

ISBN 1–4039–6430–0

Library of Congress Cataloging-in-Publication Data
Doyle, James M., 1950-
True witness : cops, courts, science, and the battle against misidentification / James M. Doyle.
    p.   cm.
  Includes index.
  ISBN 1–4039–6430–0
  1. Judicial error—United States.   2. Eyewitness identification—United States.   3. DNA fingerprinting—United States.   4. Criminal justice, Administration of—United States.   I. Title.

KF9756.D69   2004
345.73'066—dc22

                                                              2004049756

A catalogue record for this book is available from the British Library.

Design by Letra Libre, Inc.

First edition: January 2005
10 9 8 7 6 5 4 3 2 1

Printed in the United States of America.

For Margaret, Nick and Libby

Give us if thou canst
Eyewitness of what first and last was done,
Relation more particular and distinct.

—*Milton*

CONTENTS

ACKNOWLEDGMENTS

ANY LAWYER WRITING ABOUT THE LEGAL SYSTEM'S misuse of psychological research should expect to appear as a specimen as well as a commentator. In my case this will not be because psychologists have not tried to steer me onto the correct path. I should express my thanks—and also convey absolution—to many who responded to my direct inquiries, and to many more whose research I have read. Researchers who were especially helpful include Elizabeth Loftus, Gary Wells, Steven Penrod, Saul Kassin, Ron Fisher, Rod Lindsay, Sol Fulero, Katherine Ellison, Amy Bradfield, John Turtle, and Roy Malpass. The mistakes, of course, are my own.

Hundreds of police officers over the years have tried to clear away my misconceptions about their lives and practices. I'm especially grateful to Don Mauro, Paul Carroll, Ken Patenaude, Ed Rusticus, Karl Bickel, and Pat Marshall for lending a helping hand to a representative of "the dark side" on this occasion. I would also thank many current and former prosecutors who tried to help even though they held out very little hope that I would ever get things right, including especially Attorney General Janet Reno, United States District Judge James Zagel, Linda Fairstein, Melissa Mourges, Mark Larson, and J. W. Carney. Countless defense lawyers also tried to alert me to problems. Barry Scheck and George Kendall were very helpful on the national picture. Cathy DiTraglia and Jerri Merritt, my undaunted defense colleagues on the Technical Working Group on Eyewitness Evidence, also lent a hand. Richard Rosen, who defended Ronald Cotton, oriented me to the North Carolina Actual Innocence Project, and Chris Mumma helped me with the history of that effort. Ben Loeterman gave me a tour of media practice, specific and general, and granted permission to quote unpublished material. Chet Mirsky gave me a picture of Bob Buckhout in action. Jeremy Travis, Richard Rau, and Lisa Kaas helped me to understand the important work (and the precarious position) of the National Institute of Justice.

The indefatigable research librarians of the Boston Athenæum accepted every challenge with glinting eyes and were never defeated. Susan Futterman generously ran down materials on "Harry" Wigmore in the Wigmore Archives at Northwestern University, and Nan Balliott of the Roger Williams University School of Law Library guided me to several important sources. Tom Geraghty of Northwestern Law School steered me toward his very helpful research on Wigmore in a reformist mode. The WGBH Educational Foundation kindly granted permission to quote from the *Frontline* documentary, "What Jennifer Saw."

A number of stoic readers, including Stephen Ruwe, my agent at Literary and Creative Artists of D.C., Steve Jelin, and Hildegard VanDeusen cast subtle eyes over an early version of the manuscript and made many helpful suggestions. David Pervin, my editor, made stringent comments tempered by compassion that greatly improved the final product. My learned colleague, Janice Bassil, provided sage advice even *without* reading the manuscript.

Finally, Jennifer Thompson and Ronald Cotton have helped me—and many, many others—to appreciate the terrible cost that the fragility of memory can impose on its victims, and the difference individuals can make by following their convictions into the public arena.

PREFACE

"IT IS MORE IMPORTANT THAT INNOCENCE BE PROTECTED than it is that Guilt be punished," John Adams said, arguing in defense of the British officers charged with the murder of colonial demonstrators in the Boston Massacre trial.[1] Adams did not invent this principle on the spur of the moment; he drew on a venerable line of legal authority—drew, in fact on Blackstone, whose *Commentaries on the Laws of England* provided so much of the American colonists' idea of the rule of law. According to Blackstone, it was better that ten guilty men escape than that one innocent man be convicted.

Times change, and there are officials now who seem a little skeptical about Adams's assertion, and downright hostile to Blackstone's ratio. The current attorney general, for example, shows signs of regarding Adams's sentiment as one which might easily be carried too far.

But what if someone develops a toolbox for use in criminal investigations which both protects the innocent *and* punishes the guilty—a method that claims to cut the number of errors in half? Who could argue with that? Every wrongful conviction, after all, is also in practical terms a wrongful acquittal. If the wrong man is jailed, then the *right* man is left free to continue to commit crimes.

Modern research psychologists claim that they have developed just such an improvement in the way we investigate crimes—that they have derived from the scientific study of human memory a protocol for handling eyewitness identification cases twice as reliable as the traditional methods currently in use. In offering their findings to the legal system these psychologists revived an argument which is now almost 100 years old, an argument about the meaning of memory in the investigation and punishment of crime. The goal of this book is to allow readers to join that argument in progress—in fact, to join the argument as it reaches a crisis. The argument's outcome hangs in the balance in many places in the United States where initiatives such as "Innocence Protection Acts" are being fiercely debated in the legislatures.

For the last 25 years of this argument—that is, for most of my career as a criminal defense lawyer—I have been an interested bystander, occasionally even a tangential participant in this debate. I am the co-author of a legal treatise that advises lawyers about what to do in defending and prosecuting identification cases; I sometimes lecture defense lawyers on handling eyewitness cases, and I occupied the defense seat on the Planning Panel of the Technical Working Group of the National Institute of Justice, which is discussed in chapter eleven. I disclose this now because it may seem to some readers to indicate a bias—to suggest that I am predisposed to come down too heavily on the Adams (rather than, say, the Attorney General Ashcroft) side of the balance. That may be. I am content to have readers evaluate my prejudices for themselves as the story unfolds, and I have tried to be explicit about them when they might be at work. But the professional biases of a criminal defense lawyer really have very little to do with the story that follows.

The psychological researchers claim they have developed an improved method for preventing eyewitness mistakes *before they happen.* The prime beneficiaries of their efforts are innocent citizens who will never be wrongly identified—citizens, in other words, who will never need to hire a lawyer in the first place. If the researchers are right, and if they succeed in convincing the legal system to do something about it, I will never meet the people the research has protected—at least I will never represent them in my professional role. Almost 30 years of courtroom experience convinces me that for lawyers representing clients who are identified through the use of the new procedures the researchers recommend, those new procedures will actually present a daunting extra challenge.

Even so, working as a defense lawyer does provide a unique vantage point on the collision between research innovation and the criminal justice system's officials. More often than not, events have cast some defense lawyer or other in the role of instigator and translator in the discussions between researchers, cops, judges, and prosecutors.

That should not be confused (in my case, anyway) with a deep expertise in the social sciences or in the law enforcement official's daily life. For a comprehensive view of the science, readers should turn to the scientists; for investigative techniques, to the investigators. In a brief bibliographical note I have tried to provide readers with access to a number of scientific and other publications. Several of the protagonists provide regularly updated web sites, which are thick with links to further materials that will make it possible to follow the battle to its conclusion.

As this preface is written, the most popular show on contemporary television is *CSI: Crime Scene Investigation,* a drama that rightly trumpets the advances in forensic technology that will permit us to solve previously inexplicable crimes by discovering and assessing clues left at the scene of the crime. Our story is important because in eyewitness cases the memory of the witness *is* the crime scene—the witness's memory holds the key information, but that information is difficult to recover and easy to contaminate. What the psychological researchers offer is a plan for handling that evidence.

It can be argued that the significance of the argument over whether the threshold will be crossed, and the researchers' plan actually put into operation lies exactly in its small scale.

Here is just one decent, discrete, small, but definite set of improvements in protecting the innocent and identifying the guilty. Look how long its road has been; look how hard it has been to make the journey.

CHAPTER ONE

AS SURE AS I CAN BE

EARLY IN JUNE 2000, GARY GRAHAM SWELTERED on death row, awaiting execution for a murder that had been committed when Graham was 17. Graham had been on death row for more than half his life, but now the date for his execution was only days away. Graham claimed that he was innocent. The only man who could save Graham, Texas Governor George W. Bush, was campaigning for president, and that made Graham's fate a national issue. Partisans from both sides of the capital punishment debate came running. Television satellite trucks clogged the roadways around the prison in Huntsville, bringing with them their traditional accompaniments: candlelight vigils and hymns of death penalty opponents dueling with the Confederate flags and sardonic T-shirts of execution fans.[1] With life and death in the balance and a closely contested presidential campaign fascinating the country, the Graham case created the kind of classic electronic feeding frenzy which might attract, say, Jesse Jackson and Bianca Jagger. It did: Both stepped before the microphones before the drama was complete.

Among those swept up by the media whirlwind were two women who hadn't asked for attention. Each, through no choice of her own, had been an eyewitness to a crime.

The first of these eyewitnesses was a dignified, mature African American woman named Bernadine Skillern. Skillern was anxious for the return of her privacy, but she calmly faced the media and told her story, just as she had at Graham's trial. She was waiting in the parking lot for her daughter to return from the market, she explained, and she watched the murder of Bobby Lambert through her car window at a distance of only 30 feet. She had identified Gary Graham, a precocious hoodlum with a pile of robberies to his credit, as the shooter. She understood that a life was at stake, and she took no pleasure in her role, but she had seen it with her own eyes. She was certain that she had chosen the right man.

The second eyewitness was Jennifer Thompson, a North Carolina home-maker and mother of triplets. She was worried that she had interrupted the triplets' home-schooling program to come to Texas. Inexperienced, unpre-pared, with her knees shaking, she was shoved in front of a bank of cameras from around the world, and she told her story, too. She was there to bring to the Graham controversy the lessons of her own experience, an experience in which Gary Graham had played no role. Thompson was in Texas to tell the story of a brutal rape she had suffered nearly 15 years earlier, and hundreds of miles from Texas.

In July 1984, Jennifer Thompson, then a 22-year-old student with a 4.0 average at Elom College in North Carolina, was raped in her apartment by a light-skinned African American man. Two hours later and half a mile away, the same man raped a second woman. Even the North Carolina Appeals[2] Court's austere summary of these attacks conveys a sense of their brutality:

> ... the first victim was awakened by an intruder in her bedroom. The in-truder jumped on her, put his hand over her mouth and held a knife to her throat. The intruder pulled the first victim's underwear off, held her legs down and performed . . . sex on her. . . . The intruder stayed in the first victim's apartment for about 30 minutes. She was able to escape by running out the back door and running to a nearby apartment. . . .
>
> The second victim . . . looked up and saw a man in her house. When she sat up, the man fondled her breasts. The man went out the back door and around the house. The second victim went over to close a window, but the man reached through the window and pulled down the top of the garment she was wearing. She tried to use the phone, but it went dead. The man crashed through the front door and grabbed the second victim. The man pushed her down the hall to a bedroom, pulled off her clothes, threw her on the bed and sucked on her breasts. He crawled on top of her, putting his penis in her vagina. The man then left through the front door, after having been in the second victim's house for 20 to 30 minutes.

Jennifer Thompson, the first victim in the court's narrative, is blonde and tiny, five feet tall and 100 pounds. She speaks quietly, and she ends her sen-tences on the rising, interrogative lilt characteristic of girls raised in the South. Watching her describe her ordeal for the PBS series *Frontline*,[3] it is easy to see the traces of her upbringing as the adored daughter of suburban Carolina business executives.

But it is easy to see something else in Jennifer's interview, too: the iron resolve with which she survived the attack and pursued her attacker and the unflinching honesty with which she is determined to tell the story of the assault and its aftermath. No one will confuse Jennifer with the wilting southern belle of legend. During the rape, her mind was racing:

> At that point, I realized that I was going to be raped and I didn't know if this was going to be the end, if he was going to kill me, if he was going to hurt me and I decided that what I needed to do was outsmart him. Throughout the evening, I would turn on lights, even if it was just for a second, and he would tell me, "Turn that light off." And at one point, he bent down and turned on my stereo and a blue light came off of the stereo and it shone right up to his face and . . . and I was able to look at that. When I went into the bathroom, I shut the light on and he immediately told me to shut it off, but it was just long enough for me to think, "Okay, his nose looks this way" or "His shirt is navy blue, not black," little, brief pieces of light that I could piece together as much as I could piece together.

Jennifer escaped to a neighbor's house, and was taken to a local hospital emergency room where a rape kit was prepared. There, she was interviewed for the first time by Burlington police captain Mike Gaudlin. Jennifer's empathy for the second victim augmented her determination.

> Mike Gauldin came in and I heard a woman crying a few stalls down from me and I remember looking at him and saying, "Did she get raped also?" and he said, "Yes, and we think it was the same person." And that was a horrible feeling, that he had hurt two women on one night. And I can remember feeling so sorry for her because I knew how much pain I was feeling and I could only assume that she was feeling the same amount.

The qualities that strike a viewer watching Jennifer's interview struck Detective Mike Gauldin during their initial encounter: "She was so determined during the course of the sexual assault to look at her assailant well, to study him well enough so that, if given an opportunity later, she would be able to identify her assailant . . . I had great confidence in her ability to identify her assailant," Gauldin remembered. "A lot of victims are so traumatized, so overcome with fear during the course of the sexual assault itself, that it's unusual to find somebody that's capable of having that presence of mind."

Gauldin asked Jennifer to help a police artist prepare a composite drawing of the rapist. That drawing was widely circulated, and it generated an anonymous tip. An informant provided Gauldin with the name of a man with a criminal record, a man who worked at Somer's Seafood restaurant in the neighborhood of Jennifer's apartment—a black man with a habit of touching white waitresses and teasing them about sex. The caller said the man owned a blue shirt similar to the shirt Jennifer had seen on the night of the rape. Gauldin placed that man's photograph in an array of six individual mugshots of black men and asked Jennifer whether she recognized anyone. The composition of the array was fair—no one stood out unduly. Gauldin played it straight: He made no effort to prompt Jennifer, or tip her off to his suspect.

Jennifer remembers her photo identification this way:

> It didn't take me very long. It took me minutes to come to my conclusion. And then I chose the photo of Ronald Cotton. After I picked it out, they looked at me and they said, "We thought this might be the one," because he had a prior conviction of the same . . . same type of circumstances sort of.

Armed with Jennifer's identification, Mike Gauldin obtained a search warrant and set out to arrest Ronald Cotton. Cotton wasn't at home, but Gauldin did find two pieces of evidence in Cotton's room: a red flashlight like one described by the second rape victim, and a shoe with a foam insert consistent with foam found on the floor at Jennifer's apartment. When Cotton heard about Gauldin's search, he turned himself in at the police station, "to clear things up." Cotton gave Gauldin an alibi, but his alibi did not check out. Gauldin arranged to have Cotton stand in a "live" lineup.

Jennifer methodically examined the line of six black men arrayed across the front of a room in the police headquarters. "They had to do the steps to the right, to the left, and then turn around," she recalled. "And then they were instructed to do a voice presentation to me. They had to say some of the lines that the rapist had said to me that night so I could hear the voice, because the voice was a very distinct voice."

Jennifer narrowed her choices to the man wearing number "4" and Ronald Cotton, who was wearing number "5". She had the police put the lineup members through their routine again. Then she was sure: "It's number 5," she said. Later, Gauldin explained what had happened: "That's the same guy. I mean, that's the one you picked out in the photo."

"For me," Jennifer remembered, "that was a huge amount of relief, not that I had picked the photo, but that I was sure when I looked at the photo that

[it] was him and when I looked at the physical line-up I was sure it was him." She was still sure when she testified in court and identified Ronald Cotton.

She was just as sure when she faced Cotton again, in a second trial ordered by the North Carolina Supreme Court. There was a new challenge this time. Cotton's lawyers had pursued inmate rumors that the Burlington rapes actually had been committed by a convict named Bobby Poole. At Cotton's second trial Poole was brought into court and shown to Jennifer. Jennifer didn't flinch then either. "I thought," she told *Frontline*, "'Oh, this is just a game. This is a game they're playing.'" It wasn't Poole, Jennifer told the jurors, "I have never seen him in my life." She told them it was Cotton. At the second trial, the other Burlington victim testified for the first time, and she also positively identified Cotton. Cotton was convicted again, and Jennifer was elated. "It was one of the happiest days of my life," she recalled. Now she knew for certain that Cotton was never going to get out. She had forced herself to go through two trials; she had picked the right man; she had her justice. "I was as sure as I can be," she remembers.

But Jennifer Thompson was wrong.

The second Burlington victim was wrong. Mike Gauldin and the Burlington police, despite their conscientious, by-the-book investigation, were wrong. The 24 jurors who in 2 separate trials had convicted Ronald Cotton were wrong.

Fourteen years after that first night of terror—fourteen years that Ronald Cotton spent in the state penitentiary—DNA evidence proved that Ronald Cotton was innocent.

The DNA also proved that Bobby Poole was guilty: guilty of raping Jennifer, guilty of raping the second victim. Jennifer had been mistaken about that, too. And, to ratchet the horror up further, Bobby Poole was guilty of other rapes—rapes committed while Ronald Cotton was incarcerated for the crimes Poole had committed, rapes committed during the liberty that Poole enjoyed thanks to law enforcement's reliance on Jennifer's mistake.

There was nothing freakish about the Cotton/Thompson case. That is the frightening thing about it. Later in this book we will see other cases like it. We will see, to take just one example, that the DNA technology that proved that two eyewitnesses wrongly sent Ronald Cotton to prison for life plus 54 years also proved that *five* eyewitnesses wrongly sent Maryland ex-marine Kirk Bloodsworth to death row.

In fact, of the 62 wrongful convictions revealed in the first wave of DNA exonerations, 52 (83 percent) relied to some extent on eyewitness identification evidence—a total of 77 sincere, mistaken witnesses.[4] In eight of these cases an innocent man was sentenced to death. In every case the real criminal was allowed to go free. In most of the cases, the real criminal is still free.

What the Ronald Cotton case, the Kirk Bloodsworth case, and all of the other mistaken eyewitness exoneration cases have in common is that—except for the actual criminal, of course—they are stories without villains. The mistaken victims are not driven by greed, racism, or malice; they are simply mistaken. The police were not trying to "frame" anyone; they were trusting the evidence they had: evidence from a sincere, unbiased witness. A mounting body of evidence shows that the roots of the mistakes lie in the *normal* operation of human memory.

The implications are unnerving. Each year an estimated 75,000 American prosecutions turn on eyewitness identification evidence.[5] Eyewitness evidence is frequently right, and it is often the only evidence available, but DNA proves every day that eyewitness evidence can be tragically wrong. And in most cases—armed robberies, drive-by shootings, armed assaults—there will be no biological material such as the criminal's blood or semen left on the scene. There will be no DNA safety net to catch the mistakes.

The DNA exoneration cases were the signal for a new battle in an old war. For almost 100 years, research psychologists have been studying the process of eyewitness identification, and struggling to force the legal system to pay attention to their results. The researchers believe that they know how many eyewitness mistakes can occur, and they have tried to tell the courts how to catch the mistakes. At both the Ronald Cotton and Kirk Bloodsworth trials, for example, the defense offered—and the judges rejected—expert psychological testimony intended to warn jurors about frailties in the eyewitness identification process. The researchers also believe that they know methods by which many, even most, eyewitness errors can be prevented *before* they happen—that information, too, has been reflexively dismissed by the legal system.

Perhaps that was to be expected. "The life of the law," Justice Holmes famously noted, "has not been logic: it has been experience."[6] The testimony of eyewitnesses is our oldest form of proof. It predates not only DNA, but also fingerprints, blood-typing, ballistics, and forensic scientific evidence of every kind. Courts and the legal system won't tamper with identification procedures until they have concrete, experience-based proof that they were unreliable, and some confidence that replacement procedures will be better.

Still, if it is experience that the law requires, then DNA evidence has now provided it. That, anyway, is the researchers' argument. If nothing else, the DNA cases have certainly provided a fresh occasion for calculating the cost of doing nothing.

Wrongful convictions receive front-page treatment because we respond to their primal drama, to the realization "That could have been me!" Anyone, or anyone's son or daughter, might be wrongfully accused by a sincere eyewitness and imprisoned like Ronald Cotton or Kirk Bloodsworth were. Anyone might, like Jennifer Thompson, be forced to live with mistakenly depriving a man of 14 years of his life. Anyone, like the jurors in Kirk Bloodsworth's case, might send a man to death row, only to learn later (perhaps even after an execution) that their verdict was mistaken. Anyone might be victimized by a Bobby Poole, who was allowed to roam the streets because an honest but mistaken eyewitness led investigators down the wrong trail. Any honest, sincere, and *correct* eyewitness, victimized by a Bobby Poole, may be *dis*believed by some future jury if the drumbeat of DNA exonerations in faulty eyewitness cases continues unabated, and cynical jurors decide to throw the good identifications out with the bad.

In the late 1990s, after absorbing nearly a century of hostility, derision, and patronizing neglect from the legal system, research psychologists seized on the DNA exoneration cases and launched one more effort to make the case that the science of memory must count in police stations and courtrooms. The researchers believed that by applying lessons from the science of everyday human memory we will forestall both the specific horrors that fell upon Ronald Cotton and Jennifer Thompson and the general public's vulnerability that arises every time a Bobby Poole escapes justice and returns to the community's streets. They denied that the pain of Ronald Cotton, Jennifer Thompson, and Bobby Poole's other victims was just inevitable collateral damage in the War on Crime.

The researchers argued that the mystery "How could Jennifer be so wrong?" was no mystery at all; they had the answer. And they argued that by employing their answer we could do something to prevent it happening again.

The researchers had Ronald Cotton and Jennifer Thompson to argue for their side in this renewed effort.

The researchers would need all of the help they could get. They were venturing into the life-and-death context of the criminal process, where the State mobilizes its monopoly on violence to discipline and punish.

And the researchers were asking for nothing less than a revolution in how the State confronts its own fallibility.

CHAPTER TWO

THE LAWYER ALONE IS OBDURATE

Professor Munsterberg Battles Dean Wigmore

JENNIFER THOMPSON WAS WRONG ABOUT Ronald Cotton, and wrong about Bobby Poole, too. That an honest eyewitness can be so certain and still so wrong shocks most people. But it does not surprise modern psychologists; even 100 years ago it would not have surprised Professor Hugo Munsterberg, the German-born chair of Harvard's psychology laboratory.

Munsterberg always argued that a witness' honesty is no guarantee of reliability, and that a witness's certainty is no proof of accuracy. What's more, Munsterberg claimed that he had the experimental results to prove his point. His 1908 book, *On The Witness Stand*, was the opening shot in scientific psychology's war against the legal system's complacent acceptance of eyewitness testimony, and Munsterberg was the psychologists' first general. The history of Munsterberg's *On The Witness Stand* and its reception provides a template for psychological science's later encounters with the law.

In the eyes of later generations of researchers, Munsterberg's performance in the role of war leader wins a place beside Ambrose Burnside's at Fredericksburg and George Armstrong Custer's on the Little Big Horn. In this view, Munsterberg launched ill-prepared troops in a premature frontal assault across badly chosen ground and into the teeth of a strongly defended position. He threw the flower of his infant discipline against the massed batteries of Dean John Henry Wigmore, titan of Anglo-American legal scholarship, and the psychologists were slaughtered. Historians of psychology describe the resulting carnage as a "miserable failure" that laid Munsterberg's troops open to Wigmore's "scathing" counterattack, and left psychology "so vilified by legal scholars that it almost irreparably damaged early attempts to apply the behavioral sciences to the law." Munsterberg is remembered as having brought on a legendary interdisciplinary Armageddon.[1]

Whatever Munsterberg's other failings as a general, he certainly led from the front lines, not from the command bunker. Among the first casualties of his doomed assault on legal tradition was Munsterberg's reputation within his own discipline. Although Munsterberg had been the second president of the American Psychological Association in 1898, by the time of his death in 1916 he was in such thorough eclipse that no memorial notice appeared in any of the Association's publications. In a recent survey of researchers in the field of memory studies, not one would admit to using Munsterberg as a starting point, or even hazard a guess about why Munsterberg's ideas—which, after all are the same as their *own* ideas—seemed to vanish for 50 years after his death.[2]

———•◆•———

From the publication of Charles Darwin's *Origin of the Species* in 1859, the nineteenth century was marked by stylized public combats over fundamental issues. These battles captured the public imagination because of their central substance—science versus faith, tradition versus modernity—but also because of the charismatic quality of the champions who emerged to represent the opposing points of view. Huxley fought Gladstone over evolution; Whistler fought Ruskin over modern art. Perhaps the first thing to be said about the Munsterberg/Wigmore confrontation is that the two antagonists certainly deserved their places on this list. They were giants in their times, and giants characteristic of their times. It is impossible to describe either man without providing a dizzying list of accomplishments, but, in the end, those accomplishments are less interesting than the personalities they reflect—and the prodigious Victorian energy and sense of purpose that those personalities embodied.

Munsterberg was a genuinely eminent man, but not a comfortable one. There is a painting at Harvard in which William James and his colleagues are depicted gathered in Olympian congress around a small table. Munsterberg is missing. Two stories circulated about his absence. In one version, the anglophile mandarins of Harvard ordered Munsterberg painted out of the group portrait because they were offended by Munsterberg's bumptious personality and his vehement advocacy of German *kultur* on the eve of World War I. In the alternate version, Munsterberg ordered *himself* painted out because he felt his position in the painting was not sufficiently prominent.[3] Neither of these stories is very persuasive, but the fact that they were in circulation tells us something about Munsterberg anyway. On the one hand, everyone felt that Munsterberg's absence required an explanation. Why *wasn't* Munsterberg there? On the other hand, people were prepared to believe the wildly differing versions of Munsterberg's banishment. Munsterberg was the sort of man around whom such stories accumulated—and about whom people enjoyed telling stories. There is no denying that Munsterberg, judging by his photographs—glaring through wire-framed spectacles above a bristling mustache and a high, stiff collar, as though auditioning for the comic role of Herr Docktor Professor in an operetta—would have introduced a discordant note of Teutonic assertiveness into the circle of Brahmin rectitude surrounding James in the Harvard portrait.[4] As one Harvard student remembered him:

> He was a great husky German with a confident yet friendly smile that was modified somewhat by a vigorous moustache curled slightly higher on one side so that it somehow suggested hardness. When he was piqued he had a look of ferocity that students said he acquired by trying to look like the Kaiser.[5]

Munsterberg was born in 1863 (three months after Wigmore) in Danzig, the son of a lumber merchant who bought lumber in Russia for sale in Britain. If Munsterberg was not actually present at the creation of psychology as a discipline, he was there on the day after, attending Wilhelm Wundt's pioneering lectures at Leipzig in 1884, and earning a Ph.D. in Psychology there in 1885. He was thoroughly trained in philosophy and medicine, the disciplines from which psychology first emerged. He earned a medical degree at Heidelberg in 1887 and was authorized to lecture at Freiburg as a "privat docent" by 1887. By 1891 he had been invited to attend the First International Conference of Psychology at Paris. At that conference he met William James, and the two men began to correspond.

James, the founder of American psychology, was gently coaxing the new discipline out from under the wing of Harvard's Philosophy Department. The author of *Varieties of Religious Experience* was deeply convinced of the value of experimental psychology but he had no taste for experimental work himself. James saw in Munsterberg an opportunity to put Harvard on the cutting edge of the new discipline while simultaneously relieving himself of the vexing administrative duties that running a psychological laboratory would entail. James began quietly campaigning to bring Munsterberg to Cambridge.[6] James was a philosopher, of course, but he was also perfectly capable of pursuing his own interests in a highly practical manner. Among his levers was Munsterberg's powerful ambition. Appointments to the highest levels of German university life were the Kaiser's gift, and Munsterberg undoubtedly recognized that despite his talents, he was still the son of a Jew who had converted to the Lutheran Church (with no great enthusiasm). His road to the German academic pinnacle would be a long and perhaps futile one.[7]

James got his man. Munsterberg arrived at Harvard for a three-year term in 1892. Within six months he was lecturing comfortably in English, and running the psychological laboratory. He returned briefly to Germany before urgent messages from James and Harvard's president, Charles Eliot Norton, drew him back to Harvard for a permanent appointment. By this time, Munsterberg's talents were no secret. Oxford offered to appoint Munsterberg to a readership. The university at Königsberg tempted Munsterberg (who always thought of himself as a philosopher as well as a psychologist) with the chair in philosophy once held by Immanuel Kant. James succeeded in persuading Munsterberg to commit himself permanently to Harvard by issuing a call to duty liberally perfumed with flattery:

> The situation is this: We are the best university in America, and we must lead in psychology. I, at the age of 50 disliking laboratory work naturally, and accustomed to teach philosophy at large, altho I *could, tant bien que mal,* make the laboratory run, yet am certainly not the kind of stuff to make a first-rate director thereof. We could get younger men here who would be *safe* enough, but we need something more than a safe man, we need a man of genius if possible.[8]

Accepting the challenge (and the compliment), Munsterberg fulfilled his mentor's wildest hopes. He threw himself into the development of Harvard's psychological laboratory, and he threw himself into applying the laboratory's findings in the world, too.

Psychology was a very young discipline, but not so young that a fissure was not already visible between those who aspired to pure research, and those who sought relevance in the surrounding world. The first group seemed to James timorous and self-important. Their reaction to the post-Darwin revolution—measure everything—struck James as harmless, quiet employment for patient minds,[9] but not a course he wanted Harvard to follow. What James liked in Munsterberg was his freedom from academic orthodoxy, a shared recognition that the advancement of psychology in those earliest stages would be accelerated by a certain swashbuckling disregard for meticulous academic niceties. James wrote to Munsterberg in reaction to professorial criticism of the younger man's work:

But I find in you just what is lacking in this critique of Muller's, a sense for the perspective and proportion of things. . . . Whose theories in psychology have any definitive value today? No one's! Their only use is to sharpen further reflection and observation. The man who throws out most new ideas and immediately seeks to subject them to experimental control is the most useful psychologist in the present state of the science. *No one* has done this as yet as well as you. If you are only flexible towards your theories, and as ingenious in testing them hereafter as you have been hitherto, I will back you to beat the whole army of your critics before you are forty years old. . . .[10]

Munsterberg was a fantastically ingenious generator of ideas that could be subjected to experimental testing, and he found fertile fields for application of his experimental findings. He earned the title "father of industrial psychology" with experimental investigations into monotony, attention and fatigue, and social and physical influences in the work place. He earned the more encompassing title "father of applied psychology" by projecting his creativity and the rigor of the experimental method into virtually every area of everyday life. Childrearing, education, theater, vocational testing—all of these were grist for Munsterberg's laboratory. He broke new ground in every area.

Munsterberg quickly discovered a facility for popularizing his findings and publicizing them in magazines, speeches, and interviews. William James was delighted. He wrote his brother, Henry, that he had succeeded in hiring "the Rudyard Kipling of Psychology" for Harvard.[11]

That may have been true (Kipling, another lion of those times, has undergone an equivalent eclipse), but it was also true that Munsterberg turned out to be remarkably accident-prone where public relations were concerned. Once, Munsterberg managed to get himself quoted as saying that his friend, Vice-President Theodore Roosevelt, believed that the Declaration of Independence was "nothing but glittering generalities." That set off a political firestorm. An experiment in Munsterberg's Radcliffe classroom involved his students in mock jury deliberations, which generated the headline: "WOMEN ARE STUBBORN, MEN ARE FIRM." That brought on another avalanche of ridicule. Much of this was tabloid business as usual, but Munsterberg had some special talent for making himself the target of derisive misinterpretations. It is hard to believe that any other Harvard scientist could have provoked the stolid editors of the *New York Times* into running a facetious interview which (wrongly) attributed to Munsterberg the claim that he had invented an infallible "lying-machine" and began: "As soon as I heard that Prof. Hugo Monsterwork [*sic*] of Harvard had invented a machine for detecting liars in the act, I said to myself melodramatically: 'Ho!'"[12]

Munsterberg's energy in pursuing what he referred to as "*productive* scholarship" also generated sniping from fellow academics, who disliked the implications that Munsterberg's term held for their own work. (They preferred the dichotomy "pure/impure" to Munsterberg's "unproductive/productive.") The professors accused Munsterberg of opportunism: a Cornell rival claimed that Munsterberg "debased" psychology at Harvard.[13] But while Munsterberg was perfectly willing to use his intellect as a social weapon, it seems unlikely that he chose his research targets exclusively for their proximity to the main chance. He did solid philosophical and theoretical work, too: his "action" theory is a recognizable precursor of behaviorism. He collected honorary degrees from all over.

Munsterberg was a genuine protagonist in the modern movement. For example, in 1916 he published *The Photoplay: A Psychological Study*,[14] the first theoretical discussion of the new art of cinema. *The Photoplay* presents an analysis that, since its rediscovery, has been regarded as a prescient refutation of the half-baked psychoanalytic approaches to film that dominated film criticism until very recently. Munsterberg's concentration on the direct relation between mental processes and cinematic functions—the flatness of the image, the separation from reality, flashbacks, close-ups—is now regarded as positively avant garde. Among Munsterberg's Radcliffe students was Gertrude Stein, whose concentration on the sensory impact of "the words themselves" at the expense of the meaning of the words seems likely to owe something to Munsterberg's psychological approach.[15] Robert Frost was also Munsterberg's student for a semester.[16] Another of his pupils became the creator of Wonder Woman—that should count for something.

After Munsterberg's death, a friend wrote that Munsterberg was utterly guileless, "In fact a singularly unsuspicious nature, and not infrequently was imposed on by astute men."[17] Perhaps that was the problem. Still, looking back over Munsterberg's American career reminds one of Vladimir Nabokov's transplanted Europeans—Humbert Humbert in *Lolita*, for example—men so bedazzled by the unaccustomed liberty of the New World that they do not realize that aspects of their own personalities, which had been constrained by Europe, will bring on disaster when they are allowed to flower in the heady climate of the Land of the Free. Munsterberg either had no interest in, or no talent for, anticipating the effect of his remarks on distant audiences. All of this lends Munsterberg's public life a picturesque element.

But Munsterberg was also the author of a philosophical work called *Eternal Values*,[18] and there was a tension between his commitment to the German Idealist philosophers he had studied in his youth and the demands of modernity. Munsterberg's work never entirely submerges his profoundly moral orientation. He was on a mission. Robert Kargon, writing to explain the enormous popular interest in Munsterberg's *On The Witness Stand*, notes that:

> From the 1880's, then, the opinion-formers in American society were swept up by enthusiasm for natural science as a way to rationalize and control the social and political world as well as the natural. One bastion of the social and political that remained was the realm of the psychological. It was the task of the twentieth century to "scientize" and "professionalize" the self and the mind.[19]

Munsterberg made that task his own, but the seismic upheaval in the settled order of things caused by the Darwinian revolution had made the struggle between science and tradition look to some like a struggle between order and disorder. In Munsterberg's case this was mistaken. Munsterberg passionately identified himself with science, but sought to employ it as a tool for establishing a new and more efficient order. When he wrote for popular journals he wrote on issues—education, justice, the life of the laborer—where science could be brought to bear on large moral questions confronting the general public, and the expert scientist could arrange things in a rational, efficient manner.

When William James proposed to Munsterberg that while James himself preferred "free wild Nature," Munsterberg preferred "an Italian Garden where all things are kept in separate compartments and one must follow straight-ruled walks," Munsterberg replied that he also saw experience as having "plenty of weeds," but that "life's duty"

> makes us gardener, makes us to unweed the weeds of sin and error and ugliness and when we finally come to think over what flowers were left as valuable, and we bring together those which are similar—then we have finally indeed such an Italian garden as the world which we are seeking.[20]

Munsterberg was alert enough to notice, as Alexis de Tocqueville had almost a century before, that in America moral issues, perhaps all issues, inexorably gravitate toward the courts. In Europe the implications of the Darwinian theory of evolution were fought out in periodicals, sermons and debates, but in America they were fought out in the Scopes trial. By 1906, Munsterberg was ready to enter that arena with the lessons of experimental psychology as his weapons. The courts were where the action was. But beyond that, the courts offered a kind of action in which Munsterberg's science and his ideals could be combined in the service of his thirst for recognition in the world. This was not simple careerism; it was a search for fulfillment. Munsterberg thought he saw injustices, and he sought to bring experimental psychology to bear. If the process made him famous too, there was nothing wrong with that.

———•◦•———

Munsterberg began his engagement with the legal system in characteristic fashion, by provoking a barrage of attacks on himself in the popular press. Invited to comment on the notorious 1906 Chicago murder case of a young man named Richard Ivens, Munsterberg announced that he believed that Ivens' confession was false and that Ivens was innocent. Munsterberg's reasons for supposing that a suspect's confession *could* be false have been to a large extent vindicated by modern research, but his bland assertion that Ivens himself was *actually* innocent is not one any psychologist would now venture—certainly not from Cambridge, 900 miles from the scene of the crime, the defendant, and the corroborating facts generated by the criminal investigation. Ivens was hanged despite Munsterberg's efforts, and Munsterberg was warned by the Chicago newspapers that the opinions of "Harvard irresponsibles" would not be welcome: "Illinois has quite enough of people with an itching mania for attending to other people's business without importing impertinence from Massachusetts."[21]

For his next adventure, Munsterberg decided to put himself at the scene of the action.

In the summer of 1907, trailing a trunk full of psychological measuring instruments, Munsterberg journeyed to Boise, Idaho, to examine Harry Orchard, the confessed murderer of 18 people (including the governor of Idaho) who had turned state's evidence and was prepared to testify that all of his crimes were ordered, directed, and paid for by the Western Federation of Miners. Munsterberg had no plan to influence directly the trial of "Big Bill" Haywood and the other union leaders; he simply planned to experiment on Orchard to test whether a variety of procedures developed in his laboratory could cast any light on whether Orchard's new testimony was truthful. Munsterberg initially assumed that Orchard was lying. His first contact with Orchard "filled him with disgust," and he was impressed by Bill Haywood. After 100 tests and several days of experiments, however, Munsterberg concluded that Orchard's conversion and repentance were genuine—that his incriminating testimony was truthful. Munsterberg kept the information to himself, enjoyed Boise's pretty river and its dramatic view of the surrounding dun-colored foothills, then embarked on the four-day train ride to Massachusetts, cradling a parting gift from the new governor. (A " beautifully embroidered case for an Indian papoose.")[22]

On the train, in another of the incidents that indicate that to call Munsterberg "guileless" may have been an understatement, he shared his results with a reporter. "Great was his surprise and disappointment," Munsterberg's daughter wrote later, "when he perceived the next day that his extorted remarks had been wired all over the country." A flood of ridicule and invective followed. False stories surfaced that Munsterberg's examination had consisted of measuring Orchard's head. "I'll bet a dollar to two bits," one reporter wrote, "that Prof. Munsterberg has a head like a prize pumpkin." The legend of Munsterberg's "lying-machine" was born. Haywood's defense lawyers accused Munsterberg of accepting graft.[23]

But all of this seemed only to augment Munsterberg's interest in legal issues, and the public's interest, too. "Psychology and the Law" became the most demanded of Munsterberg's lecture topics in 1907–1908. He spoke on the subject in Chicago, in Buffalo, and at Cornell that year, and he began to publish the series of popular articles that were collected in *On The Witness Stand*. "Untrue Confessions" appeared in *Times Magazine* in January 1907, and was followed there by "On the Witness Stand" in March. *McClure's* published "Nothing but the Truth," "The Third Degree," "Hypnotism and Crime," and "The Prevention of Crime" during the same year. It was the equivalent of being on the cover of *Time* or *Newsweek* every other month.

Psychology and Law as a subject was launched, and it launched Munsterberg as a public figure. Munsterberg became a Carl Sagan or Stephen Jay Gould of his era—a willing commentator on anything and everything, a talk-TV pundit before his time. If Munsterberg were alive today he would be on CNN every night—Larry King's best friend, Oprah's consultant on the psychology of everyday life, Court TV's go-to-guy on the next "trial of the century." Munsterberg's biographer's observation about the attractions Munsterberg offered the media would be as true today as then:

> Psychology promised power—over self and others—in years when men and women felt increasingly powerless to control their lives, and it offered an explanation for the irrational behavior that seemed more and more to dominate public life.[24]

—◆◆◆—

On The Witness Stand[25] belongs to the category of books more talked about than read, and when one finally comes to the book itself after wading through the commentary on the legendary law versus psychology feud it provoked, it provides a number of surprises.

The first of these surprises for any reader conditioned to expect Teutonic bombast from the famously "abrasive" and "pugnacious" Munsterberg is the book's generally genial tone. Munsterberg mounts an attack on eyewitness re-liability, but the only eyewitness he attacks in any detail is himself. He begins the pivotal essay, "The Memory of the Witness," with a disarming account of his own performance as a witness to a burglary at his own home.

Munsterberg had been called from his vacation by the police after the re-port of a burglary at his home. He later testified at the burglar's trial. Accord-ing to Munsterberg, he felt no particular animus towards the criminal. He had suffered no great loss, "[a]s they had started in the wine cellar and had forgot-ten under its genial influence, on the whole, what they had come for." Mun-sterberg had a prodigious memory: he had given over 3,000 university lectures without once resorting to notes. "I was thus under the most favourable condi-tions for speaking the whole truth and nothing but the truth," he observed, "and, as there is probably no need for the assurance of my best intentions, I felt myself somewhat alarmed at seeing how many illusions had come in."[26]

In his brief testimony, Munsterberg confidently misstated under oath nu-merous observations and deductions he made when he returned to his home in the aftermath of the burglary. He was wrong about the burglars' point of entry, the wrapping of a clock packaged for removal, the number of suits stolen, the location of candle droppings, and the number of burglars. "[I]n spite of good memory and calm mood, a whole series of confusions, of illu-sions, of forgetting, of wrong conclusions, and of yielding to suggestions were mingled with what I had to report under oath."[27] He had omitted some things, twisted others, and mistakenly assigned to his own perceptions facts supplied by bystanders. But *On The Witness Stand* was not intended to be a confessional document. The theme that Munsterberg pressed was that his mistakes—like the errors of Jennifer Thompson and other mistaken eyewitnesses—while not inevitable, were *normal*:

> In short, we never know from the material itself whether we remember, per-ceive, or imagine, and in the borderland regions there must result plenty of confusion which cannot always remain without dangerous consequences in the courtroom.[28]

Munsterberg wheeled a battery of experimental demonstrations into line to prove the general applicability of his personal experience.

Munsterberg told, for example, of an experiment he had staged in his own laboratory in which he showed his psychology students a white piece of card-board with 50 black squares pasted on it, and asked them how many squares were on the sheet.

The answers ranged from 25 to 200; the answer "over one hundred" was more frequent than the answer less than 50. Only three students gave the right answer. Munsterberg ran the experiment again, this time with 20 black squares. The results were similar: "We had here highly trained, careful observers, whose attention was concentrated on the material, and who had full time for quiet scrutiny. Yet in both cases there were some who believed that they saw seven or eight times as more points than some others saw."[29]

Munsterberg also marshaled experimental results which bore very directly on the courtroom problem: a series of "staged crime" experiments. One which he cited, performed at the University of Berlin, had involved an unexpected argument ending in gunfire at the front of the classroom. The staged incident was divided into 14 segments, and the students were asked to write an exact account of the event. The *smallest* number of mistakes was 26 percent. The rate of mistakes was noticeably higher in the witnesses' accounts of the second, more stressful—and arguably more attention-getting—portion of the staged event. The mistakes included not only misstating events that had occurred, but also *inventing* events that had not. "Words were put into the mouths of men who had been silent spectators during the whole short episode; actions were attributed to the chief participants of which not the slightest trace existed."[30]

Munsterberg also anticipated (and disposed of) the argument that the experimental records showed nothing more than the incompetence of student audiences. He did this by describing[31] the convocation of an exalted scientific association made up of jurists, psychologists, and physicians which was interrupted by the sudden eruption of a clown, chased by "a Negro":

> In the middle of the hall first the one, then the other, shouts wild phrases; then the one falls to the ground, the other jumps on him; then a shot, and suddenly both are out of the room.

The dignitaries were asked to compile reports suitable for submission to the courts. Of the 40 reports handed in, all but one were mistaken about *more* than 20 percent of the relevant facts. Besides omissions, 36 statements in 40 contained positively wrong statements. In one fourth of the papers, at least 10 percent of the statements were false, in spite of the fact "that they all came from scientifically trained observers." Munsterberg pointed out that "Only *four* persons . . . among forty noticed that the Negro had nothing on his head; the others gave him a derby, or a high hat, and so on." In short, "the majority of the observers omitted or falsified about half of the processes which occurred completely in their field of vision."

Munsterberg's claim that some eyewitnesses made mistakes was one most people could grasp—conceding that mistakes happen, even if they remained unconvinced about the rate of mistakes. But Munsterberg also insisted that the experiments showed more than just that eyewitness mistakes occurred in surprising numbers. Munsterberg argued that the *nature* of the mistakes indicated that the legal system had no capacity for catching eyewitness mistakes after they had occurred. Munsterberg's warning that the legal system's traditional protections against these mistakes were entirely futile was the key feature of *On The Witness Stand*. His claim that the legal system could not sort the true accounts from the mistaken ones was something new and disturbing.

Munsterberg declared that the experiments indicated that the first of the trial system's bulwarks against error, the requirement that testimony be given under oath, was if anything positively harmful. In cases such as his own burglary trial (or the Ronald Cotton rape trial), the witnesses' sincerity was never a real issue in the first place. Why, after all, would Jennifer Thompson want to identify anyone *other* than the person she believed was the rapist? Why would Bernadine Skillern identify Gary Graham if she didn't really think that he was the murderer she had seen in the parking lot? In such cases, the oath's "seriousness and solemnity suggest that the conditions for complete truth are given if the witness is ready not to lie." This was simply misleading. The oath may suppress the intentional lie, and it may focus attention on the details of the statement. "But," Munsterberg asked, "Is it so sure that our memory works faultlessly simply because we earnestly want it to behave well?"[32] Munsterberg supported his arguments by combining a shrewd call to common sense self-observation with a barrage of experimental results. Think, he suggested, of all the times you have tried very hard but failed to remember someone's name, only to have the name slip into consciousness later, after you have moved on to some other chore. Did concentration really help you there?

He also attacked another of the legal system's revered protections against witness error: its reliance on the witness' "demeanor" as an indicator of confidence, and on that eyewitness confidence as an indicator of eyewitness accuracy. Munsterberg declared that the assertion by a witness such as Jennifer Thompson or Bernadine Skillern (or for that matter, Hugo Munsterberg) that "I am as sure as I can be" had no relevance to the task at hand. A witness's subjective sense of certainty, Munsterberg argued, is beside the point.

To demonstrate the dangers of relying on a witness' confidence, Munsterberg relayed the results of a series of experiments in which subjects reviewed a picture or an event, and were asked to give a written account in which they underlined the facts about which "they felt so absolutely certain that they would be ready to take an oath before a court on the underlined words."[33] The experimental results showed almost as many mistakes in the underlined portions as in the unemphasized portions. It was almost the same with adults as with children, and "the grown-up students of my laboratory," Munsterberg noted, "commit this kind of perjury all the time." The conclusion he drew from the psychological experiments was "that the feeling of certainty stands in no definite relation to the attention with which the objects are observed. . . . The correlations between attention, recollection, and feeling of certainty become more complex the more we study them."[34] Badgering a witness such as Jennifer Thompson to admit that she was uncertain would do no good, Munsterberg pointed out, because Jennifer would be unaware of any reason for questioning her subjective memories.

On The Witness Stand sets all of this out in tones of sweet reason. The legend that Munsterberg provoked a ferocious legal counterattack by the arrogance of his tone is mistaken. The fact is, there was more than enough in the substance of Munsterberg's critique to wound the lawyers.

The problem was not that Munsterberg's argument was weak or exaggerated, but that it contained a discomfiting core which was impossible to disregard. Munsterberg pointed out that the law, like the general public, takes it for "granted that if [a witness] is normal and conscious of responsibility, he may forget a thing, but it would not believe that he could remember the wrong thing."[35] Munsterberg made it clear that a witness could do just that: that even when a witness such as Jennifer Thompson correctly remembers something (for example, having seen Ronald Cotton's face) she can innocently misattribute the source of the memory (in Jennifer's case, believing that the source of the memory was the night of the rape, when in fact she first saw Cotton in the photo-array). According to Munsterberg, "The feeling of belonging to our past life may associate itself thus just as well with a perfectly new idea of our imagination as with a real reproduction of an earlier state of mind."[36] Even more disturbing, the experiments proved that this was the state of *normal* memory, not the effect of pathology or injury.

If Munsterberg was right, then the legal system was fundamentally dependent on a fiction—on a belief in a permanent, fixed memory faculty in humans, on the belief that memory is the equivalent of a videotape. The law assumed that Jennifer Thompson, for example, called on to identify the man who had brutalized her, simply had to "roll the tape." Munsterberg's collected experiments showed that memory is nothing of the kind; it is a complex process of perception, storage, and recall, vulnerable at every stage to suggestion, distortion, and omission. This was very bad news for legal procedure.

Munsterberg insisted that his experiments proved that the legal emperor had no clothes.

It is hard to say what would have happened if Munsterberg had simply left it at that—described a problem and suggested further work. For better or worse, "leaving it at that" was something of which Munsterberg was incapable. He pressed on. Ironically, the elements of his further efforts which seem to have gotten Munsterberg into the most trouble can best be described not as "arrogant," "abrasive" or "pugnacious," but as "lawyerish."

Munsterberg did not simply analyze a problem; he pressed a grievance. In effect, he filed suit against the lawyers. To be exact, he accused the legal system of a tort: The law had a duty to honor the psychologists' achievements; the law disregarded that duty; and the public and the psychologists were hurt by the disregard:

> No juryman would be expected to follow his general impressions in the question as to whether the blood on the murderer's shirt is human or animal. But he is expected make up his mind as to whether the memory ideas of a witness are objective reproductions of earlier experience or are mixed up with associations and suggestions. The court proceeds as if . . . experimental psychology, with its efforts to analyze the mental faculties, still stood where it stood two thousand years ago.[37]

In the face of scientific proof that Munsterberg believed was incontrovertible, the lawyers "go on thinking that their legal instinct and their common sense supplies them with all that is needed and somewhat more." According to Munsterberg, not only did the Law have a problem, but Psychology had the solution, and the Law contemptuously ignored it. The fact is, Munsterberg said:

> The Court would rather listen for whole days to the "science" of handwriting experts than to allow a witness to be examined with regard to his memory and his power of perception, his attention and his associations, his volition and his suggestibility, with methods which are in accord with the exact work of experimental psychology.[38]

Then, to redress this grievance, Munsterberg unleashed one last lawyer-like rhetorical strategy: He decided to isolate his legal and judicial adversaries in order more effectively to turn the public audience against them. Everyone else saw the indispensable contribution that experimental psychology had made, Munsterberg argued. Educators were using psychologists' teachings, and so were physicians, artists, businessmen, politicians, and clergymen.

"All are ready to see that certain chapters of Applied Psychology are sources of help and strength to them," Munsterberg charged. "The lawyer alone is obdurate."[39]

That was exactly the sort of statement that would attract the attention of John Henry Wigmore.[40]

———————•·•·•———————

John Henry Wigmore was born in San Francisco in March, 1863. He died in 1943 at the age of 80 after a taxicab accident, which occurred as he hustled from the meeting of one committee that was determined to improve the world to a second. He had attended thousands of these meetings, and probably chaired a thousand, too.[41]

Wigmore's father, an Anglo-Irish emigré from Cork, had established a cabinet-making business, which quickly expanded into an extremely prosperous enterprise dealing in fine lumber. Young "Harry" attended private schools in San Francisco, then Harvard and Harvard Law School. After a brief period of private practice in Boston, he taught for several years as the chief professor of Anglo-American Law at Keio University in Tokyo, before returning to take up a faculty position at Northwestern University School of Law in Chicago in 1893. By the time Munsterberg filed his claim against the legal profession in 1908, Wigmore had been the dean of Northwestern Law School for seven years.

As Dean, Wigmore embodied the idealized Victorian headmaster of *Tom Brown's Schooldays*. Like Munsterberg, he had rigorously stylized his appearance to fit the role he had chosen. Tall, slender, bright-eyed, with a brushed-up cavalry mustache, he wielded a long cigarette holder. He dressed fastidiously: Outdoors he wore a Homburg and carried a stick. He was an upright presence in tailored tweeds, but always eager to put aside his dignity and engage the brighter boys. Did the Law School Revue theatrical performance need a few songs? Wigmore wrote them. Did it lack performers? Wigmore sang the songs, with *brio*, while accompanying himself on the piano. And he made his charges feel that he wanted them to realize their potential. As one colleague—a psychologist, as it happens—wrote years later: "He was loyal to his colleagues as long as they honestly grappled with the problems that they had to meet and did not run away. When they dreamed a little, with their feet on the ground, and tried to make their dreams come true they confirmed him in his faith that there is more good than evil and more strength than weakness in humankind."[42]

Wigmore had already published, in 1904, the first edition of his master-work, *Treatise on Evidence.*[43] According to one authority, Wigmore's *Treatise* is not only "the best, by far the best, treatise on the Law of Evidence, it is also the best work ever produced on any comparable division of Anglo-American law."[44] By its third edition the *Treatise* filled ten volumes, and lawyers then (and now) simply referred to "Wigmore" in the same way that they once referred to "Blackstone." But the preeminence of Wigmore's *Treatise* can hide the amazing distinctiveness, even oddness, of the book and its author. Wigmore was a towering scholar, but he was also a fascinating character.

Wigmore spoke a dozen languages, and when in his seventies he planned a trip to the Middle East, he quietly added Arabic to the list. In one year, while administering the Law School and updating the *Treatise*, Wigmore read 179 non-legal books, great works and detective novels both, and he took notes on every book he read. This voracious reading in all fields was something that Wigmore believed was essential for every lawyer. He even published a "List of 100 Legal Novels" to make the point that he, with Holmes, believed that the life of the law had been experience, not arid logic.

The fruits of Wigmore's encompassing curiosity about the world are very evident in his *Treatise*. More than an astounding piece of scholarship, it also provides a kind of courtroom manual for lawyers and judges. It has an elegant analytical framework, and its level of intellectual precision is such that Wigmore is often driven to coining new words when the existing English term seems to him too hazy. One critic complained:

> Professor Wigmore presents us with such marvels as retrospectant evidence, prophylactic rules, viatorial privilege, integration of legal acts, autoptic proference, and other no less striking inventions. It is safe to say that no man, however great, could introduce into the law three such extravagantly novel terms and Professor Wigmore proposes a dozen.[45]

But beyond all of this, the *Treatise* is pervaded by the recognition that law is an enterprise carried out by people. Anthony Powell, the British novelist, always argued that certain books of reference—Powell had *Burke's Landed Gentry* in mind—can tell you a great deal about what human beings are like and how they live. Wigmore's *Treatise* has that quality. This is an observation, not a recommendation; there are more entertaining and efficient ways to learn these things than by reading Wigmore. Still, Wigmore's *Treatise*, with its rich mix of doctrine, quotation, illustration, and anecdote, bears a much closer resemblance to, say, *The Oxford English Dictionary* or Robert Burton's *Anatomy of*

Melancholy than it does to the latest productions of the professoriat in either its Law and Economics or Critical Legal Studies incarnation. The most striking feature of Wigmore's *Treatise* is its intellectual generosity. Even Felix Frankfurter, who during the Sacco and Vanzetti debates was the victim of a Wigmorean attack far more vitriolic (and unfair) than anything unleashed on Munsterberg, wrote of "Wigmore on Evidence": "It is not only a great treatise on the law of evidence, but it is a masterpiece of scholarship, conveyed through a distinguished style of writing . . . I would make his treatise compulsory reading in every university that has the ambition to turn out its graduates as competent masters of the English language."[46]

Wigmore was allergic to the cloistered professorial life; he was one of those outsized Victorian characters who were congenitally incapable of seeing a problem without setting about seeing it solved. He was an indefatigable founder of committees, publisher of articles, and organizer of conferences. Were the Chicago Police inefficient in investigating the St. Valentine's Day Massacre of feuding gangsters in a Chicago garage? He set up the country's first forensic crime laboratory at Northwestern, and created the *Journal of Criminal Law & Criminology*. Did air travel fail to fit comfortably into existing law? He founded a *Journal of Air Law*. Did the cathedral of Tréguiere, which had a monument to St. Ives, the patron saint of lawyers, need a new stained glass window? Wigmore raised the money. Were hundreds of Northwestern students and alumni serving in the Army? Wigmore wrote and dispatched by hand 20 postcards every day.[47] Wigmore was a Tory Romantic: loyal to the past, but loyal because he saw the past as the site of chivalric adventures and Great Deeds. Someone far more likeable than the venerable effigy "Wigmore On Evidence" comes through in the picture provided by a novice professor at another school:

> I heard the opening address by a tall, thin, dandy-like man with a flushed face, urging some such program as the adoption of a new Greek terminology by American lawyers. Undaunted by the apparently hostile reception of his thesis, on the speaker went as if he were ushering in a new era. So that was the great god in the flesh. I was introduced to him afterward and he acted as if he had but waited to see me. Conversant with my preoccupations at the University of Missouri Law School, he gave me such warm encouragement that I began to feel myself someone in a strange environment.[48]

Intensely conservative in many ways, Wigmore was hostile to pacifism, fearful of Communism, impatient with hyper-technical constitutional interpretations that "handcuffed" the police, and believed Sacco and Vanzetti were fairly tried and executed. But he also threw his enormous energy and prestige into the protection of the innocent. He was one of the earliest champions of the public defender and legal aid movements. As early as 1913, Wigmore was arguing for legislation to compensate wrongfully accused and convicted citizens, and he warmly praised Edwin Borchard's *Convicting the Innocent: Errors of Criminal Justice* on its publication in 1932.[49] (Borchard, a Yale Law School professor, compiled a list of wrongful convictions, most of which had derived from eyewitness error.)

Wigmore was no reflexive apologist for the legal system. He was always more than willing to criticize legal things as they were. In fact, the most frequent complaint about the *Treatise* was that Wigmore failed to pay judges their due respect. As to the Bar, well, Wigmore wrote, "The Bar is overcrowded with incompetent, shiftless, ill-fitted lawyers, who degrade the methods of the law and cheapen the quality of services by unlimited competition." "The number of lawyers," Wigmore asserted, "should be reduced by one-half."[50]

Wigmore, like Munsterberg, retained a profoundly moral orientation. The greatest legal expert on the rules of law believed that, "All the rules in the world will not get us substantial justice if the judges and the lawyers have not the correct living moral attitude toward substantial justice." Wigmore, one friend remembered after his death, "Looked upon ignorance as an evil."[51] If there was something wrong in the legal system, then Wigmore wanted to know about it, and once he knew about it, fixing it became a matter of duty. Wigmore's attitude toward duty is indicated by his response to a War Department questionnaire which he received on the eve of World War II:

Q. *Availability*
A. Can do library and desk work. Have just completed a guide to War Law for the American Bar Association.
Q. *How much time will you require . . . before reporting for duty?*
A. None.

When he answered that questionnaire Wigmore was 79 years old.[52]

———◆◆◆———

Amazingly enough, in light of the aftermath of his confrontation with Munsterberg, Wigmore was also the best friend Psychology had in the legal profession—perhaps the best friend Psychology has ever had in the legal profession.

Much of Munsterberg's message regarding eyewitness fallibility was old news to Wigmore, but it was still a message that Wigmore believed ought to be heard. One of Wigmore's students remembered lessons in the unreliability of eyewitnesses as a staple of Wigmore's classroom teaching:

> One day in another class three members of the faculty came hurriedly into his room, each shouting a different and somewhat confused statement. The Dean promptly named six students . . . and said, "I subpoena you as witnesses to make proof of these disgraceful occurrences." One after another the six students were called to testify as to the statements made by the faculty members a few minutes before. . . . Only one of the six "witnesses" had approximated in any way the correct statements of the three professors, but the jury did not believe him. He was a shiftless and somewhat irresponsible character and yet he had keen perception.[53]

As early as 1907, Wigmore was sufficiently intrigued that he sought Munsterberg's permission to reprint his writings on witnesses in *The Illinois Law Review*.[54] On the other hand, Wigmore also believed that Munsterberg's *On The Witness Stand* "greatly overstated the contributions that psychology could make at that time and then took the legal profession to task for not using them." According to Wigmore's biographer, Wigmore hoped that some psychologist "would question Munsterberg's claims or submit more solid proof of their applicability to the practice of law."[55] When no one came forward, Wigmore, unwilling as ever to allow a problem to go unaddressed, undertook the task himself, and undertook it with his accustomed maniacal thoroughness.

The February 1909 issue of *The Illinois Law Review* carried Wigmore's response to Munsterberg: The account of a mock trial, "Professor Muensterberg and the Psychology of Testimony: Being a Report of the Case of *Cokestone v. Muensterberg*."[56] Munsterberg wanted to put the legal profession on trial in the court of public opinion for its dismissal of psychology; very well then, Wigmore would put "Muensterberg" on trial in an imaginary court of law for libeling the legal profession.

In retrospect, Wigmore's goals in this article seem very clear. He wanted to challenge Munsterberg's overstatements, and he wanted to exhort the legal profession to learn the lessons that Psychology had to teach. There are indications that Wigmore took the second goal more seriously than the first. The final word in Wigmore's mock trial of "Muensterberg" is assigned to the judge, who blasted American lawyers: "In no country had the legal profession taken so little interest in finding out or using what the other sciences were doing." Counsel for the legal profession (a Wigmore proxy) brought his argument to a crescendo when he "urged earnestly, as the lawyers in Europe are urging, friendly and energetic alliance of psychology and law, in the noble cause of justice."[57] To get that enterprise off to a good start, Wigmore supplied an appendix that listed the 149 articles (only 9 in English) that Wigmore had mastered in preparation for the "trial." He also took the opportunity to announce the forthcoming convocation of a first National Conference on Criminal Law and Criminology (another Wigmorean production, his further response to the unanswered problem) as a vehicle for improved interaction between the professions.

So why is Wigmore's article remembered as a savage, bloodthirsty slaughter of psychology, psychologists, their children, and old people?

———•◆•———

The answer lies in the natural consequences of the adversary discourse which Munsterberg and Wigmore had casually (perhaps even playfully) chosen. That is fitting enough. Much of the tension in the relations between psychological science on eyewitnesses and the legal system can be traced to the peculiar characteristics of the adversary trial as a medium for interaction. The case of *Wigmore v. Munsterberg* was one in which the medium of adversary presentation really became the whole message.

The adversary trial approach brings with it a special "battle model" atmosphere. In its zero-sum death grapple between irreconcilables, one side must win all and one side lose all. It also generates its own strategic imperatives. So, for example, because Wigmore has cast himself as a trial lawyer, he ignores Munsterberg's strong point (eyewitnesses make mistakes) even though it is a point with which Wigmore himself happens to agree. The logic of trial strategy dictates that Wigmore must focus his attack on Munsterberg's weak point: his assertion that psychology has ready tools for handling the problem. And the influence of adversarial thinking goes deeper than that.

The imaginary trial of "Muensterberg," because it was imagined as a trial, embodied the legal system's endemic tendency to think of all questions of science as questions of expert testimony. The lawyers' reflex reaction is that if the scientific findings cannot be presented as evidence, then the science is useless. In order to be presented in evidence, the science must meet certain technical tests. Some of these evidentiary hurdles are matters of practical common sense. For example, if the science is so new that no community of experts has been formed to evaluate a particular "expert's" opinion, the expert is excluded. Otherwise, the court system and the jurors would be left at the mercy of the quirks and delusions of any individual calling himself an "expert." So, when "Mr. Tyro," plaintiffs' counsel (and Wigmore's alter ego), forces Prof. Muensterberg to admit that all of the psychological materials on eyewitness psychology are quite new and are unavailable in English, he wins his point, and disposes of Muensterberg as a potential witness. Tyro proves that Muensterberg's science is something that cannot be shared with a jury. At that point the average lawyer loses interest. Psychology becomes something that can safely be ignored.

But Wigmore was not the average lawyer, and in Wigmore's hands the expert witness lens also reveals a more fundamental dichotomy that divides the two professions: Psychologists and lawyers value different kinds of knowledge.

Psychological experiments, no matter how carefully performed, yield statistical, probabilistic results: they can tell you what happens eight times in ten, but not whether in any given case the defendant is one of the eight guilty men or one of the two innocent ones. That second problem—the clinical or diagnostic problem, "is this one of the eight or one of the two?"—is what the legal system is interested in. In fact, the clinical, diagnostic problem is what the legal system is called on to answer. The question for the courts is never "Will a witness in Jennifer Thompson's position be right 80 percent of the time?" but rather is *this* witness right, *this* time?" DNA evidence, for example, provides such a clinical and diagnostic result. So, for that matter, do eyewitnesses. But do the psychologists have anything equivalent to offer?

"Mr. Tyro" attacks "Prof. Muensterberg" on exactly this issue. Tyro wrings from Muensterberg the admission that psychology can offer only two candidates for solving the question of whether a witness such as Jennifer Thompson is right or wrong. Munsterberg had singled out the "individual difference" approach developed by Stern, and the "association method" advanced by Jung. Tyro has no difficult in showing that the two psychological methods are equally novel, unpublicized in English, and (even in the eyes of Stern and Jung themselves) not ready for practical use.[58] That answers the question of their legal admissibility.

But Tyro/Wigmore is acute enough to see that even if they *had* been as fully developed as *On The Witness Stand* claimed, neither method would be truly diagnostic. Stern, for example, might conduct tests to measure the capacities for perception, memory, and recall of a witness in Jennifer Thompson's position, but his experiments can only tell us (at best) that a witness such as Jennifer is *relatively* likely to be accurate a certain percentage of times. No examination can say that Jennifer is *always* wrong or always right, or *definitely* right this time. Similarly, Jung might some day be able to show that his association method has demonstrated that a witness such as Jennifer is relatively more likely to be accurate about a particular fact, but that method cannot solve the ultimate diagnostic problem of distribution of errors and correct statements. "Was Jennifer right this time?" is a question for which experimental psychology can offer no direct, categorical answer.

What Munsterberg had failed to grasp was that his knowledge about the reliability of *witnesses* was not a sufficient answer to the legal system's concern for the reliability of *verdicts*. On that subject Munsterberg had nothing—or nothing experimental—to offer. The cross-examination of "Muensterberg" revealed in humbling fashion that when it came to understanding which particular witness produced a good, and which a bad, verdict, psychologists were, just like lawyers, groping in the dark. In Wigmore, Munsterberg had an adversary who read psychology and believed in psychology, but Wigmore was a serious man, and he issued Munsterberg an astringent call to order.

Besides, the trial format in which Wigmore and his fictional "Muensterberg" wrestled exacerbated personal attributes of the self-designated champions of law and psychology in a manner virtually guaranteed to eclipse Wigmore's sincere efforts to stimulate any "friendly and energetic alliance in the noble cause of justice."

Wigmore had a strong Walter Mitty streak. After his service as a Colonel in the Judge Advocate General's office during the First World War, for example:

> Frequently he reverted to being a Colonel and became one of the Nation's greatest legal scholars playing soldier. He loved to be referred to by his military title. It seems strange, if not silly, but it was terrifically human. No boy ever lived and escaped the temptation to play soldier. He was a great man but still at heart such a boy and could never resist the temptation. The students could not help but like it, even though they smiled.[59]

Wigmore, the greatest scholar in the history of the law of trial evidence, had never tried a case. To fantasies of military glory Wigmore apparently added fantasies of courtroom swashbuckling. These are not unknown among law professors. Anyone who has watched a parade of law professors pontificating on the trial performance of the lawyers in, say, the O. J. Simpson or William Kennedy Smith trials, has seen the same impulse in action. Law professors, by and large, don't do trials. Munsterberg's proven capacity for attracting satirical caricature threw gasoline on the fire. The mock trial format might have been designed to incite Wigmore, always excitable, to go too far.

And Wigmore did go too far. Wigmore's rhetorical capacities, like Munsterberg's, were equipped with an accelerator but no brake. The substance of Wigmore's presentation was irrefutable: He proved that Munsterberg had overstated his case in virtually every respect. Psychology did *not* yet possess the silver bullet for preventing wrongful convictions. Wigmore's review of the psychological materials had been exhaustive, detailed, and accurate. Wigmore was right—*scientifically* right, not right simply as a matter of arcane legal technicality. But the method of presentation Wigmore used was something else.

Wigmore released his stand-in, Mr. Tyro, from any constraints the rules of evidence would impose in an actual courtroom. Mr. Tyro's cross-examination questions to "Muensterberg" are long, complicated, argumentative, and assume facts that are not yet in evidence. So, for example:

> Q. Very well. But in this connection, calling your attention to the fact that the German and Austrian workers published their results in psychological or legal journals, let me note that when Gotschalk, the Berlin advocate, blamed Stern "for ignoring the impolicy of publishing such theories" in that they tended unjustly to destroy popular confidence in the courts, Stern defended himself by pointing out, "I did not try to stir up any popular agitation; I offered my results simply to scientists, and to that end, I printed, not in popular magazines, but in scientific journals." Now, comparing that course, from the point of view of fairness and charity, with the course taken by yourself, have you any explanation to make?
> A. Not at present.[60]

Again and again, the wretched "Muensterberg" squirms under this treatment, only to be forced eventually to acknowledge the justice of Mr. Tyro's charges. Before long, Muensterberg is reduced to such a state that he cannot gather himself to answer at all:

> Q. Now then, my dear professor, I want you to be good enough to explain to this jury how any one could have predicted (if there are psychological laws governing testimonial error) that precisely you would commit the whimsical mistake of bearing testimony against our innocent profession, arraigned in the dock of public opinion, for neglecting to use new and "exact" methods which were and still are so little "exact" and so incapable of forensic use that even their well-wishers confess that thousands of experiments and years of research will be required before they will be practicable, if ever?
> A. (No answer.)[61]

At some points Mr. Tyro is unfair: It isn't Muensterberg's fault, for example, that *other* psychologists have conducted trivial experiments on collar buttons. At other points, the attack begins to have sadistic overtones: Surely it would have been possible to refute Munsterberg's allegations without showing that they had been repudiated by Munsterberg's childhood heroes, the eminent philosopher Fichte and the pioneering psychologist Wundt, for example—even by Hugo Munsterberg himself, whose earlier comments had undermined his pronouncements in *On The Witness Stand.*

In the end, no amount of friendly commentary before and after Wigmore's mock trial could hope to erase the image of the hapless psychologist trapped in sweaty humiliation on the witness stand that the mock trial created. Munsterberg himself once proposed experiments on the comparative ease of remembering recent events and vivid events. Did we remember vivid events better? Or were recent events sharper in our memory than vivid ones? Wigmore's mock trial of Munsterberg seems to offer some data on that issue: it was vivid, and it was remembered. William James' novelist brother, Henry, always said that a novelist must "Dramatize! Dramatize!" Wigmore had done just that, and Wigmore's courtroom drama, not Wigmore's encouraging editorializing in favor of psychology, was what people remembered.

⟶ ◆ ⟵

Wigmore imagined that at the close of his mock trial the lawyers and the psychologists would get together. "Muensterberg" was seen making appointments with the lawyers:

> Doubtless the first appointment was for that same evening; for it was afterwards credibly rumored that all parties including the counsel when seen later around a table at the University Club, appeared to be animatedly engaged in psychological experiments and . . . the jovial chorus *"Was kommt dort von der Hoeh."*[62]

Perhaps if the issue had been left to Wigmore and Munsterberg it might have been handled that way, and disagreements hashed out to the accompaniment of drinking songs and good fellowship. After all, another of Munsterberg's public relations disasters was the revelation, shortly after he threw his psychological prestige into anti-Prohibition polemics, that brewer Adolphus Busch had made enormous donations through Munsterberg to Harvard's German Museum.[63] But it is hard to believe that Munsterberg could ever have shrugged off Wigmore's assault. For all of Munsterberg's appearance of ferocity, there was the other side to him which William James, in one of his bursts of shrewdness, had recognized from the first. Writing to Josiah Royce to describe Munsterberg, James had noted that Munsterberg was "Not the heroic type but of the sensitive and refined type . . . inclined to softness and fatness, poor voice, vain, loquacious, in person rather formal and fastidious . . . desiring to please and to shine."[64] Munsterberg dropped the law from his target list.

Even so, Wigmore and Munsterberg continued to correspond, Munsterberg taking Wigmore to task over some misunderstanding on the dean's part of German academic practice, and Wigmore taking the criticism in good humor. Wigmore, for his part, was prepared to acknowledge that he had gone too far in his mock trial. Writing to Munsterberg in 1913 to thank him for giving permission to reprint segments of *On The Witness Stand* in a law school text, Wigmore assured Munsterberg that he "need have no fear that I will use the occasion to renew the sarcastic controversies of two years ago."[65]

And Wigmore doggedly continued to do what he could to promote the "friendly alliance." For years, psychology professors were assigning Wigmore's article to their students as the most comprehensive review of the state of the science.[66] The final edition of his *Science of Judicial Proof*, published in 1937, explicitly invokes psychological authority in its extensive discussion of the problems of perception, memory, and recall. Wigmore even conducted a couple of experiments of its own. "When the psychologists are ready for the courts," Wigmore asserted, "the courts will be ready for the psychologists."[67]

But that was the expression of a wish, not the description of a reality, and by the time Wigmore wrote it Munsterberg had been dead for almost 20 years, felled by a stroke in the middle of a Radcliffe lecture. The Wigmore/Munsterberg exchange had given psychological researchers one more argument for "pure" scholarship, and they retreated to the laboratory. The phrase "Law and Psychology" came to refer to clinical evaluations of insanity and competency to stand trial—to the study of the abnormal, rather than the normal operations of the human mind.

When, in 1974, psychologist Robert Buckhout resurrected the question of the psychology of eyewitness testimony he observed:

> It is discouraging to note that the essential findings on the unreliability of eyewitness testimony were made by Hugo Munsterberg nearly 80 years ago, and yet the practice of basing a case on eyewitness testimony and trying to persuade a jury that such testimony is superior to circumstantial evidence continues to this day.[68]

Buckhout's arithmetic was off—it was closer to 70 years than 80 since Munsterberg's first publications—but his bleak assessment of psychology's contribution to preventing eyewitness error in the courts was the simple truth.

The courts had decided to go it alone. If the lawyers were going to catch eyewitness mistakes, it would be through their traditional methods. That's where things stood when events forced an Alamance County jury to decide whether Jennifer Thompson was right about Ronald Cotton being the rapist. Adversary attack would have to provide the answer.

CHAPTER THREE

THE LAWYERS' ART

Bad Verdicts from Good Witnesses

EVEN WITHOUT MUNSTERBERG'S PREACHING MOST of us would have known in a vague way that some eyewitnesses will sometimes make mistakes. Research confirms this intuition. There are surveys indicating that 20 to 25 percent of real eyewitnesses choose the wrong man in police identification procedures.[1] In another recent study, 45 percent of military trainees who had undergone a high-stress interrogation chose an innocent "filler" when they were asked to identify their interrogator from a traditional lineup, even though they had spent 30 minutes with the interrogator.[2]

Still, many of these mistakes don't matter. When an eyewitness goes to a lineup and picks Number Three as the robber but Number Three turns out to be a patrolman from the traffic unit who is standing in as a "filler" in the lineup, no one is placed in jeopardy. It is only when the eyewitness wrongly identifies the man whom the police have chosen as an actual suspect that we have a problem.

How often does this constellation of factors actually align to place an inno-cent defendant on trial? Answering that question requires some extrapolation. No one compiles—or even *could* compile—precise statistics on the number of eyewitness cases that entangle innocent defendants each year. The authoritative "guilty/not guilty" that DNA can provide is only available in cases—typically sex crimes—in which the criminals leave some biological material on the scene, or are quickly captured with biological markers of their victims on their clothes or weapons. Armed robbers, drive-by shooters, and burglars will not provide inves-tigators with DNA samples to work with. In Gary Graham's case, for example, the investigators had no biological material to compare. Still, there are solid indications that, as one commentator noted about false convictions in general, the level of eyewitness accuracy "is at once both reassuring and frightening—reassuring in the aggregate, but frightening to contemplate individual cases of injustice, even if they constitute a very small proportion of all convictions."[3] The percentage that mistaken eyewitnesses contribute to the overall number of identifications may be relatively small, but because there are so many eyewitness cases to begin with, the absolute number of mistaken eyewitness cases is stunning. After all, about 6,000 people *per month* are included in identification procedures. One careful estimate (by Professor Steven Penrod, of the John Jay College of Criminal Justice in New York City) concludes that erroneous prosecutions based on mistaken eyewitness testimony number in the thousands every year.[4] There could be a lot of innocent Ronald Cottons doing hard time for someone else's crime, and a lot of guilty Bobby Pooles left free to find new victims.

Perhaps the exact number isn't that important. Just as combat remains the defining and organizing event of military life even though relatively few military careers involve actual combat, the jury trial of an innocent citizen remains at the core of the legal system, and of the society that relies on it. When a wrongful conviction pivots on eyewitness testimony—our oldest form of evidence—it raises the question whether if we can't get this case right, we can get any case right. Because we can't live without eyewitness testimony, and because eyewitnesses are usually accurate, how we live with honest eyewitness mistakes is an urgent question.

Still, as Wigmore tried to remind Munsterberg, the real harm lies in mistaken *verdicts*, not in mistaken witnesses. The legal system has hundreds of years of experience confronting the challenge of those eyewitness mistakes that might really count, and if the classic tools of the adversary system enable jurors to sort the accurate identifications from the mistaken ones, all this talk of scientific expertise provides an interesting gloss on a non-problem. Can the lawyers catch the mistakes that the eyewitnesses make? If they can catch them, or most of them, then maybe Wigmore was right, and Munsterberg, if not quite the figure of fun he became in Wigmore's mock trial, was an academic alarmist.

———•·◆·•———

Perry Mason always had an innocent client, always exposed the guilty party during the episode, and always won the case. For a defense lawyer who is determined to pursue the Perry Mason Dream, taking a case based on eyewitness testimony is a very promising starting point.

Trials have become rare events: the overwhelming majority of criminal cases are resolved by guilty pleas. The trial of an innocent defendant is even more rare. After all, one reason that there are so many guilty pleas is that most of the people the police arrest are guilty—plainly, irrefutably, even ludicrously guilty. But thanks to DNA we are now certain that eyewitness mistakes really do translate into prosecutions of innocent defendants. Of the first 80 cases of wrongful conviction uncovered by the advent of DNA technology, 63 were based on eyewitness identification testimony.[5] This should mean Perry Masonesque trials for eager lawyers: After all, defendants who are innocent are more likely than guilty defendants to turn down plea bargains and test the evidence in the courtroom. Then the eyewitness will have to convince the jury, and convince them in the face of cross-examination by the defendant's counsel.

Lawyers place a mystic faith in the power of cross-examination, which no less a figure than John Henry Wigmore himself once described as "the greatest legal engine ever invented for the ascertainment of the truth." Treatises, videotapes, Continuing Legal Education Programs, and workshops designed to teach lawyers how to operate the Great Engine abound. Lawyers see cross-examination as the crucible in which correct eyewitnesses are separated from mistaken ones.

Every generation of advocates has its new "Bible" on cross-examination, but most of the advice these Bibles contain is immemorial. Good cross-examiners seize control of the courtroom. They ask tight, leading questions which restrict the eyewitness to exculpatory information and prevent damaging rambling. ("You didn't describe his eyes" rather than "What did you see?"). They try to tell an interesting story. Above all they prepare meticulously, studying the eyewitness's prior statements for inconsistencies and mistakes which can be brought to the jury's attention. ("Didn't you say in this written statement to the police that the robber had a scar?").

Most lawyers—not to mention the legion of non-lawyers who are riveted by televised courtroom dramas—can imagine themselves kicking Wigmore's great engine into life and dominating the courtroom while rescuing the innocent client.

In fact, there are lions of the Continuing Legal Education Circuit who claim that they can show you how it is done: they will teach you how to do the Mr. Potato Head cross-examination on an eyewitness. At the trial practice seminar, the demonstration goes something like this:

An Alpha Lawyer (usually wearing cowboy boots and a Rolex watch the size of a melon) advances confidently on the eyewitness, brandishing the sketchy description the eyewitness provided the police on the night of the crime in one hand and Mr. Potato Head in the other:

Q. You gave a height?
A. Yes.
Q. And weight?
A. Yes.
Q. But that was all?
A. I guess.
Q. You didn't describe his eyes?
A. No.
[Lawyer removes eyes from Potato Head.]
Q. You didn't describe his little glasses?
A. No.
[Lawyer removes glasses from Potato Head.]
Q. You didn't describe his little moustache?
A. No.
[Lawyer removes moustache from Potato Head.]
Q. You didn't describe his ears?
A. No.
[Lawyer removes ears from Potato Head.]
Q. You didn't describe *his little pipe?*
A. I guess not.
[Lawyer removes pipe, stalks to prosecution table, disdainfully hands over naked Potato.]
Lawyer: Your witness, counselor.

Memories of Perry Mason fill the air. It's pretty hard to imagine a jury convicting *this* Potato Head (guilty or not) after such a slaughter. Everyone adjourns to the bar. The Alpha Lawyer has the most attractive student on his arm.

But does this work with eyewitnesses in real life? Certainly the appellate courts seem to think it does: "effective cross-examination is adequate to reveal any inconsistencies or deficiencies in eyewitness testimony," one noted.[6]

Or can the Perry Mason Dream turn into a nightmare for even a very good and very well-prepared lawyer?

———◆———

Ronald Cotton was as innocent as any client Perry Mason ever represented—as innocent, in fact, as you or me—and there was a point in the Cotton trial when a genuine Perry Mason moment seemed to be on the horizon.[7]

The annals of wrongful convictions are filled with drunken lawyers, sleeping lawyers, and lawyers who refer to their client as "this poor little ol' nigger man."[8] Gary Graham's lawyer, for example, could not be bothered calling two witnesses who said that Graham was *not* the shooter. But Ronald Cotton's lawyer did not fit that mold; Philip Moseley was unusually accomplished and hard-working. If you found yourself wrongly accused of a crime, you'd be lucky to have him. Moseley knew Cotton's case, and he believed in it. Moseley even went the extra mile and found a Munsterberg of his own, a psychology professor from the University of North Carolina, whom he offered to the court as an expert witness on eyewitness unreliability. The trial judge had rejected that offer without hesitation.

And Moseley managed to do one thing that few lawyers are able to do—something right out of the Perry Mason playbook. As a practical matter Perry Mason's episode-ending public service—exposing the true perpetrator right in the courtroom—is unworkable in real cases because in real cases the true perpetrators don't make themselves available. Through a combination of defense investigation, jailhouse rumor, and a clever ruse developed by Ronald Cotton himself (who managed to get a photograph of Bobby Poole to his lawyer), Bobby Poole, the actual rapist, had been found. Better than that, because Poole was in custody on an unrelated sentence, Moseley could obtain a writ and have Poole brought to court and shown to Jennifer Thompson.

So, the real rapist was brought to the courtroom, and placed between where Jennifer Thompson sat on the witness stand and where Phil Moseley sat with his innocent client trembling beside him at the counsel table. If Jennifer identified Poole, the case against Cotton would be over.

Jennifer looked at Poole from a distance of about 15 feet. She believed that she had never seen him before in her life. That's what she told the judge.

Evidence about Poole was excluded from the trial.

Since bringing in Poole couldn't persuade Jennifer to identify the right man, it would be left to the great engine to convince the jurors that Jennifer was identifying the wrong man. Ronald Cotton's defense was going to provide a pure test of the advocate's tools.

Moseley lacked one of the cross-examiner's standard tools: facts known by the witness but not voluntarily disclosed. Jennifer Thompson was not intentionally lying or withholding the truth. That is true in almost all eyewitness cases. Eyewitnesses are never aware of their mistakes (the cases wouldn't go to trial if they were) and Jennifer wasn't aware of hers. Jennifer was not a paid informant, or a business rival of Cotton's; she hadn't asked to be a victim. She certainly had a compelling reason to see the right "light-skinned black male" punished for the rape, but no reason at all to choose Cotton if she *didn't* think he was the right man. Whatever power cross-examination may have to reveal liars, that power had nothing to do with Ronald Cotton's defense; there was no "liar" involved in Cotton's trial.

But that didn't mean Moseley had no ammunition at all. To begin with, he had the simple question of Jennifer's vision. Jennifer wore glasses, but she wasn't wearing them on the night of the rape, and her eyesight was hazy. Moseley knew this, and he brought it out. The jurors heard it. It didn't matter.

Moseley had more: He could use contradictions both from Jennifer's own earlier versions of events and from the physical evidence. Although at trial Jennifer testified that she was certain that she had the right man, at the original photospread she had chosen *two* men who "looked like the robber." Moseley was able to confront Jennifer with that contradiction. It didn't matter. He was able to show that there were semen stains left on the crime scene which even pre-DNA serological testing could prove did not match Cotton's blood type. That didn't matter to the jurors either. The second woman who was raped by Bobby Poole on that night also saw Ronald Cotton in a lineup, and she did not identify him. She did not testify at Cotton's first trial, but the jury at the second trial knew about her failure to choose Cotton from the first lineup. They convicted Cotton anyway.

———•◆•———

This was bad news for Philip Moseley and worse news for Ronald Cotton, and it would probably not have been much comfort to either of them to learn that they were not alone. But to understand the context in which Ronald Cotton was convicted, it helps to peek ahead slightly at the research that probes jurors behavior in eyewitness cases. There is plenty of research indicating that these elements of Cotton's case were not exceptional. In fact, Moseley's gallant but futile efforts resonate with a consistent body of experimental results.

Jurors start with a remarkable implicit faith in eyewitnesses. There is more to this than the natural humility of "She was there, I wasn't, who am I to doubt her?" (Although it is hard to believe that sentiment doesn't play a role.) Prove the same case using eyewitnesses, then prove it using fingerprints, and the rate of guilty findings will be *higher* in the eyewitness example than in the fingerprint example.[9] Nor is that initial faith easy to undermine.

Consider, for example, an experiment in which jurors who decided an eyewitness trial returned "guilty" verdicts 72 percent of the time.[10] When jurors decided the same trial, but with the added news that the eyewitness was legally blind, the proportion of guilty verdicts plummeted. "Plummeted," that is, by 4 percent. Even when the eyewitness's blindness was disclosed, 68 percent of the mock jurors still voted to convict.

Or consider the muted impact of the inconsistencies and contradictions between Jennifer Thompson's early versions of the rape and her trial testimony. Was there something eccentric in the Cotton/Thompson jury's decision to ignore the variances? Apparently not. Researchers in one study showed mock jurors a trial in which an eyewitness was inconsistent about: (1) a robber threatening to shoot the victim, or not threatening at all; (2) wearing jewelry or not wearing jewelry; (3) being calm, or being sweaty or nervous; and (4) putting the stolen money in a bag he was carrying, or putting the money in his pocket. Examined under careful statistical control, the marginal effect of these inconsistencies on the jurors' verdicts simply disappeared.[11] Neither does contradiction by other evidence seem to have any guaranteed impact, inside the laboratory or outside. There was an early DNA case in Hartford, Connecticut, in which the jurors chose to believe the eyewitness's conviction that the defendant was the rapist, even though the FBI's lab director testified categorically that the defendant's guilt was an impossibility.

What the "jurors" in experiments seemed to look for from eyewitnesses was not consistency, but confidence: their question was, "Was the eyewitness certain?"[12] The results of these experiments can be viewed cautiously—some rely on written transcripts, others are quite lifelike, and the range of results is more complex that I have indicated to this point—but even if the experiments should be seen only to raise rather than to decide questions, their cumulative effect is daunting.

Faith in the great engine of cross-examination might be shaken a little further by an experiment in which the eyewitness was cross-examined by beginning law students before one jury, and by experienced veterans—the sort of "Alpha Lawyers" who might teach the continuing legal education program—before another jury. There was no significant difference in the results obtained by the tyros and those obtained by the pros.[13] The advocacy skills and tactics that lawyers struggle to learn, the hard-won lessons of long careers of practice had no discernible effect on the jurors' decisions in eyewitness cases. If differences in lawyer performance have no impact on juror decisions, does adversary attack actually achieve anything in helping to separate the mistaken eyewitnesses from the correct ones?

In the research on jury behavior in eyewitness cases the defense lawyers keep pushing the buttons and throwing the switches, the great engine cranks away, and yet nothing happens. Why isn't this working? The answer may lie in the process of jury decision making.

Jurors decide cases by taking the raw data generated in the trial's question-and-answer exchanges and then interpreting that data by applying general common sense principles of everyday life. If the evidence shows, for example, that there is blood on a club, then general common sense suggests that someone was struck with it. This works pretty well in all sorts of unexpected contexts: The cumulative knowledge and experience of 12 deliberating jurors is a formidable force.

One of Munsterberg's more obvious mistakes was that he clearly never grasped the adversary trial's capacity to generate data. The Cotton/Thompson jury knew that Jennifer had poor eyesight and that she wasn't wearing her glasses; that there were semen stains that did not match Cotton's blood type; that Jennifer's first photo-array identification was tentative; and that her statements had been inconsistent. When fragments of relevant fact are floating around in the world, the adversary process apparently does a decent job of rounding them up. Even in the burglary trial which Munsterberg described in *On The Witness Stand*, in which Munsterberg himself erroneously testified, the trial process brought before the jury a number of features that Munsterberg recognized only in hindsight. It was through the trial that Munsterberg learned the list of things he had not perceived or had misremembered.

And Munsterberg—perhaps as the result of his European background—was blind to the profound political importance of having important decisions made by a lay jury of citizens who are representative of their community. In fact, if Munsterberg hadn't been blind to that political feature of the trial, he probably would have been hostile to it, considering it hopelessly slapdash and untidy. Munsterberg would have preferred to turn the whole matter over to expert psychologists to measure and evaluate.

But Munsterberg—possibly without quite realizing it—had posed one question to which Wigmore had no ready answer: What if jurors in eyewitness cases were interpreting that mountain of trial-generated specific data by using "common sense" general principles that were simply, radically, wrong?

The core piece of data in an eyewitness trial—the eyewitness's statement "I remember"—could be so extremely problematic if the jurors apply the general principle, "memory is like a videotape." The Cotton/Thompson verdict could be explained by that reasoning process. If the jurors believed that there is a permanent memory capacity in humans, then they could believe that Jennifer had forgotten something she did perceive—that her videotape was damaged, or had a gap.

But the same jurors could *not* believe that Jennifer had remembered the *wrong* thing. When Jennifer's poor eyesight is evaluated using this "common sense" principle, her poor eyesight is simply beside the point. Jennifer had no reason to lie about what she saw during playback.

"Common sense" says Jennifer had to see the rapist's face well enough to record it, because if she *hadn't* seen it, it wouldn't be recorded, and it couldn't be played back. True, Bobby Poole's second victim did not identify Cotton in the lineup, but that failure simply proved to jurors that in her case, the videotape had not recorded Cotton in the first place (the light was bad, or she was too terrified) or it had decayed or been erased since. Munsterberg, however, claimed that memory is *not* a permanent record, like a videotape; he argued that in that regard common sense was simply wrong. If Munsterberg was right about this, it was not a point that Ronald Cotton's lawyer, Philip Moseley, could make simply by generating more helpful data.

Even worse, the harder a lawyer cross-examining Jennifer Thompson tried to generate data, the more opportunity he would give Jennifer to communicate—through her words, but also through her demeanor, her expressions, her body language—that she was absolutely certain that Ronald Cotton was the man who had raped her. Jennifer's confidence in her identification became another piece of the specific data that the trial produced.

What if the jurors evaluated that specific data by applying the general, common-sense principle that witness confidence shows witness *accuracy?* Munsterberg argued that "[T]he feeling of certainty stands in no definite relation to the attention with which the objects are observed. . . . The correlations between attention, recollection, and feeling of certainty become more complex the more we study them."[14] If Munsterberg was right, and confidence does *not* indicate accuracy, what could the trial lawyer do about it?

The great engine will not force Jennifer to question her own subjective confidence. In fact, it is far more likely that attempting to force Jennifer to question her own honest confidence in front of the jury would only succeed in forcing her to reaffirm it. Watching a Jennifer Thompson sustain her confidence under attack by an aspiring Perry Mason will make that confidence seem stronger to the jurors. Nor can the great engine work as a vehicle for attacking the general "eyewitness confidence equals eyewitness accuracy" principle itself. What question would a lawyer ask a witness to discredit that common sense belief? It isn't even easy to say which witness the lawyer could find to ask the question.

Lawyers can really enjoy the pleasures of the Mr. Potato Head cross-examination safely only in the classroom and the continuing legal education performance. In real trials, the Mr. Potato Head cross-examination is followed by a prosecution's re-direct examination. In that exchange, the prosecutor simply stands and mobilizes general "common sense" principles:

> Q. You remember the defense lawyer asking you whether you remembered all these facial features?
> A. Yes.
> Q. And you said you didn't?
> A. That's true.
> Q. How did you recognize this man?
> A. He had a head sort of like a Potato.
> Q. And how certain are you that this is the man?
> A. As certain as I have ever been of anything. I'll never forget that face.

Research indicates that the mock jurors believe a confident but mistaken eyewitness at exactly the same rate as a confident and correct one when viewing conditions are in the same general range. In one experiment, 80 percent of the jurors voted guilty in the correct witness case, 80 percent guilty when the witness was wrong.[15] And it is hard to blame them. The fact is, when a traditional adversary trial is over, the honestly mistaken eyewitness's misidentification will look just about the same as a correct eyewitness's choice.

This isn't always true. There are cases with tipping points: cases where the original description is wildly different from the defendant's appearance, or there are ten inconsistencies, or the exculpatory physical evidence is irrefutable, and the jurors reject the prosecution's case and acquit. These cases are often screened out before trial, but they do arise. Still, in a very broad middle range of cases, the testimony of the correct and the mistaken are nearly impossible to tell apart. You might believe that mistakes are rare or that mistakes are frequent, but they are certainly difficult to catch once they have happened.

Still, there is another answer to Munsterberg's jeremiad. Wigmore might have argued that very few "eyewitness" cases depend entirely on eyewitnesses: The legal system's faith in eyewitnesses isn't quite as abject as that, and cross-examination is not the only protection. There is almost always "something more"— some corroboration, some physical evidence, some circumstantial confirmation. The trial, after all, is only the last step in the legal process, and there are plenty of opportunities at earlier stages to screen out uncorroborated identifications.

There is documentation for this position; the fact is, there *is* always "something more" in an eyewitness case.

Unfortunately, one easy place to find examples of "corroboration" is on the list of DNA-exposed wrongful conviction cases—corroboration that turned out to be misleading. In virtually every one of the first round of DNA exoneration cases, there was "something more" than a single eyewitness identification. In some wrongful conviction cases there were multiple eyewitnesses identifying the same man; in other cases there were false alibis offered; in one case there was a false confession.[16]

Whether there is something else and whether the something else will seem important to trial jurors is heavily influenced by the fact that the jurors will see it through the special lens that the eyewitness's identification has provided. The wrongful conviction of Ronald Cotton was based on Jennifer Thompson's identification testimony, but in the Cotton case there was something else, too: There was, for example, the flashlight found under Cotton's bed. There was the foam lining of a shoe found in Cotton's house, which was "consistent" with foam fragments left at the scene of the rape. There was testimony that Cotton had "misbehaved" with white waitresses at the fish restaurant where he worked. There was the fact that Cotton's original account of his whereabouts could not be supported. None of these pieces of data was particularly sinister or inculpatory taken separately. Certainly, none of them independently proved that Cotton was a vicious serial rapist. Taken together in the transforming light of Jennifer's identification testimony, they all served to bury Cotton further under a mountain of "corroboration."

In fact, the Cotton case demonstrates that sometimes the more an innocent man thrashes around trying to free himself from an eyewitness mistake, the more tightly he entangles himself. The more Jennifer Thompson's identification was challenged, the more certain she seemed. The more alibi witnesses Moseley offered, the more guilty undertones the jurors heard. And for Ronald Cotton, even simply sitting still was no answer. After Jennifer Thompson's identification testimony, even Cotton's posture at the counsel table, seemed to at least one juror to prove his guilt. She told PBS:

> He had no change of emotions for eight days. He never changed his facial expression. This was extremely strong to me and, as time went by, I expected to see him react and he never did. And so he seemed more guilty and guiltier as time went by.[17]

You don't have to be a lawyer to imagine yourself in Ronald Cotton's place at the counsel table. Look nervous and you will seem guilty; look calm and you will seem guilty and callous. With a very small effort, any one of us can imagine turning to our lawyer and asking, "How do I look innocent to a jury that has heard an honest and convinced eyewitness say that I'm guilty?"

But perhaps only lawyers who have actually had that experience can really know what it is like to hear that question from an innocent client, and to recognize that you have no answer. Maybe only lawyers can put themselves in Philip Moseley's position, and imagine listening to that guilty verdict—recognize that "nothing is worse than defending somebody that you know in your gut is innocent and watch them go to jail. Nothing is worse for a lawyer than that."[18]

The feeling is intensified by the lawyers' knowledge that the trial jury's decision will be final, and will never be reviewed in any meaningful way. Although appeals can drag on for years, lawyers know—and most lay people do not—that the basic "right guy/wrong guy" decision made by the jurors in a case such as Ronald Cotton's or Gary Graham's will never be questioned by an appellate court. The appellate process reviews the legal decisions of the trial judges: decisions about the admissibility of evidence, or about jury instructions. The appellate process does not question the identifications of defendants made by a Jennifer Thompson or a Bernadine Skillern; the jury's decision to believe the witnesses is final. The fact is, handling an eyewitness case will cure any lawyer of Perry Mason fantasies once and for all.

The failure of cross-examination, closing argument—and all of the trial advocate's most venerated weapons—instilled a sense of desperation in defense lawyers. It goaded scattered members of the defense bar into action. They had no answers for their clients, but at least they could keep asking the questions. Eventually, as we will see in the next chapter, they resorted to an old weapon—offers of expert testimony—but applied it to a novel subject by trying to call research psychologists as witnesses before the jury. Calling an expert witness to testify is the lawyer's endemic reflex when some relevant piece of new information surfaces in another discipline. True, Munsterberg's disembowelment at the hands of Wigmore would not make this strategy look very promising, but few defense lawyers knew about Munsterberg. All they knew was that they were in trouble: Expert testimony about eyewitness fallibility was better than nothing.

The defense lawyers didn't always understand the science—in fact, they frequently lived down to the psychologists' image of lawyers as "bright people who don't like math." The psychologists who have dealt with many defense lawyers over the years tend to describe them in the terms you might use for a pack of St. Bernard puppies: endearing, exhausting, ultimately infuriating. "These lawyers," one psychologist observed, "are always asking you, 'Can't you just say *x*; can't you just say *y*?' when *x* and *y* are two things no one has ever even *thought* about testing."

In the long run, the scientists paid a price for being so fully identified with the defendant. Still, the defense lawyers are an important part of the story. The criminal defense lawyers' stubborn efforts to get expert psychologists in front of citizen juries held open the door that the legal system's officials were trying to shut once and for all on psychological findings about eyewitnesses.

CHAPTER FOUR

NOBODY LIKES A SMARTASS

Bob Buckhout Joins the Battle

THE PULL OF AN EYEWITNESS'S IDENTIFICATION IS felt long before the
jury is seated. At many forks in an investigative road, the power of the eyewitness draws investigators down one branch and away from others. Once the
fork has been passed, it is often difficult for investigators to retrace the trail, to
find their way back to the place where they turned, or even to remember that
they turned at all. In criminal investigations, time matters: Every day that
passes can benefit the criminal, and that is a fact that investigators never forget. A juror in an eyewitness case faces a difficult challenge evaluating the evidence. And the problems that a juror experiences in analyzing the facts
provided at trials are aggravated by the reality that there are usually other facts
that the jurors never get to see, because investigators have brushed past circumstantial evidence in their rush toward the eyewitness. These gaps are built
into the process.

Think what it must have been like to pursue the murderer of Dawn
Hamilton; think how important it must have seemed to catch him before he
killed again. Dawn Hamilton's death was described in the clinical language of
the Maryland Court of Special Appeals:

On July 25, 1984, police discovered the partially nude body of nine year old
Dawn Hamilton in a wooded area near Golden Ring Mall in eastern Baltimore County. The victim was found lying on her stomach with an eight inch

stick protruding from her vagina. Near the victim's head was found a large piece of concrete with a possible blood stain. The victim's skull was "fractured" and "depressed" and her scalp had "two tears" with a "very rough edge." The victim's neck had a "patterned abrasion." The opinion of the medical examiner, Dr. Dennis Smyth was that the death was a homicide and "was a result of blunt trauma to the head and strangulation."[1]

Before Dawn's body was even found, police searching the Baltimore County woods for the missing girl encountered a man named Richard Gray wandering among the trees. He wore green camouflage fatigues and carried a policeman's billy club. Gray directed Dawn's father to Dawn's underwear, which was hanging from a tree branch. Another pair of little girl's panties were found in the back of Gray's car, and there was a red spot that looked like blood on Gray's shirt. Gray appeared quite nervous, and vomited immediately after the search of his car. Before Dawn's body was found, Gray referred to her pocketbook and gestured around his left shoulder. When the body was discovered there was still a bag over Dawn's left shoulder. Gray's car was filled with rolled-up newspapers and Gray was very dirty, except for his hands, which had been meticulously cleaned. At a point when Gray could not have known that the body had been found, he told an investigator that he hoped "they get him," and that he hated to see people "abuse little children." Gray had a conviction for indecent exposure, and he had been arrested for burglary. A polygraph test was administered to Gray. He failed it.

Ten minutes away on the day of the murder, another man, David Rehill, made an unscheduled visit to the office of Dr. Gene Ostrom, the Director of the Eastern Regional Mental Health Center. Dr. Ostrom believed that Rehill resembled a composite drawing of a man seen near the scene of Dawn's murder, but more significantly in Dr. Ostrom's view, Rehill had wanted to talk about "a personal relationship" that he had with a "little girl." Beverly Raymond, a secretary at the Mental Health Center, believed that Rehill had fresh scratches on his face. Rehill had committed prior acts of violence, and had a history of alcohol and drug abuse. He had been a patient at the clinic for seven years, and Dr. Ostrom felt that Rehill was capable of the murder.[2]

Neither Richard Gray nor David Rehill was ever arrested or charged with the murder of Dawn Hamilton. The facts surrounding them were never fully developed. The point here is not that Gray or Rehill was certainly the murderer. After all, at least one of them *had* to be innocent, and as it turned out, both of them were. Twenty years after the murder, DNA found on Dawn's body was matched to an inmate who had never previously been suspected.

Still, what could possibly have turned investigators away from two such prom-ising leads?

The answer is simple: five eyewitnesses. The man who *was* charged was an ex-Marine named Kirk Bloodsworth, a waterman from Maryland's Eastern Shore. Bloodsworth was charged because he had been identified by five eye-witnesses as the man who had walked into the woods with Dawn Hamilton just before she disappeared. Once the police had placed their bet on Blood-sworth, followup on Gray and Rehill must have seemed to promise only dis-traction and confusion. Gray was never asked to stand in a lineup.

As in Ronald Cotton's case, there was also "something more" in the Bloodsworth investigation. Bloodsworth had told a friend that he had done "a terrible thing" around the time of the murder. In a police interview before the manner of Dawn's death had been publicly released, Bloodsworth had men-tioned (at least according to one detective) a "bloody rock."

Bloodsworth had explanations for these things. The "terrible thing," he explained, was breaking a promise to his wife. He thought she would never forgive him. The "bloody rock," according to Bloodsworth, referred to a rock which the police had planted on the interview room table (on the advice of FBI "profilers") in order to gauge Bloodsworth's reaction to it. Bloodsworth said he simply figured that the rock must be the weapon—why else would it be there? But the investigators, and then the jurors, saw these things through the lens that the eyewitness identifications provided. After Bloodsworth's first trial he was sentenced to death. When that conviction was reversed by the Mary-land Court of Appeals, Bloodsworth was tried and convicted again and sen-tenced to life in prison.

It is easy to see the jurors—and the investigators who discarded Richard Gray and David Rehill as serious suspects—asking themselves whether five eyewitnesses could have been *that* wrong. In fact, it is easy to put yourself in their places—viewing the autopsy photographs, listening to the testimony from Dawn's devastated family—and asking the same question.

But the five eyewitnesses *were* wrong: nine years later, DNA testing elimi-nated Kirk Bloodsworth as the source of the semen found on the Hamilton girl's underwear.

———————•◦•———————

As it happened, there was a witness waiting in the Baltimore County court-house hallway during Bloodsworth's trial who was eager to tell anyone who would listen that eyewitness mistakes happen all the time. The judge refused to allow him to testify. That ruling came as no surprise to the witness, Dr. Robert Buckhout, a professor of psychology at Brooklyn College and the creator of the Center for Responsive Psychology. For a decade before the Bloodsworth trial, Bob Buckhout, brandishing the fallen banner of Hugo Munsterberg, had conducted raids against the criminal justice system's complacent reliance on eyewitness testimony.

Buckhout was on an explicit mission to rescue Munsterberg's reputation and Munsterberg's insights from the Valley of Lost Things, but he had a temperament very different from his hero's. After Wigmore's attack, Munsterberg simply quit the field, retrieved his dignity, and went on to study vocational testing, leaving the legal system to go to Hell in its own way. Not Buckhout. Buckhout reacted to the snipings of judges and the sneers of prosecutors like the warhorse in the Book of Job, who "Mocketh at fear, and is not affrighted . . . smelleth the battle afar off, the thunder of the captains and the shouting" and "saieth among the trumpets, Ha, ha!" Buckhout enjoyed a fight.

Buckhout had an academic career before he had a forensic one, and he was quickly fascinated by eyewitness performance. As a young professor at Washington University in St. Louis, Buckhout conducted research that showed both his interest in the study of memory and an unconquerable impish streak that—along with much else—distinguished him from Professor Munsterberg. Buckhout, an enthusiastic jazz pianist, was, at least by legend, a one-time member of Woody Allen's Monday night pickup band at Michael's Pub in New York. It is hard to picture Munsterberg pitching in on the Louis Armstrong version of "Potato Head Blues." In one study, Buckhout dressed a student from head to toe in a black bag, and then sent him around to visit a number of classes. Later, Buckhout asked the students to describe the man in the bag:

> Most of their reports went far beyond the meager evidence: the bag-covered figure was said to be a black man, "a nut," a symbol of alienation and so on. Further tests showed that the descriptions were related to the needs and motives of the individual witness.[3]

The undertone of delight in Buckhout's account of these findings hints that mainstream academia might find him difficult to digest. So does the somewhat less-than-somber title he gave his report: "Through A Bag Darkly."

As it turned out, Washington University was not about to grant tenure for this sort of thing, and so Buckhout found himself teaching at California State University's Hayward campus as the tidal wave of late 1960s countercultural activism rolled up San Francisco Bay and met the counterforce led by Califor-

nia's new governor, Ronald Reagan, coming in the opposite direction. Buckhout found his Harry Orchard/Bill Heywood case in the murder trial of
Angela Davis—or it found him.

————————⋄•⋄•⋄————————

Like the Idaho trial of Big Bill Heywood, which catapulted Munsterberg into
the public eye, the murder-conspiracy trial of Angela Davis probed the deep
underlying fears of its era. Angela Davis, a young African American academic,
was a committed Marxist, and perfectly cast for her role as a heroine of the
culture wars. Davis was extremely bright, hyperarticulate, and fearlessly combative. Besides, her looks were striking—cameras loved her. She had been in
the news before her trial when California politicians, fed up with the radical
fervor at the University of California's Berkeley campus, decided to insert
themselves into the faculty hiring process. When the university's U.C.L.A.
campus offered Angela Davis, who was a member of the American Communist
Party, an appointment in the Philosophy department, Governor Ronald Reagan (among others) recognized a heaven-sent opportunity.[4]

The Civil Rights movement of the 1950s and 1960s, dominated by the
church-bred generation of the Rev. Martin Luther King and infused with the
language and spirit of the New Testament, had proven difficult for conservative forces to rebut. But by the early 1970s, glowering young radicals in the
Black Panther Party had begun to appear on posters posing with automatic
weapons. Angela Davis's commitment to Marxist analysis of the racial situation and her use of Marxist vocabulary, provided California conservatives with
the means to do what years of effort by J. Edgar Hoover had never quite succeeded in doing: now they could tie the discomfort caused by the Black Power
and Civil Rights movements to the alien ideology of the Cold War's "Evil Em-
pire," the Soviet Union. If you focused on Angela Davis, you could oppose
calls for racial readjustments without opposing the New Testament or turning
fire hoses and police dogs loose on children and old people. Reagan and his
appointees to the California Board of Regents rescinded Davis's appointment,
and took the issue away from UCLA. Litigation followed; so did rounds of
press conferences and op-ed pieces. If placing the focus on Davis served Governor Reagan's purposes, sustaining the focus on Davis also served the purposes of the moribund American Communist Party, and so a symbiotic period
of stylized public combat ensued.

Angela Davis, meanwhile, had fallen in love with George Jackson, the
charismatic leader of a group of black inmates in California's Soledad Prison.

At Soledad chaos reigned: black inmates were allegedly killed by guards, and white guards were allegedly killed by black inmates. But in Soledad George Jackson adopted an analysis of the key role of the prisons in sustaining a system of racial oppression, which he published in a vehement, eloquent book, titled *Soledad Brother*. Jackson became a celebrity. Soledad prisoners—and black California prisoners in general—began to see themselves as revolutionaries. The prison authorities took a different view. "Not everybody who says they are revolutionaries are, some are just plain hoodlums," one told the *San Francisco Chronicle*.[5] Angela Davis, then 26, and already a public figure, joined the Soledad struggle and met George Jackson. She was thunderstruck, and wrote him about the impact of the meeting:

> "I was not seeking love when I walked into a Salinas courtroom on Friday, May 8, 1970 . . . But one thing remains to be said—my feelings dictate neither illusionary hopes nor intolerable despair. My love—your love— reinforces my fighting instincts, it tells me to go to war."[6]

Trying to keep a lid on their prison system, the authorities transferred George Jackson to San Quentin prison, across the bay from San Francisco, and monitored his mail and visits.

On August 7, 1970, a black San Quentin inmate, James McClain, was on trial in a courtroom in Marin County's spectacular Frank Lloyd Wright–designed Civic Center for stabbing a San Quentin guard. Three other inmates were present in holding cells, waiting to testify for the defense that McClain could not have done the stabbing. A fifth inmate, Ruchell Magee, was testifying on the witness stand when a tall young African American in the gallery pulled a small automatic pistol and took control of the courtroom. He was Jonathan Jackson, George Jackson's 17-year-old brother.

Jonathan produced a carbine from under his coat, distributed other weapons to the freed prisoners, and selected hostages. The inmates taped a sawed-off shotgun to the neck of the trial judge and wired the hostages together. The group was led out to a yellow rental van. The hostages were put in the back; Jonathan Jackson took the wheel, and the van was driven toward an improvised roadblock set up by San Quentin guards. Gunfire erupted. Jonathan Jackson was killed; James McClain was killed. In the rear of the van there was a bloody shambles: A third inmate lay across the body of the trial judge, whose face had been blown away by a shotgun blast. The trial prosecutor, his spinal cord severed by a bullet, lay beside them. And when the rear of the van was searched, police found a series of revolutionary pamphlets and six books, three in French. Two of the books had Angela Davis's name inscribed in them. There was also a slip of paper with a telephone number written on it in Jonathan Jackson's wallet.[7]

Investigation disclosed that Angela Davis purchased the four guns Jonathan Jackson brought to the courtroom, and that the telephone number in Jackson's wallet corresponded to a telephone booth in the San Francisco airport, near where Angela Davis had purchased a ticket and taken a flight to Los Angeles three hours after the shootings. Davis was on the run. When Davis was finally arrested, the prosecutors released the inculpatory evidence to the media, and also revealed that they had seized Davis's love letters to George Jackson. The trial of Angela Davis promised the media a heady mixture of bloody violence, revolutionary rhetoric, and Elizabeth Barrett Browning—it was a story from opera, not from the crime blotter.

By the time of Davis's trial, the drama had darkened even further. George Jackson himself was dead, shot during a spectacular escape attempt at San Quentin. The prosecution alleged that Davis' passion for George Jackson had motivated her to conspire with Jonathan Jackson to plan the Marin courthouse hostage-taking. The goal of the kidnapping was to force a hostage exchange, with George Jackson's release (along with other "Soledad Brothers") as its ultimate product. But to persuade the jurors of this, the prosecutors needed to tie Davis to a series of visits Jonathan Jackson, accompanied by an unidentified woman, had made to his brother in the days immediately before the shootout. On the afternoon following one of these visits, Angela Davis had purchased the shotgun that killed the judge. The San Quentin visitors' log showed that Jonathan Jackson had signed the name of "Diane Robinson" for the woman who accompanied him on that day.

The prosecutors had to show that "Diane Robinson" was really Angela Davis. They could only make that crucial connection through the testimony of eyewitnesses.

The prosecutors had a parade of eyewitnesses to work with. Some of these witnesses—for example, San Quentin guards, who might be considered biased, or a San Quentin inmate serving life sentences for sex offenses, who might be doubted on a whole host of grounds—were easy enough for the defense to attack. But others were very difficult for the defense to deal with: specifically, the owner and employees of a service station close to the Marin County Civic Center where Jonathan Jackson and a woman they identified as Angela Davis had rented the yellow van on the day before the courtroom uprising. Like Jennifer Thompson, those witnesses were not biased. Like the witnesses in the Kirk Bloodsworth trial, their numbers gave their testimony weight. They had an extensive opportunity to observe Jonathan Jackson's companion, and they were all agreed: The woman with Jonathan was Angela Davis.

After the prosecution rested its case, the defense activated a novel weapon: Professor Robert Buckhout. He gave a masterful performance.

Buckhout attacked the videotape version of eyewitness memory at length, explaining that memory was actually a delicate three-stage process of perception, storage, and recall, which was vulnerable at every stage. He said that the typical witness overestimates the length of viewing time, and that if the witnessed events seem insignificant at the time they are seen, that insignificance will degrade memory. He said that a witness's expectations distort eyewitness memory, referring to a famous experiment in which the subjects were shown a drawing of a white man and a black man in which the white man held a razor, but where the subjects' memory moved the razor to the black man's hand. He said that social pressures inherent in the environment of a lineup or a photographic identification can lead a witness to identify a suspect in order to please authority figures. He dissected the suggestive effect of the group of photographs that the investigators had shown to a key witness: a group in which three of five of the spread of photographs shown to the witness were pictures of Angela Davis. He explained how color blindness would have made portions of one witness's account literally impossible.

On its surface, Buckhout's testimony could have been Munsterberg's own, but the surface obscures two fundamental differences. The first of these differences is Buckhout's ingrained left-American populism. Hugo Munsterberg had nothing against officials; in fact, Munsterberg might have championed the appointment of a Lord High Psychologist to evaluate and report on eyewitness testimony. In contrast, Buckhout, described by one former student as "the classic Old Lefty," was eager to have citizen jurors decide, and he welcomed the opportunity to explain the science to the jurors.

Buckhout wrung any pedagogical edge he could think of from his time on the witness stand in the Davis trial. He used graphs and slides; he brought in a tachistoscope, a device that showed the jurors how a psychologist would measure intervals when studying a witness's accuracy in reporting time. The foreperson of the Davis jury later remembered that the courtroom audience (including the attorneys and the defendant, as well as the jury) was quiet and interested. This lecture was not one that a student would sleep through, she said. The jurors thought that the material was informative and the manner in which it was presented was interesting.[8] This may have been because one consequence of Buckhout's populism was that he had treated the jurors with respect.

That was just as well: The jurors didn't consider themselves to be as igno-
rant as all that. They didn't regard Buckhout's information as a bolt from the
blue; according to the foreperson, the jurors had all been aware of some of the
difficulties involved in judging the accuracy of eyewitness identification. Buckhout hadn't rammed his findings down the jurors' throats, and the foreperson
didn't believe he had even brought out so much that was new. But she did
think that Buckhout reminded the jurors of things they might have forgotten,
and he put their discomfort into words.[9]

Buckhout's attitude toward prosecutors was less forebearing. Buckhout
believed that any government official who was responsible for prosecutions
based on uncorroborated eyewitness testimony and who did not take the trouble to learn the lessons that science taught about eyewitness unreliability must
be held morally accountable. After all, he used to argue, even Mosaic law had
proscribed the use of a single eyewitness as decisive evidence. On this point,
Buckhout gave no quarter. When the prosecutor in the Davis trial asked
whether Buckhout's testimony was not biased by Buckhout's desire to "be a
part of history," Buckhout responded, "Mr. Harris, if I started examining the
motives of anyone, I could redirect that question."[10] Buckhout was at war with
official ignorance, and he let the officials know it. He meant his attacks—and
the prosecutors took his attacks—personally.

And Buckhout, unlike Munsterberg, was fighting his battle in real courtrooms instead of on the paper field of scholarly strife. He was involved in
real cases, with real crimes, real defendants, real lives—and real careers—at
stake. After the Davis trial, one of the defense lawyers told reporter Reginald
Major that:

> I felt that Buckhout's testimony would be very helpful in attacking the eye
> witness identification by showing it as unreliable. It gave the jury a way of de-
> ciding with us, without saying that [the prosecutor's] witnesses were lying.
> When Buckhout testified I saw something come over that jury. I told every-
> body, "We've got it all, we've just won this case, this jury is completely turned
> around.[11]

Angela Davis was acquitted in a blaze of publicity. In retrospect it seems likely
that the acquittal owed more to the *zeitgeist* than to Buckhout's intervention.
But whether Buckhout had affected the final verdict or not, he had certainly
affected the course of the deliberations. When the deliberating jury reached
the key eyewitness encounter at the service station, Buckhout's testimony gave
them a framework. Their foreperson wrote that as the jurors discussed the

eyewitness testimony they recognized that the filling station episode was an al-most classic example of the possible contribution of the factors that can influ-ence eyewitness identification as enumerated by Dr. Buckhout. Insignificance, conditioning, desire to follow the leader, desire to be part of history, conform-ity, personal bias, need for approval, filling in details, and passing on a the-ory—the jurors discussed all of these factors in evaluating the testimony of the eyewitnesses.[12]

It was as though Buckhout's testimony had given the jurors permission to question the conclusions of honest eyewitnesses. After the Davis trial, the word about Buckhout's testimony got around. More and more lawyers began to believe that in eyewitness cases the defense finally had a friend, and the prosecutors an enemy: Bob Buckhout.

———————————

By 1976, Buckhout had testified 22 times about eyewitness error. ("Over the shrill objections of the opposing side," he noted cheerfully.[13]) He had been ex-cluded from testifying about 30 times. He informally advised lawyers without testifying on hundreds of other cases. Throughout the late 1970s and early 1980s beleaguered defense lawyers, who were agonizingly aware of the weak-nesses of the great engine of cross-examination, besieged Buckhout with des-perate phone calls. More often than not, Buckhout answered the summons, and, more often than not, the judge refused to allow him to testify. The lesson Buckhout took from these experiences provided the title of an essay he pub-lished in his journal, *Social Action and the Law:* "Nobody Likes a Smartass: Ex-pert Testimony By Psychologists." The title "Smartass" was one that Buckhout gloried in, and the fact that the legal system didn't love him didn't bother Buck-hout one bit. That was the nature of things. "Any psychologist who goes into court expecting to be loved will be disappointed," he wrote.[14] And so, while he continued to go to court, Buckhout did not rely exclusively on the courts' own processes for the legal system's education. He seized opportunities to build pressure on the court system in the court of public opinion.

The media were happy to cooperate. The interest in science and its mean-ing in the social world was, after all, a mass phenomenon. Munsterberg's wild celebrity ride had proven that 70 years earlier. Besides, there was a man-bites-dog aspect to many mistaken eyewitness cases, which the media found irre-sistible. So, Buckhout helped out with the case of Father Pagano, a Roman Catholic priest who was mistakenly identified by a host of witnesses as the po-lite, well-spoken "Gentleman Bandit" in a series of armed robberies. It was widely publicized. He worked on the misidentification case of Lenell Geter and Anthony Williams in Dallas, and explained the phenomenon of eyewitness error to CBS's *60 Minutes* when that program covered the Geter case. Buckhout had a flair for finding "teaching moments" in unlikely places: He knew how to choose his targets. For example, he found a case in which a butcher who had been robbed claimed that he could identify one of his own pork chops. It wasn't the Angela Davis case, or the Father Pagano case, but it made a good story—one more platform from which to explain the workings of eyewitness memory.

And, like Munsterberg before him, Buckhout was happy to intervene directly in popular media. Impatient with the glacial pace of peer-reviewed academic publications, he more or less stopped producing traditional scholarly work and aimed at the more general audience of *Scientific American*, where, in 1974, his reader-friendly tour of the horizon in his article, "Eyewitness Testimony," presented general readers (and desperate defense lawyers) with a confident attack on the "video tape" version of memory, and a comprehensive summary of the dangers that lurk in the perception, retention, and retrieval phases of eyewitness performance.[15] He published his more polemical pieces in *Social Action And The Law*, the in-house journal of his Center for Responsive Psychology ($10.00 per year; subscriptions free to all inmates) and, in a kind of apotheosis of the researcher-as-agitator mode, Buckhout helped a New York City television station to stage a mugging on the nightly news:

> The mugging film showed a young woman walking in a hallway, with a man wearing a hat, leather jacket and sneakers luring in a doorway, Suddenly the man runs, grabs the victim's purse, knocks her down and runs face forward into the camera—a total elapsed time of 12 seconds. Then the announcer presented a lineup of six men who approximated the description of the attacker. He told the viewers that the suspect might be—or might not be in the lineup. Then a special number was flashed on the screen for viewers to call in and register their choice as to which person in the lineup (numbered 1 thru 6) if anyone was the real attacker.

Buckhout and his students manned the telephones, and they recorded 2,145 caller responses. Buckhout reported the results in a *Social Action and the Law* article, "Nearly 2,000 Witnesses Can Be Wrong," in tones that can only be described as gleeful:

> [O]nly 14.1 % of our viewer-witnesses made a correct positive identification of the perpetrator. These results were the same as if the witnesses were

merely guessing since on the basis of chance (1 out of 7 including the "not in lineup" choice) we would expect only 14.3 % identifications of any lineup participant . . . there were only 10.4 % correct.[16]

Buckhout's televised demonstration of eyewitness fallibility would have delighted Munsterberg; it was an echo of the classroom demonstrations Munsterberg had relied on himself. But there are two crucial features of this sort of exercise that should not be overlooked.

The first feature provided a teaching benefit. The "demonstration" model that governed Munsterberg's experiments and Buckhout's televised mugging presentation had a definite appeal to lawyers because it offered realism—or at least what lawyers think of as realism. The demonstrations weren't real crimes, but they weren't white rats being zapped in laboratory mazes either. In fact, they used exactly the method that Wigmore himself used in his law school classroom to demonstrate the shakiness of witness memory to his students. Lawyers could see that Buckhout's staged televised mugging was the sort of thing that might happen in the real world and generate a real case. (Although you might want to adjust the scores marginally to account for the effect of a televised image, for example.)

The second point turned out to be more important. The demonstrations certainly got their audience's attention, but they were remarkably uninformative. What these efforts "demonstrated" was merely that many eyewitnesses make mistakes. They showed, in effect, that there were many Jennifer Thompsons. They offered next to no information on the more salient questions: "*Why* do eyewitnesses make mistakes?" and "*Which* eyewitnesses have made mistakes?"

The only lesson offered by the Munsterberg/Buckhout school of demonstration experiments was that we ought to be more skeptical of eyewitness opinion. The more persuasive this message became, the more frightening the problem it presented for the legal system. A radical rise in jury skepticism about eyewitness identifications would result in fewer wrongful convictions. It would also result in more wrongful acquittals.

In the hysterical atmosphere of riot-torn American cities in the 1970s, the specter of wrongful acquittals was bound to cause a reaction.

———◆———

Some aspects of the 1960s and early 1970s can look like wacky *agitprop* theater today, but that is not the way that things looked to many people at the time. It was by no means obvious in 1972 that the Black Panther party was already dissolving in dissension, or that Eldridge Cleaver would end up marketing cod pieces as a male fashion accessory. A good part of the population saw the anti–Vietnam War movement and the urban race riots of the 1960s on their televisions and diagnosed impending anarchy. Richard Nixon seized on the moment to weld anxieties about race and crime to policies ostensibly directed at law and order, and by doing so, he engineered a tectonic shift in the American political landscape that endures to this day. Psychology was not insulated from these forces. A number of respected psychologists felt that Buckhout had hijacked the discipline and put it at the service of the forces of disorder. They argued that Buckhout's position was at best unscientific, and at worst an unethical exploitation of the prestige of science. This was something beyond the dispute over "productive" and "unproductive" science; there was enough opposition to Buckhout's activities to fuel an entire conference at Johns Hopkins that debated the ethics of expert psychological testimony about eyewitnesses.[17]

Characteristically, Buckhout took a degree of wry satisfaction from his critics' attacks. They proved that he had become a thorn in the side of officialdom. "If eyewitness testimony experts were routinely asked to testify before the jury by the prosecution," he suggested happily, "I doubt that a 'Conference On Ethics In Testimony' would ever have taken place." And the attacks proved Buckhout's kinship with Munsterberg. He wrote that:

> Hugo Munsterberg was himself an object of scorn among the functionalists of his day . . . he further alienated his peers by going public, a trait which made him a kind of Carl Sagan of his day. No matter how completely such a public figure has paid his dues to the profession, much is written (and even more spoken) of his or her personal motivations to fame, power, and money.[18]

There may have been a grain of truth in Buckhout's belief that personal hostility influenced his critics. In a sense, he had earned it. Buckhout had charm and charisma, but he also had a well-developed capacity for getting under people's skins in an exquisitely annoying way. His companion in those days and co-author, Katherine Ellison, tells the story of a period during which she volunteered to drive Buckhout (by then nearly blind from the results of a brain tumor) to do his weekly grocery shopping—her only condition being that she did not want to deal with weekend traffic.

"Every Saturday morning, like clockwork," Ellison remembers, "I'd get a call from Bob saying that there was no food in the house for Stan, his cat, who was his best friend." The implication of these calls was that Ellison would be

completely within her rights if she chose to allow Stan the cat to die of starva-
tion, but that Buckhout (out of an exaggerated sense of fairness and because he
held Ellison in high esteem) would offer Ellison a chance to do the right thing.

Some traces of his talent to annoy can be glimpsed in the tone of the
scholarly attacks on Buckhout. He certainly managed to whip his adversaries
into a rage. In responding to critics from within his discipline Buckhout conveyed (with an infuriating air of tolerance) the sunny conviction that his critics
couldn't really help being fussy, dried-up ivory tower types, deaf to the call of
justice, any more than he himself could help being the citizen of a larger,
richer, more equitable world. The title he gave his rejoinder to his critics,
"Personal Values And Expert Testimony," for example, plainly implied that
this was a controversy in which one side had personal values, and the other un-
happily did not. Then, to compound the critics' annoyance, Buckhout would
select and comment blandly on the most over-the-top responses he had provoked. Buckhout was a counterpuncher of some ability. "Pachella's remarks
would seem, at first blush, to be out of character for a scholarly conference,"
he wrote about one critic, "But I am glad that he came forth as a spokesman
for the alleged undercurrent."[19]

Still, Buckhout's critics could not be shrugged off quite so easily. Two of
his principal adversaries within psychology, Howard Egeth and Michael Mc-
Closkey of Johns Hopkins University, were highly respected experimental
psychologists. They published their doubts about Buckhout's project early on,
and they organized the conference at Johns Hopkins devoted to weighing the
appropriateness of psychology's intervention in the legal arena.[20] The conference turned into something of an academic free-for-all. Egeth, McCloskey,
and their allies had a straightforward goal. They were going to do to Buckhout
and his early followers what Wigmore did to Munsterberg: consign them to
their laboratories until further notice.

Before and after the Johns Hopkins conference, in a series of articles
stretching over several years, the anti-Buckhout forces pressed a number of issues. Some of these were peripheral. The critics felt uncomfortable, for example, with the role of expert witnesses in general. Part of the discomfort with
expert testimony had its source in the position occupied by any scientist from
any field when he or she falls into the lawyers' clutches. McCloskey, Egeth,
and their colleague, Judith McKenna, observe that:

> "[W]henever an experimental psychologist gives expert testimony, there is
> the possibility that the testimony will affect the jury in some unanticipated
> and undesirable way. Jurors may misinterpret, overgeneralize, or misapply the

information presented by the psychologist, and so may come to unwarranted conclusions. Further concerns expressed in rules of evidence and appellate decisions regarding expert testimony include the possibility that expert testimony may confuse the issues in a case, or that the expert's opinions may be accorded undue weight by the jury.[21]

This is true enough as far as it goes, but it applies equally to expert witnesses from any field of expertise. Substitute "appraiser" or "neurologist" in the passage and it would still be just as true. Besides, questions of "undue weight" and "confusion" are problems for legal procedure, not psychology. Another complaint specific to the legal arena, the worry that psychology as a discipline would suffer grievous harm from any "battle of the experts" between disagreeing psychologists, could be rather easily met by the observation that battles of medical experts are endemic in civil litigation, and that medicine yet survives, its prestige intact. It's easy to imagine William James and Hugo Munsterberg dismissing these worries as too dainty to be taken seriously, and Buckhout invoked them in doing just that.

But the McCloskey-Egeth critique was based on more than amateur lawyering and professorial faintheartedness; their analysis cut to the core of Buckhout's project. The argued that, "The available evidence fails to demonstrate the general utility of expert psychological testimony and in fact does not even rule out the possibility that such testimony has detrimental effects."[22] They did not—but could have—taken for their text Buckhout's own proposed contributions to the Angela Davis and Kirk Bloodsworth cases. For McCloskey and Egeth, Buckhout's efforts to discredit eyewitness evidence in those two prosecutions typified everything that was wrong with injecting Buckhout's version of psychology into legal disputes.

————•◆•————

When Kirk Bloodsworth's trial judge queried Buckhout about what he proposed to tell the jurors, he answered:

I don't have a particularly overall general condemnation of the eyewitnesses at issue. That has never been a factor at all. My belief and sort of underlying theory is that eyewitnesses are really confronted with a difficult situation, and when the circumstances add up to a very difficult challenge to the memory system, these are the things that can happen to various parts of their testimony and various parts of their identification.[23]

McCloskey and Egeth pointed out that there was a good deal less here than it might at first seem: that, in fact, there was nothing here at all, and that Buckhout was misusing the prestige of psychology to cover the vacuum. McCloskey and Egeth represented a minority viewpoint, but they were not cranks; they could see genuine holes in Buckhout's approach.

Psychology, McCloskey and Egeth argued, just didn't work in the way that Buckhout's testimony implied. For example, Buckhout's bland reference to "eyewitnesses" glossed over the fact that nothing in the research allowed anyone to comment on the capacities or experiences of any *individual* eyewitness. Which "eyewitnesses" did all of this refer to? No effort had been made to refine, on demographic or other grounds, the translation between group norms and individual experiences. As Robert Pachella, a University of Michigan psychologist, pointed out at the Johns Hopkins conference, psychologists' inferences about eyewitness memory are "based on mean values, from averaging over groups of individuals. A completely different kind of experiment needs to be carried out in order to answer questions about how individuals, as opposed to mean values, behave under various experimental conditions."[24] There was no mechanism for generalizing between experimental results and individual events.

This observation was only one of several which undermined the two pillars supporting Buckhout's argument for expert testimony: the claim that jurors "overbelieved" eyewitness testimony, and the claim that jurors could not "discriminate" between correct and mistaken eyewitnesses. If psychologists couldn't predict in any scientific way an individual experience, and couldn't know the base rate of innocent defendants actually convicted after trials, McCloskey and Egeth argued, how in the world could they say that they knew that jurors "overbelieved" eyewitness testimony when they acted on their own common sense? How could any psychologist say that jurors couldn't tell correct from mistaken witnesses when there was no individualizing research?

Besides, Buckhout's adversaries were able to marshal experimental results that complicated the picture, which Buckhout was inclined to simplify in his lectures for jurors. They pointed out, for example, experiments in which jurors *did* acquit the innocent, and other experiments in which many of the jurors *did* understand that an eyewitness might focus on a weapon at the expense of focusing on a face.

But the backbone of McCloskey and Egeth's attack on psychological testimony on eyewitness identification—and the concern which animated it—was their reminder that the sort of testimony proposed by Buckhout to the judge in the Bloodsworth trial (but rejected) was not only overstated but dangerous: It could positively damage the cause of justice.

Even if it is true that jurors have difficulty discriminating between accurate and mistaken eyewitnesses, McCloskey and Egeth said, psychologists have no help to offer. To begin with, there were problems with the "ecological validity" of the experiments: Does the experience of a college student in a laboratory experiment reasonably approximate that of a victim of a street crime? How do we know? Even if you believe that a laboratory experiment can tell you something about what happens during a street crime, it only tells you what probably happens in some percentage of street crimes. If the result of the experiment occurs 80 percent of the time, (any many results were far less striking) the experiment still can't tell you whether this case is one of the 80 or one of the 20.[25] The only way to be certain to avoid convicting the innocent 20 percent is to acquit *everybody*, the guilty along with the innocent. Compromising and convicting only 90 percent in these circumstances would result in still convicting some innocent people while freeing some guilty ones. The issue was not the rate, but the *distribution* of mistaken "hits" and mistaken "misses."

Buckhout's critics pointed out that Buckhout and his successors had chosen to ignore the fact that "[E]xpert psychological testimony represents a 'beacon of hope' for defendants who are guilty as well as for those who are innocent."[26] By increasing juror skepticism about all eyewitnesses, Buckhout and his fellow experts were arbitrarily inflating the criteria that jurors would apply to correct witnesses to a point at which wrongful *acquittals* would be guaranteed, and all to prevent the phantom problem of wrongful convictions which, two of the critics found (after some extrapolation), only happened to "1 person every three years" even in a giant state like California.[27]

Buckhout had bypassed the basic utilitarian calculation of whether the greater good was served by more acquittals created by skepticism about eyewitness performance. The McCloskey-Egeth camp refused to accept as a matter of faith the proposition that it was better that ten guilty men go free than that one innocent man be convicted. They saw freeing the guilty as a genuine and important threat to public safety. Not only that, they suspected that Buckhout's version of the ratio might be that it was better that a hundred (or thousand) guilty men go free than that one innocent man be convicted. Buckhout in this view was guilty of trendy romantic posturing, which implicated psychology in giving a windfall to *all* of the accused, guilty or not, when everyone knew that most of the accused were very guilty indeed. It was time, Buckhout's critics argued, to "put this venerable area of research to rest three-quarters of a century after Munsterberg."[28]

———•◦•◦•———

That didn't quite happen. The McCloskey-Egeth onslaught armed judges and prosecutors with a pointed critique of Buckhout, but the controversy over eye-witness reliability survived in the courts. It survived partly because Buckhout, unlike Munsterberg, had developed an avid market for his knowledge within the legal community itself. The defense lawyers just wouldn't go away. If the legal system didn't need psychology, Buckhout could argue, why was his tele-phone ringing off the hook? Who knew better than the lawyers what the legal system needed?

And the issue survived because Buckhout agreed immediately with the charges that the state of the existing research was imperfect. In fact, Buckhout went further and argued that the research would *never* be perfect, or at least as perfect as McCloskey and Egeth demanded. No university would ever allow you to scare a human subject to death in hopes of staging an "ecologically valid" assessment of the effects of stress on eyewitnesses. For Buckhout, that was no excuse for refusing to contribute the best of what *was* available:

> As psychologists our main contribution has been and should continue to be the publication of solid empirical research findings which will aid in the un-derstanding of how any observer perceives, remembers and later recognizes the details of complex events in which he found himself a witness. . . . But, the battle over the admissibility of experts on eyewitness testimony is but a mi-crocosmic version of the battle psychologists have always had in establishing their credibility as scientists who meddle in the most basic of human affairs. While I think psychologists have a great deal to contribute to certain trial proceedings, I don't expect the battle of empirical data vs. common sense to be won in the courtroom. *We are smartasses*; while not too many people in the courts may like us, they will respect us if we are willing to step up and say the things which ought to be said within the limits of our discipline.[29]

Buckhout recognized from the beginning that he could not complete his mission by himself, and his achievement was to capture the imagination of a new generation of psychologists. His Center for Responsive Psychology be-came a place where students liked to hang out, where new ideas and new ex-periments were generated. Later, some younger psychologists would denigrate Buckhout as a "sloppy" scientist, but that criticism misses the point. Buckhout was certainly impatient with the meticulous processes of academic peer review, but that was not because he didn't know good research when he saw it. He defined himself as an encourager, a talent-spotter, a megaphone. He was extremely creative in inventing new hypotheses, extremely ingenious in finding ways to test them. He was generous with his praise of younger researchers, and he was never, never dull. He performed this self-appointed role so vigorously that the same volume of *Law and Human Behavior* that recounted the Johns Hopkins conference on Buckhout's efforts carried a plaintive article, "The Law Does Not Live By Eyewitness Testimony Alone," protesting the hold that the issue had established over young researchers.[30] Elizabeth Loftus and Garry Wells—two psychologists who will play crucial roles later in the story that follows—were both recipients of Buckhout's support. He didn't seem to be the kind of patriarch who resented his successors.

Buckhout's end was a sad one. A brain tumor was diagnosed in 1986, and it progressed steadily during the few years that remained to him. Katherine Ellison and the host of friends he had won watched sadly as his personality changed, and he gradually withdrew from the people who would have been eager to help him. He was, for whatever reason, unwilling to accept the emotional support they would have offered. His teaching suffered, and Brooklyn College began to look quietly for ways to ease him into retirement. He gained over 100 pounds. His eyesight was affected, and eventually he was virtually blind.

Through all of this, Buckhout continued to advise lawyers and to testify in court—presenting, toward the end, the poignant spectacle of an expert on eyewitness testimony groping his way toward the witness stand grasping a white cane. By then the public focus of the expert testimony debate had largely shifted to Elizabeth Loftus, whose research Buckhout had championed. That didn't seem to bother him. Buckhout was too worldly a character to be afflicted by messianic ambitions at that point, but his politics were not fashionable radical chic; they were bone-deep. He thought that people—particularly poor people—were being screwed by careless fact-finding, based on a convenient, superstitious faith in eyewitness reliability. He wanted to do what he could about it. "It kept him going," Katherine Ellison remembers.

In the autumn of 1990 Buckhout suffered a devastating seizure, and he was taken unconscious to a New Jersey hospital. He lay in the emergency room for three days because no bed was available. During the night he fell from his bed and lay unnoticed on the floor, his swollen stomach pressing against his diaphragm and inhibiting his respiration until anoxia set in. He lingered in a coma for a few weeks, but there was really no hope, and he died without regaining consciousness. At Buckhout's memorial service the lesson was taken from the Book of Amos, the same verse that is inscribed on Martin Luther King, Jr.'s memorial in Atlanta: "Let justice roll down like waters; and righteousness like a mighty stream."

At the time of his death Buckhout was due in court the following week. He didn't make it, but by then younger psychologists—including Loftus, Gary Wells, Stephen Penrod, and a dozen others—were regularly making court appearances around the country. They would face ferocious counterattacks from prosecutors, trial judges, and appellate courts, but the science of eyewitness memory was alive in the courts. It was alive in the laboratories, too: Within five years of Buckhout's death, Steven Penrod and Brian Cutler reported that there were over 2,000 published scientific studies of eyewitness memory.[31]

CHAPTER FIVE

THE BOOK ON THE STREET

The Cops, the Courts, and the Eyewitnesses

IN THE 1970S, WHILE BUCKHOUT WAS BUSY prodding the courts, the District of Columbia Metropolitan Police received a grant from the Law Enforcement Assistance Administration to construct a state-of-the-art room in which to conduct identification procedures. This room had special lighting, sophisticated photographic equipment, and a raised stage behind one-way glass. Several nights each week suspects and "fillers" were arrayed in a line behind this one-way glass and displayed to eyewitnesses, who were brought to the room individually and asked whether they recognized anyone in the line. The room was filled with cops, defense lawyers, and prosecutors. The lineups were scheduled for 7:00 P.M., just long enough after the close of the court day to allow for a generous cocktail hour, symptoms of which were usually visible here and there among the participants. The atmosphere generated those antic moments criminal justice system lifers love: the raw material for their "war stories." One night, for example, there was a demented sex offender whose non-stop obscene mouthing—visible but not audible to the audience on the other side of the one-way glass—gradually reduced his fellow lineup members to paroxysms of helpless pantomime laughter and forced the cancellation of the whole list.

Each suspect had a lawyer, and if his own lawyer didn't show up, "stand-in" counsel was appointed to represent him. The lawyers for the suspects were allowed to take turns moving their clients to preferred spots in the line before the witnesses entered the room and attempted identifications. The lawyers felt they had to do *something*, but their only idea was to make their clients as inconspicuous as possible, and by the time the last lawyer for the last suspect had rearranged things for the last time ("Please move Number 6 to stand between Number 10 and Number 3"), it seemed that a bizarre game of three card monte was being played, with humans in place of cards.

Still, facile amusement with these surreal evenings can be carried too far. Several times each Lineup Night, a witness (often a victim) stepped to the microphone and identified a man whom the police had placed in the lineup.

At that moment someone's life was changed forever.

If the victim identified a man who was not the police suspect, the chances were that the victim would never see anyone prosecuted. The authorities couldn't convict the original suspect after the victim said, in effect, "That's not him." It would seem almost impossible to convict even a new and *guilty* suspect in the face of all of the information that led the police to put the original candidate in the lineup in the first place. That evidence would have to be shared with the guilty defendant's lawyers, who could be counted on to destroy the witness with it. It might be easiest to see this problem from a juror's perspective. Even if Jennifer Thompson had not identified Cotton in the in-person lineup, would you as a juror convict Bobby Poole beyond a reasonable doubt after Poole's lawyer used Jennifer's pre-lineup, photographic identifications of Ronald Cotton, *and* the flashlight found in Cotton's house, *and* the piece of shoe found in Cotton's room, *and* Cotton's false alibi against Jennifer to defend Poole at Poole's trial?

If the victim *did* identify the suspect the police had chosen, then someone, usually someone guilty (but often someone innocent), stood in Ronald Cotton's shoes: faced with the harrowing uncertainty of an eyewitness trial.

Although it did not seem that way, Lineup Nights were carefully thought-out rituals. Each step in the process was described in detail in the General Orders of the Metropolitan Police: The lineups were done "by the book." There are 13,000 police and sheriff's departments in the United States, and all of them handle their identification procedures "by the book." Detective Mike Gauldin, for example, was operating "by the book" when he interviewed Jennifer Thompson, composed the photographic array from which she first tentatively identified Ronald Cotton, and arranged the lineup in which she identified Cotton at the police station.

Later in this story we will meet three veteran cops—Captain Don Mauro of the Los Angeles County Sheriff's Homicide Unit, Sergeant Paul Carroll of the Chicago Police and Detective Lieutenant Ken Patenaude of Northampton,

Massachusetts. Their departments were different in many ways: Los Angeles County is a sprawling jurisdiction with a chronic and bloody gang problem; Northampton, Massachusetts is a leafy college town in the Berkshires. But all three departments have a "book" on identification procedures and practices, and their books have two things in common. First, Mauro, Carroll, Patenaude, and every other cop in this country has spent their entire investigative careers trying to follow these books: The books haven't changed in any serious way for 30 years. Second, the police department books all had a common ancestor: They were all designed to meet requirements set out by the United States Supreme Court beginning with the pivotal 1967 case of *United States v. Wade*.[1] The fact that Lineup Nights around the country bore a strong family resemblance to each other could be traced to the Warren court's revolution in criminal procedure.

In the *Wade* case, the legal system did get around to trying to do something about eyewitness error, even if it was not until 50 years after Munsterberg raised the issue. When the lawyers got around to doing something, though, they did it in their own way.

————•◆•————

Until the 1960s local police practices were a local concern. It wasn't until the Warren court entered the fray that anything that might be called a "federalized" standard of criminal justice came into being.

The rights of criminal defendants are guaranteed by the first ten amendments to the United States Constitution, the Bill of Rights drafted by the original framers. They constrain the powers of the federal government. The legal basis for applying those rights—for example, the right to be free from unreasonable searches and seizures—in *state* criminal prosecutions is supplied by the Fourteenth Amendment. The Fourteenth Amendment, enacted after the Civil War largely to protect ex-slaves in the Old Confederacy, guarantees "due process of law" to all persons. The law reviews bulge with arguments over whether the Warren Court's interventions in the criminal process really comprised a "revolution." For now, it is enough to say that to whatever extent the Warren Court's tenure *was* revolutionary, the revolution was effected by defining certain of the original Bill of Rights' protections as indispensable to "due process of law," which all of the states are required to provide.

The Warren court provoked particular outrage at two points. First, the court expanded the reach of "due process of law" from the courtroom (e.g., the right to cross-examine) into the police station, and onto the street (e.g., the ban on unreasonable "stop and frisk" practices). Due process now protected not only "defendants" but also "suspects," and it controlled not only judges and prosecutors, but also the police. Second, the court determined that the "due process of law" which governed state and local practice contained not only certain rights, but also a mandatory remedy for any violation of those rights: the Warren court's "exclusionary rule." If the police obtained evidence by investigative practices that violated the constitutional guarantee of due process, then that evidence must be excluded from the trial. In *Miranda v. Arizona*, for example, the Court held that "due process of law" requires that suspects in custody must be given warnings about their rights in order to dissipate the intrinsically coercive atmosphere of all custodial interrogations. Any local cop who interrogated a suspect without giving the *Miranda* warnings violated the federal Constitution, and using a confession obtained without warnings in his trial deprived the defendant of due process of law. These were the rulings that led to anguished cries that the Warren court was "handcuffing" the police.[2]

The Warren Court recognized that certain police practices—coerced confessions were one clear example—turned subsequent trials into empty ceremonies. Some evidence was so damning that the jury wouldn't really care how you got it. It didn't take long for the court to put eyewitness identifications on its list of dangerous moments. The bar had enough experience with wrongful convictions to know that the great engine of cross-examination was no perfect answer, and the publication in 1965 of lawyer Patrick Wall's catalogue of miscarriages of justice, *Eyewitness Identification In Criminal Cases*, had crystallized that perception.[3] Two years later, in the *Wade* case, the Supreme Court announced that a pretrial lineup was such a critical stage of a criminal prosecution that defendants must have lawyers present at lineups, which take place after formal adversary proceedings have begun.

Like *Miranda*, *Wade* aimed for deterrence. If eyewitness mistakes were difficult to catch by looking back at the facts during a trial, maybe the best strategy would be to try to *prevent* the mistakes in the first place. The police would avoid unconstitutional behaviors and follow acceptable practices because they did not want to lose evidence. The *Wade* rule was preventive in two distinct ways. The presence of defense lawyers would deter the intentional rigging of lineups that generated unreliable identification evidence in the first place. If that didn't work, judges would prevent wrongful convictions by excluding evidence obtained by staging rigged lineups.

Justice Brennan, who wrote the *Wade* opinion, claimed that *Wade* is not designed to curb "police procedures intentionally designed to prejudice an accused" but at "dangers inherent in eyewitness identification and the suggestibility inherent in the context of pretrial identification."[4]

The *Wade* opinion as a whole indicates that Justice Brennan does not mean what he says; police misconduct is what *Wade* is all about. The "context of pretrial identification," after all, is entirely under police control. Every example Brennan gives of something that the new *Wade* rule will prevent is "a police procedure intentionally designed to prejudice an accused." For example, Brennan lists suspects whom the police pointed out to witnesses, or dressed in distinctive clothes, or displayed in one-on-one confrontations, or subjected to suggestive manipulation of one kind or another. Besides, the remedy that *Wade* proposes—the presence of defense counsel, who will observe and later be able to reconstruct any police chicanery at trial—does not really solve any problem *except* police chicanery. If counsel is present and counsel's presence does not deter police misconduct, then maybe the defense will be in a slightly improved position for portraying the misconduct at trial, but the *Wade* court's real hope is that counsel's presence will persuade the police to exercise a degree of self-censorship. They won't cheat if they think they'll get caught. Still, while counsel's presence might be a deterrent, by definition it can only deter the police from doing things that the police already know are wrong.

The *Wade* case tries to attack the problems highlighted by Munsterberg and Buckhout without admitting that either professor ever lived. The most striking feature of the *Wade* opinion is Justice Brennan's steadfast determination that the law can define the problem and design the solution without any reference to the psychology of eyewitness identification, or indeed to any resource other than the long experience and bracing common sense of lawyers. According to *Wade*, the legal system can eliminate many problematic identifications before they ever reach a jury, by altering unreliable police behavior. Although the *Wade* opinion goes to some lengths to suggest appropriate police procedures and to list examples from around the world, all of this learning is *legal*: it comes from lawyers' memoirs, anecdotes, and the reports of legal commissions.

Justice Brennan provided living proof of Munsterberg's charge that the lawyers complacently believe that their "legal instinct and commonsense supplies all that is necessary and somewhat more." Oddly enough, the only voice in the *Wade* opinion that we know for certain was well-read in the psychology of eyewitness testimony was that of a renowned legal eminence who had once proposed an elaborate plan for conducting reliable tests of eyewitness memory. Justice Brennan quoted this effort with approval:

At least 100 talking films would be prepared of men from various occupations, races, etc. Each would be photographed in a number of stock movements, with and without hat and coat, and would read aloud a standard passage. The suspect would be filmed in the same manner. Some 25 of the films would be shown in succession in a special projection room in which each witness would be provided an electric button which would activate a board backstage when pressed to indicate that the witness had identified a given person. Provision would be made for the degree of hesitancy in the identification to be indicated by the number of presses.

The author of this ambitious scheme was no one other than John Henry Wigmore, writing in 1937.[5] Thirty years after his evisceration of Munsterberg, Wigmore had still been doggedly working on the problem and pursuing his "friendly alliance" by developing this Rube Goldberg plan for avoiding misidentifications.

But the Supreme Court did not reveal that Wigmore's Rube Goldberg arrangement was founded on a study of psychological research. If it was a good idea, it was because it was *Wigmore's* idea, not because the venerated Wigmore had taken the time to study some psychology. The *Wade* opinion even suggested that it would be a good idea for Congress to give some thought to legislative enactment of such a plan. If standardized procedures could be instituted, the argument went, counsel's presence at lineups might be far less important—might even be dispensable.

The only Congressional activity that *Wade* provoked was the Omnibus Crime Control and Safe Streets Act, which tried to overrule *Wade* and said that *every* eyewitness identification should be admitted at trial no matter what the circumstances. This law was so blatantly unconstitutional that it was simply ignored ever after, although it has never been repealed.

—•◦•—

The term "criminal justice system" is an indispensable shortcut, but it can be a misleading one. If the criminal justice system is a system at all, it is an organic, not a mechanical system—an ecosystem like a swamp or an estuary, not an arrangement of gears and switches. It is an environment where unintended consequences often badly outnumber the intended ones.

The impact of the *Wade* ruling was in the unintended consequences tradition: In response to *Wade*, police departments around the country simply stopped doing in-person, "live" lineups.

The most convenient way to deal with the pretrial identification problem after *Wade* was to use photographic lineups: usually arrays of six police "mug shots." These photographic procedures, colloquially known as "six packs," quickly established dominance: 80 percent of initial identification procedures these days are photographic identifications. Under the cases following *Wade*, you didn't need to arrange for a defense lawyer if the lineup was held before formal charges were filed, and you didn't need a lawyer unless there was an actual face-to-face confrontation between the suspect and the witness.

Talk to veteran police officers about the "book" they operate under, and it is pretty clear that this tidal shift toward photographic procedures was motivated by convenience, not a Machiavellian desire to eliminate the defense lawyer from the identification process.

Sgt. Paul Carroll is ebullient, humorous, profane, and streetwise—everything a central casting functionary would demand from an actor playing a Chicago cop and more. The "more" in Carroll's case is a very good brain and an alertness to the processes around him undimmed by 30 years on the street. Carroll has used plenty of "six packs" to do plenty of photographic identifications, but he actually prefers "live" face-to-face lineups even though that means that there will be defense counsel present. Carroll's "live" lineup preference doesn't stem from the same sources as the ACLU's. "In live line-ups," Carroll explains, "no matter how fair you make them, the perp will always do *something* to give himself away." Besides, a two-year-old mugshot of the perp may be harder for a victim to identify than the perp himself, who will still look pretty much the way he looked last week at the time of the robbery.

Carroll ran "live" line-ups whenever he could. In many larger jurisdictions—in New York City and Don Mauro's Los Angeles County, for example—it is relatively easy to put together a live lineup. Each night's haul of arrests is big enough to populate several reasonably fair lineups; the big city legal aid or public defender offices will usually have counsel around to allow compliance with *Wade*. In a smaller place, like Ken Patenaude's Northampton, Massachusetts, it might take a very long time to come up with, say, six 5' 4" Latino youths, a defense lawyer, and a victim all on the same night in order to present a lineup that complied with *Wade*.

As James Zagel, a federal judge in Chicago and the former head of the Illinois State Police remembers it, *Wade* was not a big deal; everybody came up with a new procedure and tried to follow it. The police had managed to adapt to the far-reaching implications of the *Miranda* warnings, and they could cope with this, too. When the Supreme Court held in a later case that although the presence of defense lawyers was required at lineups the lawyers could not actually *do* anything except watch, the *Wade* case was quickly seen by the police as no real problem at all.

Besides, the stately lineup minuet that the Supreme Court envisioned in *Wade* was tangential to the life of the cop on the street. Post-arraignment line-ups had to be choreographed, and they took time. Time is a commodity that police investigators do not have.

The first interactions between the police and the eyewitness take place in an atmosphere of emergency. A 911 call comes in, or a squad car is flagged down on the street. Everyone involved knows that the criminal is still at large, and that every moment of delay raises the criminal's chances of getting away. The 911 dispatcher tries to get a description, or the beat cop does a quick pre-liminary interview. Jennifer Thompson's hysterical arrival at a neighbor's house after she escaped from her rapist, for example, generated a 911 call to the police, and the police desperately tried to gather enough of a description of the rapist to generate a "look-out" broadcast. When Mike Gauldin arrived at the emergency room to interview Jennifer for the first time, he had to deal with a second victim, a half-dozen other witnesses who had to be interviewed, two crime scenes to supervise, a barrage of radio communications to field, and most importantly, a serial rapist still on the loose. He also had lots of reports to write. You rarely see this on TV, but the police *always* have lots of reports to write, and very little time to write them in.

By the time the formal legal system got around to addressing the informal eyewitness encounters that dominate actual police experience, the member-ship of the Supreme Court had changed, and two Nixon appointees, Harry Blackmun and Warren Burger, had tipped the balance of the court. It was Blackmun, not Brennan, who wrote the majority opinion in *Manson v. Braith-waite*, in 1977, five years after Buckhout's testimony in the Angela Davis trial.[6] *Manson* is the case that has set the parameters of police identification practice in our era.

For better or worse, the *Manson* opinion does not require burdening read-ers with much arcane legal analysis. Blackmun's goal was evident: he wanted to take the handcuffs off the police. The police could use any identification pro-cedure that was not "so unnecessarily suggestive as to give rise to a substantial likelihood of an irreparable misidentification." The number of qualifiers is nearly comical. According to Blackmun, you could get away with any identifi-cation, even a suggestive one, so long as it was not "unnecessarily" suggestive, and with a procedure that created the potential for a misidentification so long as it did not create a "substantial likelihood" of a misidentification, and of a misidentification which was "irreparable." Even if the identification was ques-tionable under this forgiving standard, the question would be resolved by ask-ing whether the identification was "reliable" based on all of the circumstances of the encounter. Unless the defense could somehow show that the identification was "unreliable," the jury would hear about it, and evaluating it would be the jury's business.

The good news for the police in the *Manson* opinion was that Blackmun signaled that the police were supposed to win, and that the era of Warren court interference was dead and gone. The new majority of the Supreme Court did not believe that the due process clause required much of anything in the way of "best practices" from the police when it came to on-the-scene showups in which a single suspect is displayed to witnesses, photographic identifications, or eyewitness interviews.

The bad news for the police was that Blackmun gave them no guidance at all regarding how to handle pre-arraignment or photographic identifications. *Wade*, for all of its nuisance value, had at least done that: given the police something to build procedures and training around. According to Blackmun, the police were on their own so long as they didn't do anything grotesquely unfair. From the police perspective, the rule in *Manson v. Braithwaite* was "Be Fair!" This was a rule that was hard to argue with, but not much help in organizing day-to-day life.

Besides, the police knew that the courts might decide at some later point that you had done something wrong, and that the courts couldn't be trusted to tell you in advance what that "something" might be. So, in an uncoordinated, ad hoc fashion, 13,000 police departments set about developing their own approaches to how to handle the informal eyewitness identifications that were not governed by *Wade*. They drafted "Field Investigation Manuals" or "Standard Operating Procedures." For example, most—but not all—departments developed time limits on how long after a crime they would use single-suspect, one-on-one "show-up" procedures. You could bring one guy in handcuffs back to the victim an hour after the robbery, but not on the next day. Most departments—but not all—tried to impose some sense that lineup members should resemble each other. Very few police departments after *Wade* and *Manson* would follow the practice of the Minnesota detective who staged a lineup of five blondes and a lone African American suspect because it was "a fair cross-section of the community." Each police department cobbled together a "book" that cautioned against doing anything that was recognizably "unreliable." If it was a particularly careful department, or one that sought advice from the local district attorney, anything that the defense lawyer might later plausibly *claim* was unreliable was warned against, too.

The police did this partly to avoid legal ambushes, of course, but they also did it because while the police dislike having their decisions second-guessed by outside authorities, they don't dislike having their own procedures. This isn't just because of the quasi-military organization of police departments.

When you are out on the blazing street in East Los Angeles, or the freezing street in Chicago, with conflicting radio calls crackling for your attention, paramedics frantically treating the victim, survivors and bystanders weeping, the lieutenant back at the precinct yelling for his report, and the prosecutors screaming about what you've done with their witnesses, a procedure is a comforting thing to have. A procedure tells you what to do; it helps you to train the new guys. If you follow it, a procedure insulates you from criticism (and lawsuits) later. Jeremy Travis, the Director of the National Institute of Justice in the Clinton administration and a former deputy commissioner of the New York Police Department, makes the point that even *Miranda* warnings came to be seen that way: something easy enough to do once you were in the habit and had produced a couple of forms. "Most cops," Travis observes, "will tell you that they even *like Miranda*." Producing procedures and following them, even if it's only because "that's what the Chief wants" is something the police are good at.

These "books" of procedures were applied in thousands of cases. They were also applied for a number of different purposes. Courts and lawyers write about showups, lineups, and photo arrays as if their only purpose was to generate evidence that will be admissible at trial. In fact, generating evidence is only one purpose of these procedures; they serve several other goals which are primarily investigatory. When Mike Gauldin put Ronald Cotton in the photographic array, for example, he certainly regarded Cotton as a suspect and hoped for a "hit," but Gauldin was also prepared to have Cotton ruled out. Gauldin knew that there would still be a chance to generate and pursue other leads. This "ruling out" in the medical sense of the phrase—eliminating one plausible alternative so that you can focus on those that remain—is an important function in any investigation. Public relations can play a role, too. Sometimes, as Paul Carroll remembers, you have a police artist draw a picture of the assailant or compile an "Identikit" portrait just so "The Chief can release something to the media to show that we're doing something." The train of events which led to five Maryland eyewitnesses wrongly identifying Kirk Bloodsworth started exactly that way. Sometimes you show a witness a thick album of mug shots because you just can't think of anything else to do: you need some traction from somewhere.

The Burger court framed the amorphous "reliability" test of *Manson v. Braithwaite* as a refreshing return to common sense. But it glossed over the fact that what looked "reliable" for "ruling out" or hypothesis-generating purposes at the early stages of an investigation takes on an alarmingly different look when people's lives depended on its reliability in court.

———◦•◦•——

Justice Blackmun was careful to guard against the possibility that trial judges, faced with the distinction between street and courtroom reliability, would seize the opportunity to return to the bad old days of the Warren Court and second-guess the police about investigative decisions. He laid out a five-part test to govern the judges who must decide after the fact whether an identification was so "unreliable" that it should be excluded from a defendant's trial. The new Nixonian majority on the Supreme Court did not want to "handcuff" the police, but handcuffing trial judges was another matter. In Nixonian cosmology, "activist" liberal trial judges who lived to hamstring the police were a major cause of our woes. Handcuffing *them* was God's work.

The *Manson* test Justice Blackmun instituted has five components, all borrowed from an earlier opinion. Judges should examine: (1) the witness's opportunity to view the criminal, (2) the witness's degree of attention, (3) the accuracy of the prior description, (4) the witness's level of subjective certainty, and (5) the time lapse between the crime and the identification.[7] Every one of these subtests is an aspect of eyewitness memory that psychologists back to Munsterberg would have been eager to discuss. Blackmun would have no part of them. The Supreme Court continued its embargo of psychological knowledge.

The effect of a witness' degree of attention on the witness' accuracy, for example, was something that psychologists had studied fairly extensively. They had uncovered indications that attention was more complicated than it seemed, that when a weapon was present witnesses tended to devote their attention to the weapon instead of the assailant's face. Psychologists had studied the relationship between details in description and accuracy as well, and that also turned out to be more complicated than Blackmun seemed to think. Nor had the psychologists kept their findings secret.

During the interval between *Wade* (decided in 1968) and *Manson* (decided in 1977) two social scientists with the American Bar Foundation, Felice Levine and June Tapp, published a careful law review article showing how far psychology had come in investigating the whole range of issues involved in eyewitness reliability during the period since Munsterberg's first assault.[8] Justice Marshall's dissenting opinion dropped a citation to Levine and Tapp's article in a footnote, but that was the only indication in the *Manson* opinions that showed that someone in the legal system—Marshall's law clerks—knew of the article's existence. There was no indication that anyone in the legal system had actually *read* what Levine and Tapp had to say.

There are passages in the *Manson* opinion where it would seem that Justice Blackmun was deliberately attacking Munsterberg—if it weren't so perfectly clear that Blackmun had never heard of Munsterberg in the first place. Munsterberg, to take one example that will resurface later in this story, had explicitly warned that a witness's confidence in his or her own identification was no indicator that the witness was accurate. In the *Manson* opinion, Blackmun, without citation to any authority legal or otherwise, flatly repudiates that piece of science. Eyewitness confidence, according to Blackmun, is a key measure that trial judges must use in evaluating whether the identification is "reliable." The more confident the witness, according to Blackmun, the more reliable the identification. Witnesses like Jennifer Thompson identifying Ronald Cotton, or Bernadine Skillern identifying Gary Graham, who said that they were "as sure as I can be" essentially closed the question. They were "reliable." Their identifications would be admitted at trial.

———— •◦• ————

Manson v. Braithwaite told lower court judges to keep their hands off identification issues: Whether an identification was accurate or not was an issue for the police in the first instance, for the jurors in the last resort. The courts could play a role in deterring unlawful searches and seizures or coerced confessions by excluding evidence, but they would play no meaningful role in steering the police toward more reliable identification practices.

Some flagrantly bad identification practices must have been deterred by the *Manson v. Braithwaite* regime, but from the police perspective suffering judicial punishment after *Manson* seemed as likely as being struck by lightning. *Manson's* deterrent impact was on the order of "Don't play golf during thunderstorms." It provided guidance for infrequent and extreme situations; it provided no motivation for reexamining or reshaping everyday routines. *Manson* left Paul Carroll in Chicago, Don Mauro in Los Angeles, and Ken Patenaude in Northampton with their native desire to "be fair"; the occasional less scrupulous or overzealous investigator was left with "don't get caught." Neither of these motivations was going to change a department's procedures.

For all practical purposes, the judges had taken themselves out of the prevention business when it came to eyewitness error. The Supreme Court had let the judges off the hook. The psychology of eyewitness memory was something that the judges would be forced to confront only in the process of look-ing backward to catch an error after it occurred.

And it was still possible that they wouldn't have to confront the science of memory from that perspective either, if there were some way to hold off Buck-hout, the defense lawyers, and their desperate offers of expert testimony. In the late 1970s it looked as if things would turn out that way.

The prosecutors had regrouped after the first wave of experts, and they had begun to contest the admission of expert testimony on eyewitness psy-chology. The prosecutors had McCloskey, Egeth, and a cadre of allies on their side in this battle, and it was a battle the prosecutors didn't even have to win on its merits; a tie would do.

The legal standard for the admissibility of novel scientific evidence was that any novel science had to be "generally accepted" in the scientific commu-nity. The prosecutors could very reasonably ask how anyone could claim this stuff was "generally accepted" when respected experimental psychologists were calling conferences to contest whether testimony about it was even *ethical?*[9]

For all of Wigmore's encouragement of a friendly alliance and all of Buck-hout's agitation for attention to experimental demonstrations of eyewitness fallibility, no state appellate court had criticized a judge for excluding expert testimony on the science of eyewitness memory, and many appellate courts had upheld the exclusion of experts. There was every reason to think that trial court judges—worried, like McCloskey and Egeth, that this new science would extend a "beacon of hope" to legions of guilty defendants who might otherwise just plead guilty and get it over with—would follow the appellate courts' lead.

CHAPTER SIX

WE TOOK LOFTUS SERIOUSLY

Elizabeth Loftus and the Science of Memory

ON THE DAY AFTER THANKSGIVING, 1987, seven-year-old Billy Chambers wandered away from his parents in a Las Vegas casino, and a man grabbed him. It was a few minutes, but only a few minutes, before Billy's parents missed him and began to comb the casino and adjacent hotel.[1]

A casino patron reported that he had seen a young boy, looking "sort of dumbfounded," being held by the wrist and led down a hallway by a man whom the patron took to be the boy's father. For the next two days a desperate Las Vegas police force tried to find Billy Chambers. The FBI was called in. Five eyewitnesses reported having seen Billy. Four eyewitnesses reported seeing him with a man. The descriptions of the kidnapper varied widely. Two of the eyewitnesses separately identified different hotel employees, but both of the employees had unshakeable alibis: neither could have been the kidnapper. For a month, frantic efforts to find Billy and his kidnapper continued. Finally, on December 30, a hotel caretaker saw a pair of children's eyeglasses near a trailer about 200 yards from the hotel. Billy Chambers' body was found hidden under the trailer. He had been suffocated.

The Las Vegas police retrieved a computer printout of all the guests at the hotel on the day of the kidnapping. They quickly focused on guests who had stayed on the second floor, the floor where Billy and the unidentified man had been seen, and they secured drivers' license photographs of the males. Only one guest, Howard Haupt, bore any resemblance to the descriptions given by the eyewitnesses. Haupt's room had been quite close to the area where an adult male had been seen pulling Billy down the hallway.

Haupt submitted voluntarily to being photographed and fingerprinted, and the police compiled a "six-pack" of photographs that included Haupt. One witness said Haupt was "closest" but that witness was not certain. The witness had seen so many "mugshots," he said, that "It's starting to get foggy." Other witnesses—a blackjack dealer, the bystander who had seen the man with Billy, and another woman—ultimately chose Haupt's photograph. Haupt was arrested and charged with first degree murder.

It was a strong eyewitness case, but Haupt insisted he was innocent, and Haupt's lawyer, Steve Stein, put Haupt through three polygraph tests. Haupt passed every one. Now Stein was skeptical about the state's case. Although there were five eyewitnesses who made identifications, and they all expressed great confidence, every one of the eyewitnesses had originally picked out someone else. It was only after a series of police interviews and staged encounters with Haupt that they finally identified him as the murderer.

Still, Stein knew that just because he didn't believe in the state's case against Haupt that didn't mean he could beat it at trial. Stein was haunted by the Perry Mason nightmare. So he called a young University of Washington psychology professor, Elizabeth Loftus, whose articles on eyewitness vulnerability in popular journals such as *Psychology Today* had been widely circulated among desperate defense lawyers. She was busy, but she was also a sucker for a sad story, and she agreed to take a look.

What Loftus found, and what she told the jury at Haupt's trial, was that during the delay between the kidnapping and their identifications:

> all of the eyewitnesses were exposed to a number of sources of postevent information that could have affected their original memory of the man and the boy. They studied artist sketches, they were shown numerous photos, mug shots, and photo lineups, and they were exposed to extensive television and newspaper coverage of the kidnapping and murder. The original memory, decimated by the passage of time had become increasingly vulnerable to these postevent information sources.[2]

Loftus noted that witnesses's confidence in their identifications had increased; that their descriptions of the kidnapper had changed over time to resemble Haupt; that they had been exposed to photographs of Haupt before they made in-person identifications; that they had seen but *missed* Haupt in the earliest procedures. All of this supported a narrative consistent with the innocence of Howard Haupt. True, there were five eyewitnesses, but all of them had experienced things that Loftus believed might have changed their memories. Loftus could not prove that the eyewitnesses were definitely wrong; but she could argue on the basis of her research that they were not definitely *right*.

Over fierce prosecution objections, the trial judge allowed Loftus to testify, and throughout fierce prosecution cross-examination she stuck to her findings. The memories of the witnesses and the witnesses's confidence in their memories, she said, could have been changed by things they learned during the course of the police investigation, and without the witnesses realizing that a change had occurred.

The first vote of the jury was nine for acquittal, two for conviction, one uncertain. Then, it was ten for innocence and two for guilt. Finally, after 3 days and 20 hours of deliberation, the jurors returned a verdict: "Not Guilty." Haupt threw his arms around his lawyer; Billy's parents sobbed in the front row.

Later Haupt's lawyer talked with the jurors and asked them about the impact of the expert testimony.

"We took Loftus very seriously," they said.

It was beginning to dawn on prosecutors and judges that if jurors were going to take Loftus and her science seriously enough to acquit people like Haupt in the face of testimony from multiple eyewitnesses, then the officials had better begin to take her seriously themselves.

———————•·◆·•———————

Readers of this sort of book have to be wary of documentary filmmaker Ken Burns's syndrome: the tendency to tell the complex story of the Civil War, or baseball, or jazz, through the lives of a few great figures. This technique avoids drowning readers in a Homeric catalogue of scientist's names, but at the price of overlooking the accomplishments of some, inflating the reputations of others. After all, science is a collective enterprise, which generally advances incrementally, step-by-step and experiment-by-experiment, not by claps of thunder and shouts of "Eureka!!" Still, if anyone deserves the Ken Burns treatment in the history of psychology's effort to make itself heard in the criminal justice system it is Elizabeth Loftus. St. Paul famously described faith as "the evidence of things not seen." Loftus showed empirically that eyewitness evidence was sometimes exactly that—that Jennifer Thompson and other eyewitnesses were honestly giving "evidence of things not seen," and that for the legal system to believe eyewitnesses uncritically was an exercise in faith, not reason.

Elizabeth Loftus has been a public figure for 30 years, and it can be hard to remember that there was a time when failing to take her seriously was even an option. These days she is a polarizing figure as well as a public one. She is taken so seriously in some quarters that she has received the William James Award of the American Psychological Association, so seriously in others that she has received death threats for stubbornly asserting that there is no proof that "recovered memories" of childhood sexual abuse are not sometimes "false memories." Anyone with a passing interest in the psychology of everyday life can probably remember seeing Loftus on Oprah, or Larry King, or Court TV. She has received a deluge of honors. She has been elected to the American Academy of Arts and Sciences and designated one of the 100 most important psychologists of the twentieth century. Her curriculum vitae is a 34-page list of accomplishments that rivals Munsterberg's or Wigmore's. Like Munsterberg and Wigmore, Loftus combines a genuine scholarly eminence with a magnetic attraction to controversy.

Although everyone takes Elizabeth Loftus seriously today—some people as a heroine, others as a menace—in the 1970s there were prosecutors who didn't see her that way. They could have called Loftus by her titles, "Dr." or "Professor, " or by the nickname her friends and family used, "Beth," but prosecutors discussing her testimony liked to talk about "Lizzy Loftus," sometimes "Dizzy Lizzy Loftus." The implication was that what we confronted here was just another lovable, California-bred ditz. Individual prosecutors who actually believed this portrait would discover at their cost that it was radically mistaken, but it seemed plausible at the time for a number of reasons.

One reason was the endemic sexism of the criminal justice system in the 1970s. The criminal courts were still a largely all-male world, and "girls" were not expected to be taken seriously. Buckhout, who had spotted Loftus's potential early, seemed a familiar enough sort of character in this environment. But Buckhout was big, imposing, combative. Loftus was young, pretty, even sexy, and far from communicating adversary challenge, she radiated an overwhelming friendliness from behind her heavy-framed glasses. This was an era when no one had quite decided what garb professional women were supposed to wear in court: the choices ranged from peasant dresses to severe navy suits accented with mock bow ties, and Loftus tried the whole range. The effect knocked the system slightly off balance, more so than had Buckhout. For all of Buckhout's populism there was always something in his tone of Knowledge speaking to Ignorance. Beth Loftus had lots of information to impart, but she always imparted it as if it were just a tremendously interesting piece of gossip that she had overheard only a few minutes ago and completely by accident. She may have spent her life teaching but she presented herself more as a fellow learner than as an authority. She seemed eager to share, not to preach.

And Loftus presented an unfamiliar problem to the criminal justice system in part because she expressed almost too neatly the distinctive moral upbringing of girls that Carol Gilligan posited in her *In A Different Voice*. Munsterberg was driven into controversy with the criminal justice system in order to win his profession its rightful share of respect, and Buckhout made war in the courts in order to vindicate the rights of minority defendants. Loftus was animated less by concern for legal rights than by a deep and self-renewing reservoir of empathy for people who were falsely accused, their families, and the lawyers who have to defend them. Few people in the courts had seen anything quite like her: a dedicated and meticulous social scientist who led with—and was often led by—her heart.

Elizabeth Fishman was born in Los Angeles in 1944, and grew into a self-described typical boy-crazy teenager. But when she was 14, her mother, who had been treated for depression, was found drowned in a swimming pool in circumstances that were never fully explained. Her father remarried, and her step-mother seemed to "Beth" and her brothers to favor her own children. Loftus started to study mathematics partly because it was something she could talk to her distant and chilly father about, but she quickly showed an enormous aptitude for the field. In college at UCLA she discovered psychology, and she continued on to graduate study in psychology at Stanford. The discipline was a new love, and while she was at Stanford she found another, Geoffrey Loftus, who was also studying psychology there. The two young graduate students married, and Beth received her Ph.D. from Stanford in 1970.[3]

Geoff and Beth Loftus ended up together on the faculty of the University of Washington, and they became something of a golden couple: a pair that dispelled the atmosphere of white coats and lab rats which had hung over experimental psychology. He was as handsome as a movie star, and rode a motorcycle; she was pretty and convivial. She kept a picture of herself in her office, posed beside Geoff's motorcycle in the ribbed stockings which were for a moment the height of late 1960s style. The whole effect was attractive; one article called them "the sexiest academics around."[4] They were both ambitious, highly intelligent, and nimble speakers. And they were both careful and creative scientists, making interesting discoveries in a field—the study of memory—with a proven fascination for the general public. Neither Beth nor Geoff Loftus seemed driven by any Munsterberg-like frenzy for publicity, but like many other psychologists of that period, both were moved by an influential presidential address by Dr. George Miller, the president of the American Psychological Association. It was the duty of psychologists, Miller had argued, "to give Psychology away," to make the psychologists' knowledge available to the community at large. It was more or less in that spirit that Beth Loftus published in the December 1974 issue of *Psychology Today* an article, "Reconstructing Memory: The Incredible Eyewitness," which led to the flood of desperate letters from lawyers and inmates that enmeshed her in the issue that was to consume her for the next 20 years.[5]

Lots of inmates write lots of letters, and lots of them protest their innocence. Veteran lawyers reflexively treat these letters with skepticism. The reflex they triggered in Beth Loftus was different: Her reflex was to empathize with and act on the feelings of the letter writer.

Anyone—not just prisoners, but *anyone*—could mobilize Loftus's instinct to listen and sympathize. The salesman in the next seat on the plane, the guy who fixed the phone, the graduate student in a different field, all of them found a friendly and sympathetic audience. This sympathy could extend to adversaries as well as friends.

Once, Loftus spoke on a panel at a continuing legal education program in Chicago. The format was "point-counterpoint" and her interlocutor was a woman prosecutor from the Southwest. Beth and Geoff Loftus had just divorced, and everyone involved with the program knew that this break with the man whom Loftus openly described as the love of her life had left Loftus in a fragile state. The prosecutor launched an attack that in its length, tone, and gratuitous jeering references to Geoff Loftus earned a place in the Churl's Hall of Fame. The onslaught continued for so long that the time allotted to the third, "neutral" member of the panel was exhausted by it, and the audience (of prosecutors and defenders both) sat gaping like the dumbstruck theater crowd witnessing the debut of "Springtime For Hitler" in *The Producers*. That night, at the faculty dinner, other faculty members lined up to speak with Loftus and express their sympathy and outrage. Loftus didn't want either; she had spoken with her assailant.

"The poor woman," she said. "Did you know that her doctor-husband has left her after thirteen years for a younger woman, and without any notice. It is so awful for her. And her poor daughter. I gave her some names of people who can help." The two became friends. When Michael McCloskey, the Johns Hopkins professor who had joined in attacking her science and (at least by implication) her ethics needed references for promotion and tenure panels, Loftus enthusiastically supplied them.

She could feel the pain of crime victims and their families, too. It is impossible to read her account in *Witness for the Defense* of the death of Billy Chambers and the sight of his mother and father sobbing in the courtroom without recognizing that Loftus is one of those people who actually proceed by asking themselves, "How would *I* feel if that were me?" When she was asked to testify in an Israeli trial on behalf of accused concentration camp guard "Ivan the Terrible," she refused: not because she thought her eyewitness memory evidence was irrelevant, but simply because she thought her testimony would cause unbearable pain in the survivors who listened.[6]

Still, the people explicitly asking Loftus for help were defendants, not victims, and their letters were irresistible. When she had been a student member of the disciplinary committee as an undergraduate at UCLA, she had been known as "second chance Fishman"—she just couldn't stand the idea of someone who was innocent being railroaded. She described the impact of their pleas this way:

> To understand why I entered this arena and why I now continue to battle against a growing horde of scalpel wielding opponents, one only needs to examine the foot-high stack of letters I've received over the years. . . . While each of these letters nags at me long after I have answered it, I know intellectually that I must keep in mind that many convicted prisoners are guilty but maintain that they are innocent. . . . Yet some convicted prisoners are in fact innocent. . . . How many are there? . . . It seems like a natural place to think about whether psychology might play some useful role, and if so, to give some psychology away.[7]

She started to provide expert testimony because she couldn't *not* give expert testimony. Usually she did it for expenses. Calls from desperate lawyers kept coming in, and the lawyers became one more set of people to be empathized with and to be "given" psychology. Before long, Loftus was not only testifying all over the country, but lecturing to defense lawyers all over the country as well. She had always had energy, and she had always worked hard, but now she had become a workaholic fueled by "Helper's High." The schedule was creating tension in her marriage: it was more likely that you would reach her in The Admiral's Club at O'Hare Airport than at home. Partly to try to spread her findings on a wholesale basis rather than in individual lectures 50 lawyers at a time, she published her findings in a successful general audience book, *Eyewitness Testimony*, in 1979. That step backfired: It only accelerated the demands on her time. Now the media wanted to hear from her, too, and after every media appearance there was a whole new flood of phone calls from lawyers and letters from inmates. Periodically she would resolve to cut back, but then another letter would arrive: "Dear Professor Loftus, My husband has been sentenced to fifteen years for a crime he did not commit . . ."

Throughout all of this, and even during bitter adversarial legal proceedings, Loftus's generosity and friendliness were unshakeable. This misled some people, who took her for a pushover. In fact, she was not prepared to be abused. The administrators of continuing legal education programs where she had lectured for free were amazed when she kept after them for months to get a few dollars cab fare reimbursed. And prosecutors who had been assured by their colleagues that they were dealing with Miss Professor Hippie-Dippy were in for a harsh awakening. The kindly demeanor which seemed to some advocates to be a sign of courtroom vulnerability was misleading. One prosecutor learned this when he asked Loftus, "You don't care much about victims of sex abuse do you?" Only to be pitilessly leveled when Loftus without a second's hesitation answered, "Yes, I do. I've been a victim of sexual abuse myself,"[8] simultaneously boosting her own credibility and obliterating her interrogator's.

Beth Loftus's genial exterior concealed her fierce loyalty to the data. Attack her personally, and she would try to understand why you were doing it. Attack her findings, and you would get what you deserved. She had a tremendous amount of knowledge and she was spreading it. She was also defending it with vigilance and determination.

Empathy wouldn't let Loftus do otherwise. Loftus was perfectly aware that the research had a long way to go, but how could researchers withhold the results they did have in the face of that foot-high stack of letters from victims of misidentification and their families? Loftus lived in a context in which, as she titled one response to McCloskey and Egeth, "Silence Is Not Golden."[9]

Attractive personal qualities did not earn Loftus the American Psychological Association's William James award and membership in the American Academy of Arts and Sciences. She earned those accolades with a display of rigorous science, beginning with a series of deceptively simple experiments she designed and performed in the mid-1970s. The impact of these brilliant experiments can't be overstated. Professor Daniel Schacter, Munsterberg's successor as the head of Harvard's Psychology Department, now simply calls them "classic."[10]

In one experiment, a group of students viewed the film of an automobile accident.[11] Immediately afterwards they were asked a series of questions about the event. Half of the students, chosen at random, were asked, "How fast was the white sports car going when it passed the barn while traveling along the country road?" The other half was asked only "How fast was the sports car going while traveling along the country road," without any mention of the barn. In fact, there was no barn in the film; the reference to the barn was false information inserted as part of the experiment. Later, every student was asked individually if he or she had seen a barn.

Nearly one in five of the students who had been exposed to the false "barn" question answered that they had in fact seen a barn. In a later experiment, when half of the students were straightforwardly asked whether they had seen a barn, most answered "No." But when after an interval they were questioned again, even the group that had been asked about but *denied* seeing a barn in the first round showed an increased likelihood of saying that they *had* seen a barn when the question was repeated.

The eyewitnesses to the Loftus car crash movie had not simply forgotten something: they had remembered a barn where there was no barn. This was no blank spot on the tape; this was evidence of eyewitness reports of "things not seen." Loftus' experiment had shown that eyewitnesses do not simply "roll the tape" of a past event; there could not have been a barn on anyone's original tape.

And in another study, Loftus found that witnesses can do more than add a new memory to supplement an old one.[12]

In this second simulated accident experiment, a red Datsun was shown traveling along a side street toward an intersection. Half of the experimental subjects saw a version in which there was a "Stop" sign at the corner; the other half saw a film in which there was a "Yield" sign. Later, they were all asked a list of questions. One question on the list assumed the existence of either a "Stop" sign or a "Yield" sign. For half of the test subjects, the assumed sign was consistent with the sign they had actually seen. For the other half, the question assumed the existence of the alternative. That is, half of the people who had seen a "Stop" sign were asked a question presupposing that the film had shown a "Yield" sign. Later, everyone was asked to report whether they had seen a "Stop" sign or a "Yield" sign.

People who had been asked the consistent question (e.g., people who had seen a "Stop" sign and were asked about a "Stop" sign) answered correctly 75 percent of the time. But people who had been asked the inconsistent question (e.g., who had seen a "Stop" sign but were asked about a "Yield" sign) remembered the *wrong* sign 59 percent of the time.

It seemed that more than half of the eyewitness memories had been not only added to, but changed by erroneous assumptions in tangential questions.

Not only that, one more experiment seemed to indicate that memories could also be changed by the phrasing of questions which did not even contain a false assertion of fact.[13] After another auto accident film, the subjects were asked questions about what they had seen. Some were asked how fast the cars were going when they "smashed"; others how fast the cars were going when they "collided," "bumped," "contacted," or "hit." A week later the subjects who had been asked about the "smashing" cars were more likely to report that they had seen broken glass.

In fact, there was no broken glass. When the subjects were asked to estimate the speed at the time of the crash, their estimates escalated with the verb used in the question: faster for "smashed" than for "bumped."

The results of these studies left many things about the basics of memory unsettled. Some psychologists theorized that the new, "post-event information" which the questioning process supplied had actually "altered" the witness's memory traces. Others argued that the two memories—for example "barn" and "no barn"—coexist, that the false information only makes the true memory less accessible, although it may still be recovered at some later time. A third group claimed that the "post-event" information does not alter the underlying memory trace but confuses what the witness reports as to the source of the memory. Part of the extraordinary contribution of the early Loftus experiments was the spur they gave to the exploration of one of the most fundamental questions about the human mind: the question whether memory traces are permanently stored in the brain.

But although the results of the Loftus experiments posed many questions for basic study, they also comprised one of those rare bodies of work that had enormous simultaneous impact both on the very basic science of memory and on a particular immediate application of the science in the real world.

The early Loftus experiments made it clear that from the first moments of an eyewitness's interaction with the criminal justice system, the memory of the witness is under assault from the questions, suggestions, and assertions of well-meaning, helpful cops, lawyers, and bystanders. Every criminal investigation carried as an inescapable byproduct of its search for answers a barrage of "postevent information." How did Mike Gauldin find things out from Jennifer? He asked her questions. How did he get her to identify someone? He showed her pictures.

Loftus's experiments showed that Gauldin's well-meaning questions, and the pictures of Ronald Cotton which Gauldin employed in his scrupulous, "by the book" photo array, had the power to alter Jennifer's memory.

———— •◦• ————

The results—the end products—of the early Loftus experiments have an important place in the story of psychology's efforts to help the legal system to confront the mystery "How Could Jennifer Be So Wrong?" But the scientific *method* Loftus used to gather those results had an impact that in a way was even more crucial. Loftus cut her field loose from the "demonstration" model which Munsterberg and Buckhout had used to support their public advocacy, and she steered it onto a fundamentally different course.

Munsterberg's mock shooting starring the clown and "a Negro" and the televised mugging that Buckhout helped to stage in New York focused on the performance of eyewitnesses: How often eyewitnesses were right, and how often they were wrong. Their supporters could argue that the demonstrations were pretty realistic, but their detractors could always find something in a demonstration that happened differently from the way things happen in real life. This argument had formed one axis of debate during the attack on Buckhout at the Johns Hopkins conference on "Ethics In Expert Testimony."

At this point, psychologists might have been drawn toward devising more and more elaborate and realistic demonstrations of eyewitness performance as the best way to make psychology helpful in protecting the innocent against eyewitness mistakes.

For a number of reasons, that was a loser's game. To begin with, it is simply impossible to be realistic enough. Every university maintains a human subjects committee to monitor the ethical limits on experiments that could do harm to the tested individuals. No one will allow you to frighten subject-eyewitnesses to death (or force them to undergo a rape) in order to gauge their performance in a "true" crime situation. Besides, even if you were allowed to treat humans like lab rats, your critics could point out that whatever you had learned from frightening one eyewitness to death could not be generalized on any *provable* basis to other eyewitnesses in the distinct contexts of their own experiences. That one eyewitness missed the real robber or identified the wrong man told you nothing about what the *next* eyewitness would do in a situation which might be pretty similar but could not be identical.

Loftus did not take the bait offered by the "more realistic" option. Loftus changed the subject from the amorphous question "How good are eyewitnesses?" to "What are the factors that impact eyewitness performance?" Instead of studying the performance of eyewitnesses as a general matter—and doing nothing more than arguing over the level of skepticism their accounts deserved—Loftus did what scientists do. She recognized that eyewitness performance depended on many factors; she isolated a particular factor; she conducted controlled, double-blind experiments to reveal the influence of the factor; and she subjected her results to statistical analysis to eliminate the possibility that her results represented merely random chance.

In Loftus's "barn" experiment, for example, everything was held constant except the wording of the question put to randomly selected witnesses. One group was told about the nonexistent barn; a control group was not. With everything else held constant, the influence of the "post-event information" in the questions that assumed the existence of a barn stood out in high relief. The results could be analyzed statistically to show that the influence of the questions on memory was not simply noise in the data, but the real thing.

And the Loftus experiments could be repeated over and over again. The results could be "replicated" or "falsified" in ways that Munsterberg's and Buckhout's eyewitness performance demonstrations could not. The more often the Loftus experimental results could be replicated, the greater the force of the Law of Large Numbers in establishing their validity. If other scientists replicated her results, the results were more persuasive. But more importantly, if her results were false, they could and would be *shown* to be false: they were susceptible to the scientific method. By becoming *less* "realistic" Loftus had become more "scientific"; by becoming less superficially "relevant" she had become more fundamentally important. This was social science at a rigorously empirical level.

One immediate impact of this shift was that eyewitness research, with its striking combination of basic science and immediate application, became respectable within academic psychology in a way it hadn't been since Munsterberg. Gary Wells, a psychologist who will play a pivotal role later in this story, can remember his graduate thesis advisors gingerly warning him to steer clear of Buckhout and the whole eyewitness issue, which was identified with Buckhout, if he hoped to make a career in academia. Loftus changed that. Careers in psychology, as in many academic fields, are launched (or sunk) by the decisions of the editorial boards of a handful of peer-reviewed journals, who subject submissions to searching—even nitpicking—evaluation before accepting them for publication. Loftus's early work joined Buckhout's in blazing a trail to the courtroom, but Loftus also blazed a trail into the prestigious journals.

As soon as the eyewitness area became respectable within Psychology, it became exciting for young researchers. The timing couldn't have been better. Cognitive Psychology in the 1950s—surviving during a period dominated by a preoccupation with behavioral studies—had organized itself around an information processing metaphor inspired by the arrival of the computer. This led to a preoccupation with meticulous, minutely detailed experiments with "memory drums" and other arcane equipment. This marked the resurgence of the approach which Munsterberg and William James had derided as "brass instrument Psychology." By the early 1970s this vein of research had begun to seem increasingly stale and mined out—boring to do, and difficult to explain to anyone outside the most rarefied segments of the academy.

Even if you did succeed in explaining to your neighbors or your inlaws what you did, they were likely to respond with a mystified "But, *why?*" The whole atmosphere of the 1970s screamed for "relevance"—coming of age with Martin Luther King, Jr. and John F. Kennedy on your television every night was somewhat different from today's situation—and the information-processing approach seemed doomed to spiral further down into utter irrelevance. Loftus opened a fresh line. Her work pointed out a way to do useful work on basic questions, to have it recognized within the discipline, and to have it make an impact in the broader world, too. Besides, in the 1960s and 1970s, to serve the cause of Justice was a hope many people shared. This was a promise Munsterberg himself would have been glad to offer.

The promise was quickly spread both outside and inside the field. Loftus had a hard time saying no to speaking engagements and requests from lawyers, and she had a hard time saying no to the media as well. The television producers in particular loved her. She was young and attractive, and her quiet, friendly style was perfectly suited to the demands of their "cool" medium. The abiding public fascination with the psychology of memory, which Munsterberg had exploited, and the "man bites dog" freshness of individual local stories of misidentification put Loftus's name on the Rolodex of every news editor in the country. When they called, Loftus would answer. Her answers were compact, clear, and described shocking news about familiar experiences in everyday language.

All of this coalesced: Loftus became a star. There was an explosion in psychological study of eyewitness psychology.

———◆———

The change in experimental approach that Loftus exemplified changed the legal landscape in unexpected ways.

The prevailing test for the admission into evidence of expert testimony about novel scientific knowledge required that the science involved be "generally accepted" in the relevant scientific community.[14] This test, first announced in a case involving an early lie detector system, was designed to manage the admission of expert testimony from fields in which the judges themselves were not expert, and to protect the legal system against abuse by every Professor Wacky who came along peddling an imaginary self-invented science. This test had a built-in time lag, which would bar genuine scientific evidence that happened to be on the cutting edge, because no relevant scientific community had yet had time to "generally accept it"; but it also ensured that there would be a pool of scientists available to police mavericks within a field.

This "general acceptance" test is sometimes written about as if the individual conclusions of individual scientists had to be "generally accepted"—as if, for example, when Buckhout and McCloskey disagreed, there was no "general acceptance" and the expert could not testify. But a moment's look at the legal system's habitual practices makes it clear that this was not really the case. Every medical malpractice jury hears testimony from at least two medical doctors who disagree with each other over particular conclusions, but medicine is not ruled out as an appropriate subject matter as a result. What had to be "generally accepted" was the basic explanatory theory of the science that was offered. As long as the medical community agreed on its general explanatory theory and method, it didn't matter that two doctors disagreed on a particular diagnosis, because courts can resolve the doctors' dispute by referring to the basic explanatory theory and method to which everyone agreed.

By retreating from the "realism" of the Munsterberg/Buckhout demonstration experiments, Loftus made it clear that although she, McCloskey, Egeth, and other opponents disagreed about the appropriateness of testifying, they did *not* disagree on the general explanatory theory or the basic method of experimental psychology. The general explanatory theory and the basic method were "generally accepted." In fact, McCloskey himself provided an unusually clear example of this when he published accounts of experiments intended to debunk Loftus's speculation that original memories might be permanently lost.[15] What his experiments actually accomplished—in legal terms—was quite different. Along the way to rebutting the inferences Loftus had drawn from her experiments, McCloskey had actually *replicated* the experimental *effects* that Loftus had achieved. In other words, they were both doing science, and doing a form of science that they both accepted. They were, in effect, like two doctors reading the same charts but disagreeing over a diagnosis, and yet both still practicing medicine. In that situation, there was no barrier to the courts using their science in trials.

By 1977, Frederick Woocher, a Stanford University law student with a background in psychology, had published in the *Stanford Law Review* a comprehensive argument in favor of the admissibility of expert psychological testimony about memory.[16] Now defense lawyers—who for trial litigation purposes recognize no distinction between "research" and "plagiarism"—simply went to their copying machines with Woocher's article and Loftus's *Eyewitness Testimony* and gave judges an authoritative claim that they were utilizing "good science." Loftus had turned the tide in the scientific journals, and it was turning in the law reviews, too.

The psychologists felt they were ready to face Wigmore's test: that they were "ready for the courts." Defense lawyers encouraged by this scientific confidence began banging on courthouse doors with psychologists in tow, demanding the right to produce expert testimony. Some times they were successful, but more often not.

Whether the courts were "ready for the psychologists" turned out to be a different question. The courts certainly didn't seem to feel any pressure to *get* ready.

The leisurely pace of judicial adjustment to advances in the sciences has many explanations, but the primary explanation is the structure of appellate judicial review. When trial judges excluded expert testimony about eyewitnesses, they knew that the appellate courts that reviewed their choices would not reverse the exclusion simply because the appellate court might have handled things differently. Reversals happen only when the appellate court finds that the trial judge had committed a gross "abuse of discretion." This very lenient standard protected the trial judges in the Kirk Bloodsworth and Ronald Cotton trials when they ruled that expert psychologists would not be allowed to testify about the frailty of eyewitness memory. Inertia, innate conservatism, unfamiliarity with and hostility to science, and law enforcement bias may all have played a role in trial court refusal to make use of the psychological findings, but the "abuse of discretion" standard eliminated any pressures on an individual lower-court judge to find a way to include the new scientific findings. Under the abuse of discretion standard, the old way was still the safe way. Why make waves?

Many judges hoped that they could simply send the professors back to their laboratories and be done with them. As it turned out, the judges could send the researchers back to their laboratories, but they could not be done with them. When judges excluded testimony based on an assertion such as "Jurors know this already!" the response they got from the researchers was not a Munsterberg-like washing of hands, but something more like, "*Interesting! Let's do a study! We'll test that claim!*"

To their amazement, the judges' own propositions became objects of study for the science they were rejecting. Can cross-examination reveal eyewitness error? Lindsay studied that. Do jurors have accurate common sense understandings? Deffenbacher studied that; so did Penrod. The judges' "common sense" did not fare well in any of these empirical examinations.[17]

In 1983, the Arizona Supreme Court became the first state supreme court to find that a trial judge had abused his discretion by refusing to allow Loftus to testify as an expert on eyewitness identification. The dissenting judge predicted where this would lead:

Once we have opened the door to this sort of impeaching testimony, what is to prevent experts from attacking any real or supposed deficiency in every other mental faculty? . . . I have great reluctance to permit academia to take over the fact-finding function of the jury. Although clothed in other guise, that will be the practical effect. With little to distinguish this case from the general rule against admitting expert testimony on eyewitness identification, we are left with no guidelines to decide the deluge of similar issues which are sure to result.[18]

In 1984, the California Supreme Court ignored this warning and followed Arizona. Loftus was being taken very seriously indeed.

And by this point Loftus was also taken very seriously by the prosecutors—but taken seriously as a danger, not seriously as a scientist. Ninety-nine percent (or more) of the prosecutors asked to assess the science of eyewitness identification in the late 1970s and early 1980s would have responded succinctly: "It's bullshit!"

Still, if you were an alert prosecutor you had to feel that when the prosecution could lose an eyewitness case like Howard Haupt's, it could lose *any* eyewitness case. There was really no reason to think that anyone other than Haupt had killed Billy Chambers, and now Haupt was walking around free. Loftus had even testified for Ted Bundy. What if the prosecutors had lost *that* one? In the minds of the prosecutors the psychology of eyewitness identification was utterly bogus, totally identified with the defense lawyers, and a bona fide threat to accurate fact-finding.

The Warren court's "constitutionalizing" of criminal investigatory procedure gave the prosecutors a key seat at any table where reform in police procedures would be debated. There could be no conversation between the researchers and the police investigators without the lawyers listening in. The prosecutors could stop things dead.

But although prosecutors and judges were now taking the science seriously as a courtroom menace, no one—including the defense lawyers, who were doggedly offering it in court—was yet taking seriously the most fundamental implications of the Loftus findings.

———————•·◆·•———————

Loftus showed that the mind of the eyewitness was for every practical purpose a part of the crime scene. There was evidence in the witness's memory trace. Like a drop of blood or semen, that memory trace evidence could be found, but it could be lost or overlooked if you used the wrong methods on the scene.

And the memory trace could be contaminated: Your methods of questioning, or crime scene "showups" of a single suspect, could introduce post-event changes into the memory just as surely as spilling coffee on the blood splatter or mishandling test tubes in the crime lab could contaminate the blood sample.

There are two important differences. If your blood sample was contaminated, your chemical tests might find the contaminating substance, and you could go back and test some uncontaminated portion of the sample. No test can tell you whether a memory trace is contaminated. Once a memory trace is contaminated, there can be no *un*contaminated sample left to test; the contaminated memory will be all that you have.

CHAPTER SEVEN

THE WAY WE LOOK AT SEEING

The Accelerating Study of Eyewitness Memory

WHEN SAUL KASSIN WAS AN UNDERGRADUATE at Brooklyn College he signed up to make a few bucks by filling out a questionnaire. He noticed that the research assistant presiding over the session was really pretty cute: so cute that 30 years later Kassin can still remember her first name.

He was wistfully admiring her charms when a man rushed into the room and stabbed her.

It wasn't until Kassin's own career in experimental psychology was well along that, while reading through a compilation of past studies, he discovered that the mock stabbing had been one of Bob Buckhout's experiments, and Kassin himself had been an unwitting subject.

Following in Buckhout's footsteps was not one of Kassin's ambitions. At Brooklyn College Buckhout had been a well-known figure, but an anomalous one. William James Hall at Brooklyn College was a headquarters for experimental psychology as a hard science, and people there respected Buckhout as a social activist but didn't take him terribly seriously as a scientist. Kassin belonged to the generation of psychologists who wanted to be serious scientists and were drawn to the study of eyewitness memory by the explosion of research following Loftus's basic experiments. Like many of his peers, Kassin was quickly approached by criminal defense lawyers looking for expert testimony.

Virtually the first time Kassin testified, the prosecutor attacked him with questions drawn from a mock cross-examination McCloskey and Egeth had

included in their *American Psychologist*[1] attack on Buckhout, Loftus, and the
ethics of expert testimony. Like everyone else in the field, Kassin had followed
the debate, and talking to lawyers about the issue gradually piqued Kassin's curiosity. Could McCloskey and Egeth and the prosecutors who adopted their
arguments be right? They claimed that everything on the Buckhout/Loftus
list of "discoveries" about eyewitness memory was either scientifically ques-
tionable or already widely known, and that nothing Buckhout and Loftus were
testifying about was *both* scientifically valid *and* new to jurors. Kassin found
himself wondering exactly what—in the legal system's own terms—was "generally accepted" about the psychology of eyewitness memory. He also found
himself wondering which things on the "generally accepted" list might surprise jurors.

So, in a move characteristic of the challenge-and-response relationship
between the lawyers and the psychologists, Kassin decided to do a study. In
fact, he and his colleagues did three studies.[2] In 1989 and again in 2001, they
asked a pool of psychologists working in the field to evaluate a series of propositions about eyewitness psychology to see who "accepted" which propositions. In the middle, in 1992, they put the same series of propositions to
ordinary prospective jurors.

Kassin asked the scientists questions about each proposition on his list. To
take the first proposition—"The presence of a weapon impairs the accuracy of
eyewitness testimony"—as an example, Kassin first asked whether the experts
thought the proposition was reliable: 87 percent of the experts in Kassin's 2001
study, an increase over the original 1992 result, stated that it was. Kassin and his
colleagues then asked whether the expert personally would be willing to testify in
court based on that statement: 77 percent said that they would. Next, the experts
were asked whether they believed that the "weapon focus" statement was supported by a body of peer reviewed research: 97 percent of the experts felt that it
was. Finally, the experts were asked whether they believed that the "weapons
focus" conclusion would fit with jurors' intuitive, common sense notions of how
eyewitness memory worked. Only 34 percent of experts thought that it would.

By using this procedure, Kassin developed a list of factors in eyewitness
cases that over 80 percent of his experts believed were reliably based on published, peer-reviewed experiments. The Kassin surveys provide benchmarks
for the growth of the field and its relation to the "common sense" of jurors.
There is no better way to appreciate the explosion of research that followed
Loftus's reorientation of the field than to read Kassin's surveys.

In one sense, there was nothing new about these findings; Munsterberg
had predicted most of them 70 years earlier. What was new about them was

that now they were *findings*, not speculations or educated guesses. Kassin's pool of experts had asked the questions that Wigmore demanded that they ask, and asked them in careful peer-reviewed experiments.

They did not see anything like a videotape process in the answers. What the experts saw through the lens of their research was a resounding refutation of the videotape conception of memory. The science taught them that an eyewitness identification depended on a fragile three-stage process. An eyewitness had to see, to store what had been seen, and to retrieve what had been stored. The process was vulnerable at every stage.

———————•◦•———————

The process that the research illuminated was anything but simple. Numerous aspects of every crime event turned out to have a powerful, and sometimes surprising impact on the ability to identify the criminal later.

For example, one "perception phase" factor which experiments revealed as influential was knowledge that a crime was occurring. Experimental subjects did better if they knew that a crime was going to occur, apparently because they paid better attention. This wasn't particularly surprising; but the research also showed that it mattered *how* the witness learned that a crime is in progress. When the subjects learned that a crime was in progress only because a robber suddenly brandished a gun, for example, witnesses will tend to focus on the gun, degrading their ability to perceive. Kassin found a "general acceptance" among experts that this "weapons focus" tendency was genuine. A majority of the experts Kassin polled—although not the 80 percent of experts required to meet Kassin's "general acceptance" threshold—agreed that although the stress inherent in a crime situation may sometimes enhance alertness, *very* high levels of stress will actually impede perception and memory.

The race of the witness matters, too. After reviewing pioneering research spearheaded by Roy Malpass, a psychologist at the University of Texas at El Paso, Kassin's experts were convinced that when the race of the criminal was different from the race of the victim, the process of identification became markedly less reliable. People turned out to be significantly better at identifying members of their own race than members of other races. This involved more than whites' primitive notion that "They all look alike." Malpass had not stopped at clichés; he had tested other explanations and qualifications.[3] The experiments found this "cross-racial" effect in witnesses of all races: whites did worse identifying blacks than they did identifying fellow whites, but blacks did worse identifying whites than they did identifying fellow blacks.

There was also general agreement that what the witness sees and remembers can be profoundly influenced by what the witness expects to see. Race was operating in the background here, too: One of the early experiments testing the effect of expectations and bias had suggested that witnesses to a drawing with a white man holding a weapon and an African American standing beside him showed a tendency to remember the weapon as being held by the *black* man—correctly remembering the existence of the weapon, but wrongly remembering its holder.

The psychologists' research-driven doubts about the "camera" phase of the process were nothing compared to their doubts about the "tape" on which the camera's product was stored. According to the consensus of the experts, the storage of eyewitness memories was far more complex than common sense would indicate. If there was a "memory tape" at all, it was an unstable one.

Over 80 percent of the experts agreed that memory did not decay slowly and at a gradual, steady rate. Their experiments showed that memory begins to decay rapidly and at an accelerating rate, and after a surprisingly brief period. A graph of this loss of memory would not be a straight, gently sloping line, but a dramatic downward "forgetting curve," a line that looked as if it were falling off a cliff.

Over 90 percent of the experts in Kassin's latest (2001) survey agreed that during the storage phase the eyewitness's memory was vulnerable to contamination by "post-event" information. In other words, many things on the "tape" might not be things that the eyewitness saw during the crime, but bits of specific data which had found their way into memory from other sources. Virtually all of the experts agreed that witnesses' memories could be changed by information conveyed by the wording of questions, as in the "smash"-versus-"bump" example, which in Loftus's early work produced a memory of nonexistent shattered glass.

These findings had seismic potential for the criminal justice system. During the hours between a crime and an identification, the memory of a witness is subjected to an extraordinary barrage of information: from other witnesses, from police, from family members, and sometimes from the media. During the months between the crime and the trial that barrage continues—and meanwhile, the "forgetting curve" operates to weaken the original memory. This can result in complete confusion in the witness' mind about the *source* of his or her memory.

An example of this source confusion, sometimes called "unconscious transference," which was well known within the psychological community was the story of an Australian psychologist, Donald Thompson.

Thompson was arrested and charged with rape, and to Dr. Thompson's shock the witness actually chose him from a lineup. Fortunately, he had an invincible alibi: At the time of the rape he had been in a television studio, broadcasting a panel program which also included an assistant commissioner of police. Still suspicious, the police investigated and learned that the victim had actually been watching Thompson on television at the time that the rape occurred. She was quite right that she had seen Dr. Thompson before, but she had wrongly—and unknowingly—transferred her memory of Thompson's face to replace the face of the rapist. That was why she had chosen Thompson from the lineup.

This kind of anecdote would have been enough for Munsterberg, who would have rushed into print with it. It was not enough for his heirs; they rushed into the laboratories. There, they generated a body of experimental findings that led to another extraordinary consensus: 95 percent of the experts agreed that a witness who had seen a mug shot of a defendant in a photo-array was more likely to identify the same man in a subsequent "live" lineup, whether the initial photographic identification was right or wrong. A Jennifer Thompson at a lineup could correctly remember seeing Ronald Cotton's face before, but the *source* of her memory could be her view of the photographic array, not the night of the rape. The police routine of showing mugshots to witnesses, in other words, provided post-event information of unusual salience. A photo-array process that had been regarded as a routine preliminary screening turned out to be the last genuine chance to retrieve uncontaminated memory. By the time the in-person lineup came around, the witness would be remembering the face the witness had seen in the mugshot.

The depressing—even alarming—message of this science was that there was no guarantee that the "tape" would be uncontaminated. This growing body of data seemed to prove Munsterberg's original assertion that witnesses could incorporate into their current memory of past events intervening facts, conjectures, and illusions that had no basis in the witnesses' own experience.

The researchers were also developing a body of "generally accepted" conclusions about what could go wrong at those replay stage procedures. The "mug shot" bias discussed earlier is one example. A second is the influence on eyewitnesses of the instructions they are given at lineups. The people chosen as lineup "fillers," the number of fillers, the format in which the fillers were presented—all of these were shown to have the potential to create mistakes.

Compare Kassin's 1989 survey with his 2001 version and two trends stand out. The first of these is the phenomenal deepening and elaboration of the research. By Kassin's 2001 survey, over 95 percent of the scientists surveyed believed that the proposition "Police instructions can affect an eyewitness's willingness to make an identification" was reliable enough to support courtroom testimony. More important, 95 percent also believed that proposition was founded on a solid basis of peer-reviewed empirical research. The quickly tested intuitions that Munsterberg offered and the sparse experiments Buckhout had marshaled were supplemented in the aftermath of Loftus's redirection of the research by a wealth of replication, elaboration, and clarification. By 1995 Brian Cutler and Steven Penrod, two veteran leaders in the field, published *Mistaken Identification: The Eyewitness, Psychology, and the Law*, and found over 2,000 scientific publications on the psychology of eyewitness identification.[4] A handful of experimental trees had become a substantial forest of research. Cutler and Penrod were able to base a careful and comprehensive view of the entire issue on actual experimental results. The imaginative leaps and speculative bridges thrown over wide gaps that had characterized Buckhout's polemics were no longer necessary.

These experimental results concealed a mountain of effort. Each ten-page article recounting an experiment in a learned journal was the product of intense and often wearisome labor in the decidedly unglamorous surroundings of university psychology labs in places like Alberta, Plattsburgh, El Paso, and Ames, Iowa. Each experiment had to be designed. Dozens—sometimes hundreds—of citizens or undergraduate students had to be coaxed or bribed into taking part. Methods for randomly selecting the participants had to be designed to control any impact of the selection process. The tests themselves had to be conducted under "double-blind" or other conditions that prevented contaminating the data. The results had to be compiled, collated, and statistically sifted to be certain that they had any significance at all. Sometimes the experiments resulted only in more confusion. This laborious process frequently resulted in nothing at all. Still, these dead ends didn't seem to discourage anyone.

Kassin's surveys indicate that by virtue of these experiments the psychologists could argue that they were ready to cash the check that Munsterberg had impetuously written 80 years earlier.

Kassin's survey looked at from a historical perspective reveals a less obvious, but more influential trend. Psychology was now also prepared to carry Mun-

sterberg's war into Wigmore's own territory. Psychology's deepening understanding of eyewitness performance was sharpening psychology's critique of
the legal system's own eyewitness evaluation practices. Wigmore's quarrel with
Munsterberg was that when Munterberg's messianic claims were carefully examined, Munsterberg offered lawyers nothing about whether *any particular*
witness was right or wrong. Munsterberg had not added anything to the legal
system's capacity to make an after-the-fact diagnosis of whether it was prosecuting the right guy.

But by the time of Kassin's second survey, it was evident that a respectable
body of scientists believed that the legal system's own traditions of after-the-
fact analysis—the traditions Wigmore had been defending—were themselves
shot through with error. The most obvious and the most fundamental example
of this particular vindication of Munsterberg was the research on the value of
an eyewitness's confidence in the identification.

In *Manson v. Braithwaite*, Justice Blackmun had formally enshrined a witness's confidence in his own identification as one of the factors that a court
must consider in deciding whether that identification was reliable. From the
legal system's point of view Blackmun was simply restating a fact of nature.
Practically speaking, when a Jennifer Thompson or a Bernadine Skillern says
"I'm as sure as I can be" about a Ronald Cotton or a Gary Graham, that has always been pretty close to the end of the issue for the legal system, acting either
through its judges or its jurors. It would be difficult to point to a factor that
the legal system valued more than eyewitness confidence.

But the scientists—or at least 87 percent of Kassin's group—believed that
confidence was *not* a good indicator of accuracy. And by 2001, 97 percent of
that group believed that distrust of witness confidence was justified not by the
one, lonely, Munsterbergian experiment which had shown subjects confidently
underlining their mistaken memories, but by a solid and growing body of controlled, empirical research. Not only that; for his 2001 survey Kassin added a
new statement about confidence malleability: "An eyewitness's confidence can
be influenced by factors that are unrelated to identification accuracy." Ninety-
five percent of the experts agreed with *that*.

Kassin's experts, in other words, were urging legal fact-finders to drop one
of their most trusted tools: the confidence of the witness, expressed either
through direct "I'm certain that's him" sorts of statements or more subtly
through the confident demeanor of the witness.

The stakes in the expert witness controversy by this point were very high.
If expert witnesses convinced jurors to toss the confidence measure aside, the
law enforcement authorities could offer very little with which to replace it and

still acheive a guilty verdict. If the psychological experts got in front of the juries, they would succeed in persuading them to adopt their new propositions. This fear was reinforced by spectacular examples like the Angela Davis and Howard Haupt acquittals, but there was further evidence for it in Kassin's own surveys.

———————◆◆◆———————

Kassin's surveys refuted McCloskey and Egeth's categorical statements that there was nothing valid in the research that was new to jurors. On a number of well-proven propositions, there was a statistically significant divergence between what most jurors believed and what a consensus of the experts believed.

But Kassin's survey of juror preconceptions had not proved the opposing categorical statement: It wasn't true that *no* juror believed what the experts believed. Nearly twice as many experts as potential jurors agreed with the central statement "confidence is not a good predictor of his or her identification accuracy." Still, that did not mean that no jurors agreed with that statement. In fact, almost half of the prospective jurors agreed that confidence and accuracy were not directly related.

You couldn't expect that every individual juror knew that confidence does not automatically equal accuracy. But it would be equally unreasonable, maybe more unreasonable, to assume that no juror on a twelve person jury was aware of that proposition. Every *jury* would probably have at least one juror who agreed with the experts.

An expert's testimony, in other words, might fall on very fertile ground. If you were a prosecutor, you had to fear that a tiny minority of jurors, dazzled by an expert's testimony, could react just as the Angela Davis jury had to Buckhout's testimony and persuade their fellow jurors to acquit. Even if the members of this minority couldn't persuade their fellow jurors, their own votes could deadlock the jury and bring things to a standstill.

CHAPTER EIGHT

THE GOVERNMENT WINS WHEN JUSTICE IS DONE IN ITS COURTS

Three Prosecutors

IN JANUARY 1993, A MAN KNOCKED ON THE DOOR of an apartment in upper Manhattan belonging to the parents of "Gina Lopez," who was home alone with her three-year-old daughter. (The names of victims and witnesses in these accounts have been changed.[1]) The man told Gina that he was a plumber, sent by the superintendent to check the pipes. Gina opened the door, and he went through the apartment, apparently checking pipes and fittings. Then he produced a gun, pistol-whipped Gina, and demanded cash. He removed her jewelry, then demanded that she remove the jewelry that the toddler was wearing and hand it to him. He sexually assaulted her: forcing her to put his penis in her mouth, and raping her. The child was still in the apartment. The rapist escaped and Gina called the police. She said the rapist was a light-skinned Hispanic. She was able to describe his height and weight and a greenish tattoo on his hand.

The following month in the same Manhattan precinct, Lois Ramirez was at home in her apartment with her 14-year-old daughter, Tina. There was a leak in the apartment, and when a man knocked at the door and said that he had been sent by the super to fix the leak, Lois let him in. The man asked Lois to show him where the bathroom was, and she led him down the hallway in that direction. A few moments later, Tina, Lois' daughter, heard a loud, sharp sound coming from the direction of the bathroom. The man came out and told her to help her mother. When Tina went to the bathroom, she found her mother lying on the floor—she had been shot in the face. She was dead. The murderer made Tina remove the jewelry from her mother's hand and turn it over to him. Then he fled. Tina's description of his height and weight matched the description given by Gina Lopez. Tina, too, had seen a tattoo on the murderer's hand.

Early in April, Phyllis Post was running a shower in her apartment a few blocks away from the Lopez home when there was a knock on her door. She answered it in her robe. The man at the door told her that the super had sent him to check on a leak. Since there had been a leak, and Post had been running the water, she let him in. The man seemed to check the pipes and radiators, but when he turned around he had a gun in his hand. He demanded money, and took it from her. He hit her in the face, forced her to undress, then sexually assaulted her, in the same manner as Gina Lopez's attacker. He left after threatening to kill her if she reported the crime. Phyllis, too, described a Hispanic man, and her description of his height and weight matched the descriptions given by the other victims. The rapist had been wearing a long-sleeved shirt, and she could not see whether he had a tattoo.

It wasn't until nine years later, in July 2002, that the New York Police Department showed photo arrays to Gina Lopez and Tina Ramirez, during separate interviews.

The circumstances of these identification attempts were about as unpromising as could be imagined—in fact, if you had been reading the psychological research, the circumstances seemed close to hopeless. The original viewing conditions were traumatic. A weapon was used, which often draws the witness's attention into a limited focus and away from the offender's face. The descriptions the women had given at the times of the crimes were laconic. Nine *years* of "post-event" information had been processed through the women's memories since their fresh descriptions had been given. For nine years the "forgetting curve" had been running its downward course.

But each woman identified a man in the photo array. And each woman identified the same man, a convict who by then was serving 20 years for a series of armed robberies in the Bronx.

They were right. The rape kits collected from Gina Lopez and Phyllis Post contained sperm with DNA matching the convict's. The same DNA procedures that had shown that Jennifer Thompson was wrong showed that Gina and Phyllis were right. Two eyewitnesses had made correct identifications after nine years.

Frontline did not appear to document these DNA confirmations of correct identifications. Elizabeth Loftus was nowhere in sight. Hordes of psychologists did not descend on the talk shows to explain how these eyewitnesses could have been accurate. Just as no commission is summoned when a space shuttle does not crash, no one pays much attention to the psychology of eyewitness accuracy when the eyewitness is right. Two eyewitnesses had identified the right man after nine years, and no one noticed. That drives prosecutors crazy.

In the cases of Gina, Phyllis, and Tina, the prosecutors have DNA to back up their victims, but the prosecutors know all too well that there will be other cases when an eyewitness would be all the evidence they have. If no one believes eyewitnesses, vicious murderers and serial rapists will be set loose.

After all, Jennifer Thompson *could* have identified the right person, Bobby Poole. If she had, the prosecutors would have been forced to rely on the jury's faith in Jennifer, or Poole would have gone free. And we know what Poole did when he got free: he committed numerous vicious rapes while Ronald Cotton served his time.

Oddly enough, two women who play leading roles in this story of the legal system's reactions to the eyewitness research had both been widely discussed as members of Bill Clinton's short list for attorney general. They were similar in many ways: strong-willed, politically experienced career prosecutors. One, Linda Fairstein, was the dynamic head of the Manhattan district attorney's sex crime unit. The second, Janet Reno, became Bill Clinton's third and final choice for attorney general.

There is a tradition of placing the criminal justice system's actors on an ideological spectrum defined by crime control enthusiasts at one end, due process addicts at the other: Justice Rehnquist and Clint Eastwood to the south, Justice Brennan and Henry Fonda to the north. Stanford law professor Herbert Packer epitomized this view in his influential book, *Limits of the Criminal Sanction*, published at the height of the Warren court controversies in the late 1960s, and people have used it ever since. According to Packer, everyone who works in the system or writes about the system lies *somewhere* on the straight line between those two poles. At the crime control pole, they care most about suppression of crime. They want efficiency in pursuing that goal, and they will tolerate a high rate of error. At the due process pole, they care most about individual autonomy and the need to constrain official power. Crime control adherents see their due process adversaries as mischievous bleeding hearts, perpetually throwing up pointless obstacles to the apprehension of criminals. Due process enthusiasts see crime control advocates as faceless *apparatchiks* operating a conveyer belt that carries away the innocent—and the Constitution—along with the guilty.[2]

The prosecutors' antagonism towards the psychological eyewitness research frequently is treated just that way: dismissed as the primitive reflex of crime control automatons. According to this view, the prosecutors' settled hostility to what the psychologists preach simply follows the criminal justice system's Lifer's Creed: "Since we know that 80 percent (or 90 percent, or 99 percent) of them are guilty, we know what to do 100 percent of the time—lock 'em up." Anything that might complicate the process is illegitimate.

John Griffith,[3] then a Yale Law School professor, once pointed out that the followers of the crime control and due process models have a great deal more in common than it seems at first. According to Griffith, the crime control and due process models actually represent only minor deviations from one, large unified model, which due process zealots and crime control preachers *all* love deep in their hearts. Griffith called this the battle model: a model in which the criminal justice system was the field for a zero-sum battle between the irreconcilable state and individual, in which one side must win—and one side lose—everything. The only difference between Packer's two "polar" models is that the balance of advantage in the battle is different: crime control is weighted toward the prosecutors and the cops, due process toward the individual defendant. Every reaction to every proposal in the criminal process is simply a reaction to a change in the balance.[4]

Even if Griffith is wrong about this, ideological pigeonholing obscures more than it explains—at least if ideology is thought of exclusively as a catalogue of policies or prescriptions to which a person has sworn allegiance. A more useful way to look at ideology in the criminal justice system is to remember that whatever else ideology is, it is, as developmental psychologist Erik Erikson noted, "the social institution that protects identity."[5] Where one stands on *Miranda,* or the death penalty, or lawyers for indigent defendants, can sometimes be best explained as a response not to "What policy seems most efficacious?" or even to Griffith's "Who wins?" but to "What kind of person do I want to be, or seem to be?" This is particularly true among the criminal justice system's lawyers.

Some young men and women drift into work as public defenders or prosecutors just to get a couple of years' trial experience before moving on to civil practice, but these are foot soldiers; they are not the lawyers who stick around to make policy. The members of that second, more influential group of lawyers *chose* to be a prosecutor or a defender early in their careers. In fact, they chose the role early in their lives—just as they emerged from the protracted adolescence of law school—and in large part they chose it as an answer to the second question: What do I want my new identity to be?

Young criminal lawyers want to escape the stultifying peonage of the life of an associate in a large law firm; that was certainly not the kind of person you want to be. You want to be the sort of person who risks the courtroom battles you've been watching on TV all your life. Most of all, you want a more meaningful career—to fight for justice, to bring the outer world of criminal justice into line with the inner world of ideas and values. You want, to use the defense lawyers' favorite term for their own role, to be a "champion of justice." But it is justice you want to champion. This is the ideology of the prosecutors too: contriving wrongful convictions is not on a young prosecutor's agenda. No one leaves law school and chooses a job as a prosecutor because he or she wants to convict the innocent.

Still, wrongful *acquittals* are more real, and more painful, for some lawyers than they are for others. Linda Fairstein has had plenty of opportunity—30 years worth of opportunity—to imagine just how bad a wrongful acquittal could feel. These days, Linda Fairstein is well known as the glamorous author of highly polished best-sellers, translated into 14 languages, and loosely based on her own experiences as a prosecutor. She is consulted by directors and actors; a frequent pundit on cable TV talk shows; and, with her husband, who is a powerful New York lawyer, she is a reliable presence on the social circuits of both New York and Martha's Vineyard.

Fairstein never fit the mold of the typical young assistant D.A. drifting through the beginnings of a workaday professional career. She was the daughter of a prosperous Westchester family; she had been an English major at Vassar and then attended The University of Virginia's law school. She talked her way onto the Manhattan D.A.'s staff in 1972 over District Attorney Frank Hogan's objection that the crimes his office handled were "too tawdry" for a lady of her background to prosecute. She headed the sex crimes unit for 25 years, and during that period she played a leading role in revolutionizing the way in which sex crimes are prosecuted in the United States. On Fairstein's watch, New York eliminated its archaic corroboration requirement in rape cases, and instituted a workable "rape shield" law. She was a powerful and articulate voice in both campaigns. She had experienced her share—some would say more than her share—of limelight. Standing between Fairstein and a reporter's notebook or a camera was supposed to be one of the most dangerous locations in New York. But she had put in her time in the trenches, too. She had gone to court and taken her lumps.

Defense lawyers will sometimes deride prosecutors they dislike for being "on a mission," by which they mean too moralistically or ideologically driven to see the simple realities in front of their noses. Fairstein quickly found "a mission," but it did not have the effect of blinding her to realities. If her non-fiction book, *Sexual Violence*, is any indication, Fairstein's mission kept her vision rather sharp.[6]

Fairstein's experience of simultaneously handling individual cases and keeping her eye on the larger problem of the criminal justice system's cavalier treatment of woman victims may be what saved her from subsiding into the burnout which overtook, for example, Larry Kramer, the 30-something Bronx Assistant D.A. of Tom Wolfe's *Bonfire of the Vanities*. Kramer mourned, "Look at these cases he was handling! Pieces of shit! Garbage collection!"[7] That never happened to Fairstein. Even at the beginning, Fairstein had the novelist's instinct for individual details. She was ambitious and liked publicity, but ambition and the skillful management of publicity all happened to work perfectly in advancing the larger cause, while simultaneously earning her some vehement detractors.[8]

Besides—in an odd echo of Beth Loftus's experience—the vividness of those individual histories energized Fairstein on her mission. The individual cases and the mission had a synergistic effect. The nature of Fairstein's particular "mission" kept her focused on the facts of her individual cases because her mission was to force the system to attend to the individual stories of the women whose brutalizing experiences she was trying to redeem in the criminal process. She pursued the mission by learning and telling compelling stories. As Fairstein once told *Cosmopolitan:*

> Everyday I came face-to-face with women who have been violated and trau-
> matized. The question that I'm always asked is, how could I possibly stay in a
> job that seems to outsiders to be such grim work? The answer? I get tremen-
> dous satisfaction from helping victims regain their dignity and sense of well-
> being. You always hear people say that it's a bad idea to take your job too
> personally, but I believe just the opposite—that you can reap enormous re-
> wards from being emotionally involved in what you do.[9]

Women who became sex crimes prosecutors in Fairstein's pioneering generation knew their complaining witnesses at a deeper level of empathy than did most of the male prosecutors working their way up toward the homicide bureau. For many of those women, empathy was why they had taken the job. Besides, in the sex crimes unit, Fairstein operated within a structure that made empathy workable. The first head of the Manhattan District Attorney's Sex Crimes Prosecution Unit (SCPU), Leslie Crockett Synder, revolutionized the prosecutors' routine when she insisted that assistant district attorneys on the SCPU handle their cases "vertically"—that is, from arraignment through sentencing rather than on the relay race tradition of passing the case (and the victim) from assistant to assistant as it progressed from indictment, through motions, to trial. A SCPU prosecutor's opportunity to know and empathize with her victims was unique.

But the same empathy that kept you from thinking of your job as "garbage collection" could be a source of pain.

Fairstein remembered one young victim many years later. The girl was a project kid. She wasn't articulate. Her description of her assailant was way off: internally inconsistent almost to the point of incoherence. She couldn't describe a single specific facial feature. But 11 weeks after the rape, when she saw the suspect for the first time she broke into uncontrollable trembling. You knew—you just knew—that she had picked the right man. There was no DNA in those days to back the victim up. She was right, but there was no way to show it in a courtroom. The defendant was acquitted. Within months he had raped and stabbed to death a 23-year-old woman.

———◆———

From the front line prosecutors' perspective, *every* jury acquittal is a wrongful acquittal. After all, if you weren't convinced that you had the right guy you wouldn't be in trial in the first place. For a prosecutor who cares about victims— present and future—those wrongful acquittals are intensely frustrating. And from the prosecutors' perspective, eyewitness cases always threaten acquittals.

Seen from the outside, the prosecutors' role seems aggressive, proactive. That impression is exactly what attracts many young prosecutors to the job. At the early stages of a given case—during a grand jury investigation, for example—the prosecutor's role really is aggressive. But the experience of being a prosecutor during a trial is actually defensive: once your opening statement is over, you sit there and you watch your case attacked. The best you can do is hope that the defense doesn't dismantle your case altogether, that there's enough of your witness left after cross-examination to support a guilty verdict. You feel more like a punching bag than a sword of justice.

Statistically, the defense lawyers' "Mr. Potato Head" cross-examination is an exercise in futility that makes no real impression on the jurors, but if you are a prosecutor absorbing the hits at the counsel table it doesn't feel that way;

it feels as if the defense lawyer is scoring points left and right. Even in eyewitness cases that seem very solid, the defense can always find something to say, and once the defense has found something to say, other prosecutors' dazzling statistical success is not much comfort. No matter how right the eyewitness is, no eyewitness case feels perfectly invulnerable. The description is off by a couple of inches, or a few pounds; the lighting was bad; the races are different. The defendant has a gold tooth, but the victim didn't mention it. "Isn't that *a reason for a doubt*, ladies and gentlemen?" the defense lawyer will roar. For the prosecutor it feels—usually, as it turns out, wrongly—as though you are about to fail the victim and all of the defendant's future victims in an uniquely exposed and public way. You signed on to be a champion of justice, and if you signed on to be a prosecutor it's quite possible that your decision was influenced by a desire to play for the winning team. Signing on to be a prosecutor is like giving your heart to the Yankees, not to the Red Sox or the Cubs. Now, here you are—about to lose to some smug defender. In the highly publicized cases, the feeling is even worse.

Imagine how you would feel if you were prosecuting Bobby Poole without DNA, and you felt your case slipping away.

This vulnerable moment is exactly the point at which psychology offered to enter the picture and pile on to you and your victim—psychology with its claims about eyewitness unreliability, which could be exploited by a sanctimonious defense lawyer. The defense lawyer, who probably knows that his client is a guilty pig, baby-steps his Dr. Lab Rat through a bought-and-paid-for performance. In New York, where Linda Fairstein was prosecuting, it didn't help that psychology was entering in the abrasive person of Bob Buckhout, who was conveniently placed to conduct gleeful raids on New York prosecutors from his headquarters at Brooklyn College. Chet Mirsky, a defense lawyer who used Buckhout as an expert in New York during the early 1980s remembers the effect Buckhout had on the New York prosecutors. "You just had to put Bob Buckhout's name on a pleading," Mirsky says, "And they went *completely nuts!*" And if the psychologist the defense offered *wasn't* Buckhout, the chances were that the "expert" would offer incoherence or incompetence in place of Buckhout's abrasiveness. Buckhout at least knew what he was talking about, even if he was, in the prosecutors' opinion, on an ego-tripping "mission" of his own.

So, when Fairstein was asked recently about her reaction when she first ran into the psychological research in the 1970s she remembered it clearly: "It's bullshit! People recognize people."[10]

It wasn't that Fairstein denied the possibility of eyewitness mistakes; that possibility was the reason that in the SCPU an eyewitness case might be subjected to searching evaluation by ten lawyers in a skeptical brainstorming session. Fairstein herself has written eloquently about the harm done by false charges of rape. But once the prosecutors had evaluated the case by their own criteria, the parade of psychologists which the defense lawyers kept trying to get in front of juries had nothing to offer except smoke and mirrors. Take the psychologists' so-called expertise about witness confidence, for example. Fairstein's first mentors in the D.A.'s office had cautioned her that you often ran into witnesses who were "certain but wrong," and she had taken the lesson to heart. But you couldn't talk about confidence without talking about individual witnesses; confidence, among other things, was a character trait. Some people were confident about everything; some people were tentative about everything. Nothing you learned in some laboratory in Iowa was going to help decide what *this* witness's confidence means in *this* case.

Some witnesses were just better witnesses than others. You had to distinguish between someone who had glimpsed a drive-by shooting in the dark, and a sex crime victim like Gina Lopez who was forced to see her rapist up close and for a substantial period of time. There were individual differences between victims, too. Fairstein remembers a rape victim who was a graphic artist: you couldn't understand her testimony until you understood what a visual person she was. The psychologists couldn't do that. The best the psychologists could say was that some eyewitnesses made mistakes. So what? The prosecutors knew that already, and they had taken it into account. Did the psychologists think the prosecutors were idiots? Or moral imbeciles?

But if the psychologists had nothing to add, that didn't mean that the psychologists couldn't subtract something important.

A working prosecutor is painfully conscious of the vulnerabilities of even correct eyewitnesses. They have seen—or heard about on the office grapevine—rapists and murderers who were acquitted in eyewitness cases after their confessions were thrown out for *Miranda* violations and the eyewitness froze on the stand. They've met eyewitnesses whom they were sure were right but who just couldn't talk about their experiences.

In such a case—where you certainly had the right guy, but were likely to lose—the jurors' old conception of memory as a videotape can be a valuable resource. One of the things that bothered Fairstein about fabricated charges of rape was that the juror skepticism that fabricated charges of rape created spilled over into the trials of sincere rape victims, diminishing their persuasiveness. Jurors' *general* skepticism—skepticism from outside the boundaries of the particular case on trial—was the prosecutor's enemy. In a sense, a lost case anywhere contributed to an aggravated burden for every victim, everywhere. It wasn't that prosecutors themselves still believed in the infallibility of eyewitnesses, or that anyone wanted to deploy that pre-Munsterberg understanding of memory to convict the innocent.

But, paradoxically, the fact that the prosecutors *did* know that eyewitnesses were not infallible seemed to prosecutors to make lecturing jurors about eyewitness fallibility less important. Prosecutors like Fairstein made enormous efforts to screen out mistakes. Because of these efforts the possibility of error was an entirely abstract and academic matter. On this basis, prosecutors feel that the one-in-a-million chance of a wrongful conviction based on eyewitness testimony shouldn't be used to destabilize thousands of eyewitness rape cases every year.

In fact, the prosecution's screening efforts made a lot of academic talk about eyewitness fallibility in real-life courtrooms a destructive distraction—not just an abstract and academic distraction; a real world, cost-you-the-case distraction.

Not only was the eyewitness psychology "bullshit"; it was dangerous bullshit. Simple adversary competitiveness naturally aggravated the prosecutors' feelings. If you had chosen to fight for justice on the prosecution side, you identified yourself with the institutions of the state—not, the way a public defender might, with the besieged individual—and you expected to win. But the prosecutors' hostility to eyewitness expert testimony was more than an adversary's panic at the thought of a courtroom defeat; it was anger at justice cheated. It was anger at traumatized flesh-and-blood victims left to look over their shoulders for rapists who were acquitted and sent back onto the streets of their neighborhoods because of academic theorizing.

It took a terrible effort for a sex-crime victim to take the witness stand. It was frightening to confront her assailant, and revisit for a public audience the intimate details of her harrowing experience. The victim already faced an uphill battle against the procedural protections—the presumption of innocence and the beyond-a-reasonable-doubt burden of proof, for example—which protected these cretinous defendants. To tip the balance even further with the speculations of these laboratory denizens, based on a couple of distant and freakish wrongful convictions, seemed insane. It would send more and more victims home with "not guilty" ringing in their ears, with their stories repudiated by jurors.

———— ◆·◆·◆ ————

Structuralist historians contend that individual historical figures are no more than the spume on the sea of history: that Napoleon and Wellington, for example, are trivial symptoms of deeper material forces that shape their cultures.

The story of psychology's battle to make itself heard in the legal system poses a counter-argument: a call for attention to individual biographies. If anyone other than Janet Reno had been attorney general—or if Janet Reno had been a different sort of person—when the law-versus-psychology battle was reopened in the 1990s, the story would have taken a very different turn. In Janet Reno's biography, her parents loom very large.

When Janet Reno was first mentioned as a possibility for appointment to the office of attorney general, she took herself out of consideration. Her 79-year-old mother was dying of cancer in Florida, and Reno wanted to be with her. The phrase "quite a character" doesn't begin to do justice to Janet Reno's mother, Jane Wood Reno.[11] If a movie had been made of her life, it would have been a vehicle for Katherine Hepburn or Rosalind Russell in one of their most harum-scarum, Emancipated Woman moods. As her daughter's biographer puts it,

> Outspoken, outrageous, absolutely indifferent to others' opinions, Jane Wood Reno was truly one of kind. She drank beer like it was soda, eschewed a bra, and wore flowered housedresses and sneakers everywhere she went. Later, Jane would jazz up her outfit with a floppy hat with flowers when she accompanied her daughter to political affairs.[12]

She loved to walk outside during hurricanes, feeling the storm against her face. She was a pioneering journalist, and an early civil rights activist in a Florida which, to put it mildly, was not receptive. She wrestled alligators. Long before "environmentalism" was a word, she marched on a six-day hike along Florida's east coast beaches and championed the cause of the Everglades. She was named an honorary Princess of the Seminole tribe for her writing in support of Native American rights. Once she surprised the children by slipping peacock eggs under the chickens. The descendants of the exotic birds— all called "Horace"—still stalk Janet Reno's yard. When her own children tried to explain what "character" Jane Wood Reno resembled, they turned not to Hepburn or Russell but to the irascible Mr. Toad of *The Wind in the Willows*, "who was irresponsible and difficult, but he was not bad . . . convinced in the ultimate rightness of everything he did."[13]

Jane Wood Reno raised a clan described by one friend as "omnivorous readers, omnivorous talkers, and omnivorous communicators."[14]

She built a home for them with her own hands too on the edge of the swamps that surrounded Miami. She took a year to learn how to build it; then a year for the actual building. She took particular pride in the chimney, which she built after rescuing the bricks from a burned-out homesite and reading a federal pamphlet, "How To Build A Fireplace." The house was just the way she wanted it:

> In an era still innocent of air conditioning, the completed house was sited and designed to take advantage of breezes. Jane would not hear of fans, as they created unnatural wind currents. A fifty-foot screened porch—half the house's area—ran along the front of the house. Inside, there were no ceilings, the better to let the hot air rise to the sloping, cypress-beamed roof. For a classical touch, the pitch of the roof matched that of the Parthenon, which Jane had visited while on a college trek to Greece.[15]

Jane Reno died, in the house she had built, in December 1992, but not before the 160 mile per hour winds of Hurricane Andrew devastated Dade County that August. Janet Reno remembered her mother's response to the cataclysmic storm:

> About three in the morning, as the winds began to howl, my mother woke up. Old and frail and dying, she went and sat in her chair, folded her hands in her lap, and although trees were crashing around the house and the winds howled, she sat there totally unafraid. For she knew how she had built that house. She hadn't cut corners. She hadn't compromised her standards. She'd built it the right way.[16]

When the storm was over, Dade County looked like a battlefield, but the Reno house had lost "one shingle and a couple of screens." Janet Reno told her mother, "Old woman, you built one hell of a house."

When it came to withstanding tempests, the first days of Janet Reno's term as attorney general seemed to indicate that Jane Wood Reno hadn't done too badly with her elder daughter, either.

———◆·◆·◆———

Janet Reno was sworn in as attorney general on the twelfth day of the siege of cult leader David Koresh's compound in Waco, Texas. The FBI, which was managing the siege, was already growing impatient. The special operations teams, the sharpshooters, and other forces could not be maintained at their highest pitch of performance over long periods. The FBI said that the situation inside the "Branch Davidian" compound was deteriorating. Koresh was not responding to overtures. There were reports—no one quite remembers their source—that children inside the compound were being beaten.

Reno struggled for maneuvering room between the two very bad choices that seemed to be the only ones on the menu: acquiescence or armed attack. She consulted military specialists and asked them to critique the FBI's plans. They tinkered with them, but approved the basics. By the fifty-first day of the siege, Reno decided that there was no alternative to action, and she notified President Clinton that she had decided to go ahead. He asked whether it wouldn't make sense to wait another few days, but authorized her to use her judgment.

Reno ordered the FBI to proceed. The FBI's plan involved the gradual introduction of tear gas, but gusty wind quickly dissipated the gas, and FBI sharpshooters watched helplessly as cult members used the interval to set fire to the compound. There were no firefighters on hand, because the FBI agent in charge had determined that Koresh's weapons made the scene too dangerous for them. The flames, fanned by the wind, quickly consumed the Branch Davidian buildings: 75 bodies were discovered in the smoldering ruins.

Twenty-five of the dead were children.

For the first 24 hours following this debacle, President Clinton was nowhere to be found; he left the attorney general to face the cameras. The first questioner asked whether the president had approved the raid. Reno answered: "I approved the plan, and I'm responsible for it. I advised the president, but I did not advise him as to the details." At about midnight that night Clinton mustered the courage to make a private telephone call consoling Reno. By the next morning the reviews of Reno's "stand up" acceptance of responsibility were in. People admired her for her forthrightness; she received a spontaneous standing ovation when she dined in a Washington restaurant. Clinton nerved himself to offer her public support the next morning, but there were still others who found her a tempting target. Detroit Congressman John Conyers, for example, ambushed Reno at a committee hearing. "I'd like you to know there is at least one member of Congress that isn't going to rationalize the deaths of two dozen children." Reno didn't flinch:

I haven't tried to rationalize the deaths of children, Congressman. I feel more strongly about it than you will ever know. . . . But most of all Congressman, I will not engage in recrimination. I will look to the future and try to learn everything I can from this situation to avoid tragedies such as this in the future.[17]

It was a very characteristic performance. Reno had behaved much the same way in the aftermath of the Liberty City riots in Miami. She took responsibility. She took her medicine. She did her public duty. Whatever private agonies

Reno felt, she did not mobilize them as public weapons. She wouldn't ask for sympathy.

———————◆·◉·◆———————

James Richardson was an African American in Arcadia, Florida, a fruit-picker, who had been convicted and sentenced to death in 1968 for poisoning his seven children. In 1989, he stood in a courtroom, listening as a Florida special prosecutor argued for his release. Richardson, the special prosecutor told the judge, had not received a fair trial.

"Can I shake the white lady's hand?" Richardson asked his lawyer.

The lawyer relayed Richardson's question to the special prosecutor, Janet Reno, then the Miami Dade State's Attorney, who had been assigned by the governor to investigate Richardson's case.

"She said she appreciated the gesture," the lawyer later told the *Washington Times*, "but felt it would be inappropriate. But she asked me to tell Mr. Richardson that it was not meant as a rebuff but only her way of maintaining her own professional code."[18]

Reno was willing to argue for Richardson's release while the trial prosecutor yelled that her report was "a phony boondoogle and fraud."[19] The interesting thing is that she was completely willing to stay within her professional role, and to deny herself the pleasures of a congratulatory handshake that many lawyers—not to mention many elected politicians—would have found literally irresistible. Virtually any politician one can name would not only have accepted the handshake, but sent for the photographers first. Reno felt it was wrong to accept personal congratulations because she was only doing her job. She was arguing for Richardson not because she was a special individual, but because that was what The Prosecutor does in such a situation.

Reno enforced Florida's death penalty law so uncomplainingly that the Florida lawyer who oversaw death cases for Florida's Republican governor said, "If she was opposed to the death penalty, I never knew it." Reno's office had obtained death sentences in many cases, and when she became Attorney General she authorized many federal capital prosecutions. But in fact, Reno made no secret of her feeling that capital punishment was pointless, unavailing vengeance, and nothing more. She told everyone that: plainly, straightforwardly.

But she made no parade of ambivalence. For all that you can tell from the outside, she *felt* no ambivalence. She had private convictions, and she had a public role. She did her best in both. She would follow the law. She would do what she could to protect the innocent. She would not whine about private doubts. By taking that stance, Reno drew abuse from both sides of the capital punishment debate. As far as anyone could tell, she didn't care.

But in the James Richardson case Reno had experienced something few prosecutors have the opportunity to experience. She had been personally responsible for investigating a wrongful conviction, and for righting—to the extent that anyone could—the wrong that had been done to James Richardson. Cynics would say that it helped that it wasn't one of Reno's own cases she was overturning. Even so, Reno later described the freeing of James Richardson as one of the greatest moments of her life.

———•◆•———

Janet Reno was America's first woman attorney general, and it was inevitable that media accounts of her background would be dominated by her mother's flamboyant adventures and her own public persona. Still, there is an aspect of Reno's early life, usually submerged beneath those stories, which should be noted here.

As Paul Anderson, Reno's biographer, points out, Reno had a father, too. For 40 years, Henry Reno was the cop-beat reporter for the *Miami Herald*. During Janet Reno's childhood:

> Most mornings, Janet awoke at about six to the sound of her father on the telephone: "Hi, this is Reno of the *Herald*. Do you have anything going?" Henry would start calling police departments—what reporters call "cop shops"—at 5:30 A.M., checking on overnight arrests, burglaries, the occasional murder. When he reported to work, it was to the Miami police headquarters, not the *Herald* newsroom, preferring to have his desk among cops.[20]

Twice each year, Henry took his kids on his rounds. He was a popular man. He brought doughnuts to the station house on Sundays and he brought home-grown roses for the courthouse secretaries. For 40 years, he haunted the cop-shops. "He knew the people who made the system work—clerks in the medical examiner's office, fingerprint technicians, dispatchers—and they passed him the nitty gritty details of the most interesting cases."[21] He loved to show off the badge he had been given for being an honorary Miami police officer.

"His information was always good," one younger investigative reporter said, "but his loyalties were mixed."[22]

Janet Reno's first contacts with the criminal justice system—unlike, say, Hugo Munsterberg's, or for that matter, Linda Fairstein's—did not come in the context of the courtroom battle. Her introduction came through her father's affectionate but illusionless life among the police.

This was an unusual window for a lawyer. Henry Reno—and through him, his daughter—were in where the cases started, before the suspects had been winnowed out. They had to see that the police weren't knights or monsters, polymaths or morons; they were just regular people. Most of them were doing their best, and some of their bests were terrific. They used to come to the Renos' for the eclectic open houses that the Renos held every Sunday, drink coffee, tell stories, hang out.

Years later, Janet Reno remembered one of the lessons she took from the experience. A good homicide or sex crimes detective, she said, had just about every good quality a man could have: intelligence, dedication, compassion, judgment, courage. They were great people.

Like his daughter, Henry Reno could negotiate the conflicting demands of a professional role and a private code. In the nature of things, the *Herald's* cop-beat reporter was expected to be able to fix people's parking tickets. Henry always took the tickets, but then he'd stop by the clerk's office and pay the tickets out of his own pocket. This might have shown a desire to play a colorful role. But it seems more likely that it indicated an awareness that turning down the request would have required saying to every hopeful traffic violator, "I'm more honest than you are, and so I can't do as you ask."

Henry Reno was not inclined to put on moral airs, and he recognized that telling other people that they should pay more attention to right and wrong was really a very delicate business.

———◦•◆•◦———

Neither Linda Fairstein nor Janet Reno had the experience that J. W. "Jay" Carney had 15 years after he left the Middlesex District Attorney's Office in Massachusetts and became a leading defense lawyer in Boston. He received a call from a lawyer investigating the claims to innocence of Dennis Maher, a defendant whom Carney as a prosecutor had convicted in a series of rape cases 19 years earlier. The lawyer wanted Carney's help in finding evidence that might support Maher's claim of innocence. Carney, by this point a defense lawyer to the marrow, remembered the Maher trials: Maher's trial lawyer had been ineffectual, but it wouldn't have mattered, the testimony of the numerous eyewitnesses had been confident and compelling. The convictions had been easy; so easy, in fact, that Carney had always had an inexplicable, queasy feeling when he remembered Maher, but he attributed that queasiness to the hapless defense mounted at the trials. Carney helped Maher's new lawyers track down the evidence. A month or so later, he got a call: the DNA tests proved that Dennis Maher had been innocent all along. Carney had sent an innocent man to prison for 19 years.[23]

Carney insisted on seeing Maher and apologizing personally, and Maher accepted his apology. But talking about the case later, after Maher was released, Carney remembered another encounter with Maher.

Immediately after Maher's conviction—within a month—Carney had visited the Massachusetts maximum security prison at Walpole. It was purely routine: Carney's boss insisted that all assistant district attorneys take a tour of Walpole so they would at least glimpse the consequences of their actions, and Carney was fulfilling that annoying obligation.

Purely by coincidence, Carney's tour led him down a hallway, where, rounding a corner, he literally bumped into Dennis Maher, serving the first days of his life sentence.

"He looked at me in this terrible panic," Carney remembers. "The look on his face: I'll never forget it. He must have thought I was pursuing him."

"And when I think of that look now," Carney said, "I think, nineteen years! Nineteen *years!* We're about the same age, and I keep thinking about the things that have happened to me in nineteen years. Marriage. Kids. Law School. Nineteen years."[24]

CHAPTER NINE

DNA TO THE RESCUE (OF SOME)

KIRK BLOODSWORTH WAS AN HONORABLY DISCHARGED Marine with no criminal record, but when he was sentenced to death for the murder of Dawn Hamilton, the Baltimore County courtroom erupted in wild applause.

The verdict and sentence were overturned on appeal, and Bloodsworth was tried and convicted by a second jury. This time he was sentenced to two consecutive life terms in prison without possibility of parole. Nine years later, in June 1993, Bloodsworth reached his lawyer, Robert Morin, by telephone, to ask Morin the same question he had asked every day for a week. This time, Morin had news. Morin told Bloodsworth that independent DNA tests conducted on a semen sample from the victim's underwear had confirmed what Morin's own expert had previously found: Bloodsworth could not have been the source of the semen.

"Tell me again," Bloodsworth said. "Tell me again."

The Baltimore County district attorney dropped the case, and Bloodsworth was released—too late for his mother, who had died five months before Bloodsworth was freed. The district attorney offered no apologies. She could not even bring herself to concede that a mistake had been made, or that Bloodsworth was innocent.

"I am saying there is not enough evidence to convict him," she said.[1]

But another career prosecutor, Janet Reno, reacted differently to the Bloodsworth story. By this time she was Bill Clinton's attorney general—his third choice for the post. She had already been buffeted by the Waco shootout and was feeling her way through the unfamiliar terrain of pathologically partisan Washington.

Reno read the account of Bloodsworth's acquittal in the *Washington Post*, in an article listing the first 16 DNA exonerations. Walter Dellinger, an assistant attorney general, raised the subject later that morning in a conversation at a staff meeting.[2]

"We ought to be able to learn something from this fellow's case," he suggested. "Let's see what we can do."

"Let's see what we can do," Reno agreed.

There is an old joke among physicians that the surgeons are lucky, because the surgeons get to bury *their* mistakes, and until the advent of DNA the same was generally true of the criminal justice system. If the criminal justice system's mistakes were not literally buried—and some of them were—at least they were tucked away in penitentiaries, where their protestations of innocence could be dismissed as the whining of bad losers. No one was enthusiastic about giving up that immunity—although Janet Reno appeared to be ready to give it a try.

The United States Department of Justice includes a research arm, the National Institute of Justice, and Janet Reno's brainstorms often landed on the desk of the NIJ's director, Jeremy Travis. Travis was an acute social scientist, but more important, a battle-scarred criminal justice bureaucrat. He had been a deputy commissioner for legal affairs in the New York Police Department, and he knew the real world of the system. His job at NIJ was the leveraging of a tiny pool of resources to make big changes.

The NIJ was founded on analogy to the National Institutes of Health. The NIH funds, marshals, and disseminates cutting-edge medical information; the NIJ would do the same with promising forensic technologies. The NIJ also had a substantial social science component: assessing recidivism rates and parole strategies, for example. Unfortunately, the analogy to the National Institutes of Health had never been extended to include an equivalent level of funding; compared to the National Institute of Health, the NIJ was a pygmy. Still, it was there. The NIJ's "customers" were not limited to the federal law enforcement agencies; NIJ aimed to provide research, education, and training to the 13,000 state and local law enforcement agencies, which dominate American criminal justice.

No forensic technology was more promising, or more technological, than forensic DNA. Everyone on every side of the criminal justice system could see the power of DNA as a tool for solving crimes. And those who were slow to see it had the O. J. Simpson case to help them get started.

Janet Reno's term as attorney general coincided with a number of media-driven criminal justice crises, which gave added impetus to research and reform. The murder of seven-year-old JonBenet Ramsey in Colorado, for example, had focused attention on the horrendous problems that investigators could create for themselves by botching a crime scene. The O. J. Simpson case also had crime scene problems—for example, bloody fingerprints on Nicole Brown Simpson's corpse which had somehow been allowed to be washed off without comparison—but also DNA collection and handling problems. Meanwhile, the steady drip of DNA exoneration cases indicated that something more systemic than these spectacular examples might be going on. Reno recognized that somewhere in this mess was a potential impetus for change, but it fell to Jeremy Travis to find a vehicle for giving that impetus effect. That was fine with Janet Reno.

Janet Reno speaks of her experience with Travis in tones of wonder.

"I would give Jeremy something impossible to do," Janet Reno said, "And he would never complain. He would just get it done."[3]

————◆◆◆————

Travis quickly realized that the first step was to figure out exactly what there was to know about the DNA cases. The National Institute of Justice contracted with Institute of Law and Justice, a private research group in Alexandria, Virginia. Four of the institute's staffers—Edward Connors, Thomas Lundregan, Neil Miller, and Tom McEwen—were put to work on gathering from news accounts, court opinions (and rumors) a list of cases in which convicted defendants were exonerated by DNA testing.

They came up with 28 cases. A list was good to have, of course, but Travis was not content to stop with a list, and it was decided to publish a pamphlet surveying the available cases and their potential lessons. That paperback pamphlet, *Convicted By Juries, Exonerated by Science: Case Studies In The Use of DNA Evidence to Establish Innocence After Trial,*[4] quickly became one of the most talked about publications in the criminal justice system. Travis had seen to it that this new "Green Book," as it was called, became an event rather than one more list.

The Green Book's impact owed a great deal to its format. The raw numbers, 28 wrongful convictions for rape or murder, would certainly have had an impact of their own, but the Green Book's authors went beyond the numbers and included capsule summaries of each of the 28 miscarriages of justice. Ronald Cotton was there; Kirk Bloodsworth was there—and Terry Chalmers, and Leonard Callace, and Charles Dabbs—an amazing catalogue of undeserved punishment and shattered lives, a total of 197 years served in prison by innocent men. All of the cases had gone to trial, and in every case, it was possible to

see why the conviction would have looked plausible, even inevitable, to the jurors who evaluated the evidence. In most of the cases—although there were
several that involved law enforcement misconduct—it was easy to see why the
police and prosecutors at the time would have been certain that they had the
right man.

By far the leading common feature of the wrongful conviction cases was
eyewitness identification testimony.

This was helpful in advancing one prominent policy goal. At this early
stage in the history of DNA evidence, the reception that DNA would receive
from the courts was still in doubt. If nothing else, the Green Book identification cases demonstrated the superiority of DNA evidence of identity to the
methods traditionally employed. Judges might be motivated to permit lawyers
to mobilize this new science in courtrooms now that it could be compared to
its traditional competitors.

But was there more to the DNA findings than that? A feature of the
Green Book format helped to provide an answer. Reno and Travis were determined to go beyond the list of exonerations and the capsule summaries of the
cases, and to include commentaries from various actors in the criminal justice
system.

For one of these commentaries, they reached out to what the police like to
call "the dark side"—the criminal defense lawyers—and sought a contribution
from Peter Neufeld and Barry Scheck.

———————•◆•———————

No criminal case held the nation's attention the way O. J. Simpson's case held
it. The O. J. Simpson case was the public's introduction to the uses and mis-
uses of DNA technology, and the master of ceremonies for that introduction
was a former Legal Aid lawyer from the Bronx, Barry Scheck.

Barry Scheck and his fellow Legal Aid alumnus, Peter Neufeld, have
been described as such a close team that they resembled "a single brain
locked within two querulous bodies." Their collaboration deserves an entire
book, and in fact Scheck and Neufeld have told their own story, with brio, in
Actual Innocence,[5] the book they co-authored with *New York Times* correspon-
dent Jim Dwyer. Nothing that follows here can substitute for reading that account of innocent men saved from wrongful convictions by Scheck's and
Neufeld's efforts and the efforts of the families, students, and investigators
who worked with them. Still, there are aspects of their operations that should
be emphasized.

In the aftermath of the O. J. Simpson case, Barry Scheck tended more and more to become the public face of the Scheck-Neufeld team. Unlike some of the "celebrity lawyers" the media unearths, Scheck was the real thing: a deeply experienced former public defender, not a blowhard who happened to have stumbled onto his one big case. In fact, Scheck's career is the exact inverse of that sort of celebrity lawyer's: Scheck was as much a victim of his one big case as he was a beneficiary. Scheck's role in the Simpson trial has opened doors for him, but in another sense it has become a blight, obscuring his genuine brilliance and his indefatigable work ethic.

One example of Scheck in a tactical setting may help to demonstrate his real-world acuteness. Scheck defended Louise Woodward, a teenaged British nanny, in a Massachusetts trial in which she was charged with killing the infant son of two Massachusetts doctors. In a heartbreaking irony, the child had been taken to the emergency room of Boston's Children's Hospital where his parents had been on staff. Children's Hospital is a leading force in child abuse prevention, and it was the headquarters of Dr. Eli Newberger, a renowned expert in the field of pediatric trauma, and a man who gave every sign of believing that his Nobel Prize, while inexplicably tardy in arriving, was just over the horizon. The prosecution in "the Nanny Case," as it became known in Boston, was waiting confidently to parade Dr. Newberger and his Olympian medical conclusions before the jury.

But the prosecution made the mistake of underestimating Scheck, and the prosecutors put on their case in chronological order, beginning with the young emergency room physician who had treated the unresponsive child when the ambulance arrived. At that point, Scheck simply hijacked the case, and instead of waiting for Dr. Newberger, an experienced and supremely self-confident witness to testify, as 90 percent of lawyers would have, Scheck put in *Scheck's* medical theory during his cross-examination of the fledgling emergency room doctor. Eventually, of course, the jury did get to hear from Dr. Newberger, but the first medical information they received—the frame through which they would see all later medical information including Dr. Newberger's—was the information Scheck generated for them in his bold grab for initiative in the first day of the trial. And the information Scheck generated was the product of his fanatical study of the medical situation: he displayed a hard-won and perfectly genuine mastery of the scientific material, light years beyond the reach of any show-boating lawyer you are likely to see holding forth on TV.

Scheck's talents unsettle those who are uncomfortable around very smart people, and they cause distrust among people who identify him completely with the Simpson case. They imagine that Scheck's brains are at the service of the obviously guilty, and likely to produce spectacular perversions of justice. In the Nanny case there were people who found Scheck's manner abrasive, too. Some fraction of this was simply the chalk-on-blackboard effect that the endemic dialectical approach of natives of Greater New York has on people raised in gentler environments. But there were also people who were upset by aspects of Scheck's direct approach, which Scheck himself may have seen as an implied compliment. Scheck had a tendency to cut to the chase: "Look," he seemed to say, "I'm a smart guy and this was obvious to me, and *you're* a smart guy, so it will be just as obvious to you, too."

The fact that Scheck was usually absolutely right about what he was saying was not always mitigating in the eyes of hostile listeners; in fact, it often heightened their anxiety. These problems were exacerbated by the fact that his subject matter wasn't limited to policies; it inevitably implicated personal values. As Janet Reno once remarked, when you are talking to cops, judges, and prosecutors about questions of wrongful convictions and miscarriages of justice you are trespassing on very tender areas—trespassing on areas where people have worked their whole lives, generally for low pay. Scheck's face-to-face approach was well within normal limits—in fact he was typically quite respectful, polite, and modest—but Scheck was in a hurry, and it may be that he was not as careful about hurt feelings as Reno would have recommended.

The most important thing about Scheck's journey, however, was *where* he was hurrying. Here, too, the contrast between Scheck and Neufeld and the typical, one big case TV lawyer is striking. Scheck and Neufeld were not frantically moving to their next big case; they were trying to multiply the impact of the science for the benefit of legions of people they would never meet.

They did this, first by giving a name—"The Innocence Project"—to the pile of files and letters from inmates which had been accumulating on their desks since their first successes.[6] Working with lawyers, law schools, law teachers, and journalists around the country, Scheck and Neufeld began to piece together a network of people and institutions who were prepared to dedicate the time and effort necessary to begin to litigate claims of innocence with the new tool that DNA presented. This helped pull a constellation of widely scattered and superficially disparate cases into a form with a focus. Now, not only would individual inmates have an easier time finding representation, but the patterns and common features of their cases would be seen more easily, and someone—generally Scheck or Neufeld—would be in a position to comment coherently on those patterns and features for the media when the next exoneration case came around. At this point, every exoneration case was a big local story, and The Innocence Project could knit that local story into a national one. Behind every dramatic press conference stretched hours of grinding labor, but Scheck and Neufeld had developed the capacity to inspire the law student and journalism student foot soldiers who helped to get that grunt work done.

Scheck and Neufeld refused to be blinded by the cases they had already won with DNA, or by the future cases that allies in their spreading network of Innocence Projects would win; they insisted that attention be paid to the legions of cases—murders, robberies, shootings, burglaries—where you couldn't count on biological material being left behind for testing.

When the NIJ offered the "Green Book" as a forum, Sheck and Neufeld seized the opportunity to demand that officials examine what DNA told us about cases where there was no DNA. Look at this list of exonerations, they said. What about the thousands of cases where there are false confessions, but no DNA? How did the false confessions happen? Look at the cases where jailhouse snitches lied. What about all the other cases we don't see here, where there are jailhouse snitches, but no DNA? And look at all the *thousands* of cases where there are eyewitnesses, but no DNA? Is there something systemic going wrong? Shouldn't we at least ask ourselves that question?

Neufeld and Scheck pried loose from the FBI laboratory, which was doing most of the law enforcement DNA analysis in the country, the fact that in about 25 percent of the FBI comparisons of the DNA of "prime suspects" submitted by state and local investigations, the prime suspect was *eliminated!*[7] Scheck and Neufeld argued that the 28 cases included in the "Green Book" were a beginning point, not a conclusion. "There is a strong scientific basis," they said, "for believing that these matters represent just the tip of a very deep and disturbing iceberg of cases."

Scheck and Neufeld made the point that the "Green Book" cases presented not just cause for alarm, but an immense opportunity. They wrote: "Perhaps there has never been a richer or more exciting set of cases for criminal justice researchers to explore in terms of shedding light on how law enforcement methods impact the crucial problem of factual innocence."

The great thing about the DNA cases was the magic lens they provided. To understand what was happening in whole genres of cases, you only had to look at a DNA case as if there were no DNA. The Green Book cases made that thought experiment almost unavoidable: You could look at a DNA exoneration case and see clearly how it looked before DNA, and how it looked after DNA technology was applied. The same case, perfectly controlled, except for the one change: DNA, or—like many, many routine criminal cases—no DNA.

One of the cases you could look at in this way was Jennifer Thompson's and Ronald Cotton's.

———•◆••———

Early in 1996, the Public Broadcasting Service documentary series *Frontline* had a problem. A lot of money had been handed out to a senior producer along with the assignment "Find something new to say about the O. J. Simpson case." The producer had returned—many, many, dollars later—and announced that in the considered opinion of everyone involved in the project, there was nothing new to say about the O. J. Simpson case. Absolutely nothing. Anyone who was inclined to argue the point was invited to produce an example: no one could.

Simply admitting that the money was gone and scrapping the whole project was a distasteful alternative for a host of reasons, so *Frontline* turned to Ben Loeterman, a Massachusetts-based producer, and more or less begged him to come up with *something*. He had a reputation for being good on his feet, and for being able to cope with a short turn-around time.

Loeterman started to fish around.

It seemed to him that one of the issues that the O. J. trial—or at least its outcome—had raised was whether DNA technology, which had been touted as the miracle drug of criminal justice, was now damaged goods. Had Barry Scheck's success in defusing the prosecution's DNA evidence in the Simpson case undermined the utility of DNA for future cases? Loeterman had learned of other cases in which released defendants, supposedly exonerated by DNA, were rearrested for new rapes committed after their releases. Had DNA become the rapists' friend? During the course of asking around about this potential "hook," Loeterman began to pick up rumors about some sort of project, deep in the bowels of the Department of Justice, which was supposed to be assessing where things stood with DNA. Loeterman had stumbled across the early stages of the project that would ultimately turn into the "Green Book" on DNA exonerations.

Loeterman's success as a documentary producer—he had won several Emmy awards by this point—can be traced to his recognition that a documentary producer is a not a data compiler, but a storyteller. He was very good at telling stories. But beyond that, Loeterman even took a delight in the reporter's challenge of "getting the story," which seemed more characteristic of the frenetic, press-pass-in-the-hat-band era of *The Front Page* than of the cloistered halls of the Public Broadcasting Service. He got on the telephone;

he prodded Barry Scheck and Peter Neufeld for leads and contacts, and he got to work on sifting through the exoneration cases for a tale to tell.

Loeterman came up with a primitive list of the first round of DNA exoneration cases. As he was finishing, the Department of Justice's "Green Book" was formally issued. With money tight, Loeterman culled his list to the East Coast cases so that he could keep the airfares under control, and he started collecting documents and calling prosecutors, police, and defense lawyers involved in the cases on his list. He quickly found that nobody felt particularly eager to help out; in fact, everyone was on his or her guard. The trial prosecutors generally weren't tempted by the prospect of appearing on television in the role of convictor of the blameless; the defense lawyers didn't relish appearing as failed champion of innocence. There was a promising case in Philadelphia, but Loeterman couldn't pry the elements of a filmable story loose. Every case he looked at seemed to have insurmountable problems.

Loeterman had worked his way down the coast to North Carolina before he ran into Rich Rosen, the law professor at the University of North Carolina who had finally cleared Ronald Cotton. Rosen told him the Ronald Cotton story straightforwardly, and brought in his co-counsel to fill him in on details. They talked to Ronald Cotton, and advised him that it would be all right to sit for an interview with Loeterman. The appellate defense lawyers even steered him to the district attorney, and the district attorney seemed reasonably responsive, too—the Cotton conviction had happened on his predecessor's watch, and the current D.A.'s only role had been to accept what the DNA told him was the truth.

Loeterman took a glimmer of hope and the bare outlines of the Cotton/Thompson case back to Boston with him and consulted a mentor, veteran *Frontline* producer Ofra Bikel. Interviewing Ronald Cotton had been like pulling teeth, Loeterman explained, but he did have some decent footage, and maybe he could make something of it. The cop who had conducted the original investigation, Mike Gauldin, was the perfect portrait of confused decency, terribly troubled by what had happened. Jimmy Stewart could have played him.

"But, Ben," Bikel asked, "What does the *woman* say? The story is in what *the woman* says."

Loeterman knew that Bikel was right. He admired Bikel tremendously, and he'd had the same thought himself more than once on the way back from North Carolina. Rosen, Mike Gauldin, and the District Attorney had all been very vigorous in their praise for Jennifer's courage, honesty, and intelligence. They all seemed to think that she was something special.

The problem was that Loeterman didn't really know who "the woman" was; he had only her maiden name, and she had married since. The court records weren't easy to gain access to in a rape case, and besides they were no help when they only showed "Jennifer Thompson" as the victim's name. All of the North Carolina cops and lawyers involved on both sides had been extremely scrupulous about protecting her identity. The only crumb of information that Loeterman had was that when he had asked how the victim was doing, one of the North Carolina people mentioned that he had seen "Jennifer" at a local mall with her new triplets and that she had been doing fine.

At this point, fate intervened. In fact, a wacky level of coincidence appropriate to Shakespearian comedy took a hand. By pure chance, Loeterman's wife worked in a specialized arts-related field, and she had an associate in that part of North Carolina. That associate had a friend, and the friend had married a woman named "Jennifer," and Jennifer and the friend had just had kids—the right number of kids. Loeterman poked around a little more and convinced himself that he now had "Jennifer Thompson's" married name.

That was progress, but it wasn't an interview, and without the interview there was no documentary. There was no reason to hope that a rape victim would willingly make a television appearance for the purpose of admitting that her eyewitness identifications had sent an innocent man to prison for a decade.

Still, Loeterman had one last card to play, and he sat down at his computer to write a letter to Jennifer in which he played that card. He sent it by overnight delivery, and he tried to time the delivery so that it would arrive at a quiet moment when she would have time to think it over without an audience.

Loeterman's hole card was this: in a prior *Frontline* emergency, he had compiled a documentary, *Angel On Death Row*, which had examined the stories of the real-life victims of the Louisiana murderer who had been the focus of the Susan Sarandon-Sean Penn movie, *Dead Man Walking*. There were echoes of that project in this one. *Dead Man Walking* had focused its drama on the death row ministry of Sister Helen Prejean, and the victims of the crimes had been left on the margins of the story. The same was true of the media coverage that the film's release had generated. Loeterman's reporter's nose and a certain contrarian skepticism about what the right-thinking mainstream saw as the heart of the story led Loeterman to find those victims and to interview them. He mobilized that experience in writing to Jennifer:

> I understand completely that many years later you now have a new life and
> would like nothing more than to forget what must have been a very dark
> episode. . . . I appreciate that many people who know you now may know

nothing of what happened then. I am, of course fully willing to protect your privacy. . . . By coincidence, in my last film I met a young mother, 32, who had had a similarly terrifying experience of being kidnapped and repeatedly raped. I don't know why she agreed to talk with me. But what I do know is that since doing so two things have happened: she feels like the weight of a dark secret has been lifted from her, and the unforeseen outpouring of support she received for having done so has had a tremendously positive impact on her.

Loeterman provided Jennifer with a copy of his *Angel of Death Row* tape, and with the name of the victim he had interviewed as a kind of reference. He said, in effect, "Check me out. I'm not an exploiter." And he provided Jennifer with a reason for speaking:

> We have serious questions about whether the system in its reliance on scientific evidence may be freeing guilty men to commit further crimes against innocent people. How much weight should DNA be given in balancing the scales of justice? Talking with you would give us tremendous insight into these questions. . . . Any serious examination of this subject must, we think, include the views of someone who was a victim.[8]

Although Loeterman could not have known it at the time, this was the sort of call to duty that Jennifer Thompson could not resist. Two days later, Loeterman's telephone rang: It was Jennifer Thompson, and Loeterman was on his way back to North Carolina. One of the first things everyone learned about Jennifer was that she is an extremely decisive person.

Loeterman interviewed Jennifer in her kitchen. The interview was not routine. One plus was that Jennifer was simply a much more telegenic victim than any producer had a right to hope for, and more articulate than many professional television pundits. But Jennifer was not about to play the passive victim, lending herself to the ministrations of the inquiring journalist, and grateful to be on TV. Anything Loeterman got from Jennifer he would get because Jennifer had decided that telling it furthered her own determined efforts to avoid being either forgotten or caricatured. Jennifer was not prepared to be used, and Loeterman was mildly surprised to find that she had taken him up on his suggestion and checked him out by calling the victim in the *Angel Of Death Row* interview and quizzing her about Loeterman. Loeterman even found himself wondering whether Jennifer wasn't prepared to use *him*, if that's what getting her message across took. Still, in the end, the interview's unpredictable moments created a healthy tension. The anger and hurt came through.

Jennifer had watched Ronald Cotton's post-release interview on *Larry King Live*, and it disturbed her:

> But all of a sudden, me as a victim who suffered a horrific crime, a crime that a lot of people can't understand, all of a sudden we are almost like thrown away and the victim then becomes the man who has been released out of prison and all of a sudden, his victimization is just, it's hailed and everyone feels sorry for him and it is just, it's terrible. We took away years of his life, which I am not trying to deny any of those things, but the same amount of years have been taken away from me. His bars were made of metal. My bars are emotional.[9]

Nothing in Jennifer's lengthy interview quite delivered the stereotype of the pathetic victim who is usually paraded before the cameras. She was still tormented by the terrible price of Bobby Poole's crimes, and of her own mistake, and she wanted to tell her story, but she wasn't asking for pity. She had experienced a terrible trauma and it was always with her but she had learned to "live around it," and she was functioning—a great wife and great mother. She had no interest in recycling clichés; she had given her experiences independent thought.

Loeterman filmed the interview in a moody chiaroscuro, which set off Jennifer's expressive, wounded face and emphasized the drama. But those efforts were superfluous. Jennifer dominated the program. Ronald Cotton's segments had been poignant, but his stoicism had a muted impact. Besides, everyone had heard some exonerated inmate's side of a wrongful conviction story by then. No one had ever seen a victim like Jennifer.

This wasn't simply a matter of charisma, although Jennifer certainly has charisma to spare. The startling thing about Jennifer Thompson is the absolute congruence between her most deeply held thoughts and emotions and her expression of them. Her hurt was deep inside, but it was also right there on the surface. Here it is, viewers: pain—anguished, devastating, chronic pain, but pain without self-pity. She felt her guilt in her bones, and she expressed it with no extra emotion or rhetorical gestures. Here it is, viewers: guilt—awful, unadorned, heartbreaking, enduring guilt, without histrionics. It had the clarity of the performance of a great actress, except that Jennifer was not acting; she was just *being*. When she watched the coverage of Ronald Cotton's release she said:

> I remember feeling sick, but also I remember feeling just an overwhelming sense of just guilt that if indeed we had made a mistake and I had contributed to taking away 11 years of this man's life, and if indeed we had been wrong—I

felt so bad. I fell apart. I cried and cried and I wept and I was angry at me and I beat myself up for it for a long time.[10]

Loeterman closed his program with one final question: "When you think of the rapist, who do you see?" In the final cut, Jennifer sits quietly for a moment, looking steadily at her interviewer with her large hurt eyes:

> I have to accept the answer that's been given to me and put faith in our system that the DNA tests, the science, tells me we had the wrong guy. I just wish I had some answers. I still see Ronald Cotton. And I'm not saying that to point a finger. I'm just saying that's who I see. And I would love to erase that face out of my mind. I would do anything to erase that face out of my mind, but I can't. It's just—it's in my head. Sometimes it's more fuzzy than others because my mind now says, "Well, it's Bobby Poole." But it's—it's still the face I see.[11]

The camera lingered for a moment as Jennifer sat in silence, staring out her kitchen window. It was a haunting ending. It wasn't the story the Loeterman had come looking for, but he had the sense to realize that Jennifer's version was even better.

Frontline's "What Jennifer Saw" was broadcast in February 1997. The *Frontline* publicity people saw to it that the broadcast network talk shows learned what they had. This time, the mainstream commercial media wanted Jennifer Thompson, the mistaken victim who was ready to speak out—one of a kind. Pretty soon the story was all around. Jennifer endured a reasonably intelligent interview on *Good Morning America,* then a farcical interaction with *Oprah's* fatuous "Dr. Phil." The relationship between DNA exonerations and eyewitness unreliability was out in public for good. As Barry Scheck and Peter Neufeld continued to dole out their latest DNA exoneration cases, Jennifer's experience was there for the new cases to resonate with—a little knot tied in the memory of news editors around the country, trying to find a hook for their own local wrongful conviction case. The Cotton/Thompson case had fresh features to it, but it also called up the ghost of hundreds of books, news stories, and films of wrongful identifications: films like *Northside 666,* or *The Wrong Man,* which dramatically intensified the existential fear of wrongful convictions. From the media's point of view, it was perfect.

But "What Jennifer Saw" did not provide the complexity of Elizabeth Loftus's memory experiments; by its nature, the television format could only contribute to the generalized skepticism about all eyewitnesses that the Buckhout and Munsterberg demonstrations had created, and there were psychologists who were very critical of it for that reason. If a witness as good as Jennifer could be mistaken, the coverage seemed to imply, you can't trust any of them. But was *every* witness who was as good as Jennifer mistaken, or was this a freakish event? It was at best two steps forward, one and a half steps back. Jennifer Thompson had dispelled generic misconceptions about her personal experience, but it wasn't clear what anyone could do about it.

If there was an answer to that question it wasn't yet clear to the media—even to the Public Broadcasting Service.

◆・◆・◆

Laboring to follow up on the Green Book's impact, Jeremy Travis put together a series of "The Future of DNA" meetings, and invited a variety of potentially interested parties to brainstorm what should happen next. Usually, Dr. Richard Rau, who was the NIJ's Project Monitor for the DNA effort, would draft (with Travis' help) someone from a relevant field to serve as moderator of these sessions to try to prod people into thinking of new approaches.

During one of these meetings, as the process was winding down, Attorney General Janet Reno entered the room unannounced. Although Reno is over six feet tall, she is a less imposing figure in person than she seems on television: more slender, even prettier. Still, she was accompanied by a security man, which caused a stir, and the most powerful law enforcement official in the United States will project an aura no matter how much she might hope to avoid that effect. Everyone in the invited group tried to go on with business as usual, and succeeded for a time. After a while, however, there was a lull in their conversations.

At this point the Attorney General of the United States spoke up from the back of the room.

"I'd like to hear," she said, "what Gary Wells has to say about these eye-witness identification cases, and what we can do about them."

CHAPTER TEN

BREAK OUT SHOT

Gary Wells and The System

IN 1976, 20 YEARS BEFORE JANET RENO MADE her request from the back row, Bob Buckhout placed a telephone call to an obscure Ph.D. student at Ohio State named Gary Wells. Buckhout left a message saying that he wanted to invite Wells to speak on a panel at a conference of the American Psychological Association (A.P.A.) in Washington.

That call put psychology on the road toward solving the mystery of how Jennifer Thompson could have been so wrong and to showing what practical steps could have prevented Jennifer's mistake.

Buckhout and Wells had never met, and when Wells picked up his messages he thought that the one from "Buckhout" was a practical joke. Calls from well-known professors to lowly graduate students didn't happen in academia; graduate students were to be seen—when that was absolutely unavoidable—but not heard, and they were certainly not to be solicited for public lectures by their elders and betters. It wasn't until Buckhout called again later in the day that Wells finally accepted that he was really being sought out by Buckhout, the celebrity professor who was bearing the banner of psychology onto the battlefield of eyewitness testimony.

The understanding within the A.P.A. in that era was that graduate students did not make presentations unless they had an A.P.A. member—an actual professor—as a sponsor or co-author. So, Wells approached an Ohio State faculty member—the only one who was thought of as marginally "graduate-student-friendly"—and asked him to sign on to a presentation. Wells innocently presented Buckhout's invitation to the faculty member as a great opportunity.

"I'll sign on," the faculty member shrugged grimly, "but you may not want to do this program with Buckhout, and if you *do* decide to do it, just do the panel and clear out. Don't let Buckhout latch on to you. He's not publishing anything important of his own. He'll use you to boost his credibility, and he'll wreck your career."[1]

The whole eyewitness thing, this elder said, was a dead end. The best thing for Wells to do was to extricate himself from it as quickly as he could, and get back to his work on attribution theory.

Wells did the A.P.A. program despite this warning. He didn't clear out after the panel either; he spent some time with Buckhout. He thought Buckhout was charming. His stories were vivid and compelling, the stuff of real-life battle "in the trenches" on behalf of idealistic zealots and victimized Negroes against the unscrupulous State. The way Buckhout told the stories was fascinating, too. Buckhout was a charismatic figure, and he wasn't a monologuist; he involved his listeners. Buckhout's conversations always turned into exchanges. By some alchemy that wasn't quite visible, he made his listeners—even battered graduate students—feel free to challenge and debate him. Buckhout's own statements were black and white: he saw good guys and bad guys. The system was running these crooked lineups and ignoring psychological findings in order to get the little guy. This Manichean style made Buckhout's conversation compelling, and if it provoked questions, that seemed to be fine with Buckhout. Buckhout's Center for Responsive Psychology had become a popular student hangout at Brooklyn College because of this atmosphere, even though the tenured faculty was inclined to look askance at the whole project. The question that Buckhout's war stories of rigged lineups and tragic misidentifications provoked for Gary Wells was "Why do the cops do it?" Wells was interested in possibilities that Buckhout did not concede existed: Was it possible that the police just didn't understand what they were doing? Was ignorance, not corruption, at work? Buckhout heard these questions out, but didn't seem persuaded, or even interested. Nevertheless, the encounter had a heady effect on Wells: he was hooked.

Wells had rejected the advice of his Ohio State mentor, but he did not forget it. It echoed in his mind when Buckhout began to call him for material for his mimeographed publications, or to suggest that Wells should become an "affiliate" of the Center for Responsive Psychology. Wells had the uncomfortable feeling that his Ohio State mentor's dire warnings were right after all, that he was being drafted into a movement.

If drafting Wells was Buckhout's goal, Wells would have justified a very high draft pick. Buckhout was really a very acute talent-spotter.

"People were always telling us that Science was about asking good questions," one researcher remembers, "And Gary asks better questions than anybody else." Wells had been fascinated all of his life by the same tension that had animated Munsterberg and the other heirs of the nineteenth-century scientists: the tension between faith and proof. Wells liked solving puzzles, investigating things until you found the truth and could prove it. Even better from Buckhout's activist perspective, Wells's talents as a scientist were only a starting point. The fact is, Buckhout *was* founding a movement—or at least, continuing Munsterberg's movement—and if you were running a movement, you needed someone just like Wells. Wells liked working with people, and he didn't mind sharing credit. Like Buckhout, he was happy to help his assistants and deputies along, to launch new allies into the field, to coordinate and encourage. Wells even had an interest in how eyewitness investigation worked in law enforcement. During the summer after high school he had taken a private detective course, and it had piqued his interest in eyewitness procedures.

Better still, if you were Buckhout and planning a struggle with the status quo in the real world, Wells would provide a colleague who loved strategy and tactics. He had grown up in a home where there wasn't much money, married his high school sweetheart when he was 17 and she was 16, and had a kid right away. Wells had worked his way through college playing pool, and eventually he reached international ranking. He played all the time. Wells loved the game: the angles, the concentration, the need to see the whole table, to plan many shots ahead. Strategic and tactical thinking were part of his wiring. When Wells wasn't playing pool, he played chess for recreation, but the attraction of pool wasn't the same purely cerebral pleasure that chess offered. For Wells, pool was a case of a vocation and an avocation perfectly aligned. Wells had to learn how to hustle to support his family, and besides, he loved the rackety, eclectic company of pool players. To this day some of his closest friends are drawn from the wildly assorted individualists who play serious pool.

And like most people who came of age in America in the 1960s, Wells wanted to see justice done. He was not a radical; in fact, he had a sturdy, Midwesterner's skepticism about movements and causes. But no one was sealed-off from 1960s idealism. Wells was a scientist who put science far above politics, but he was also one committed to the idea that psychology could play a role in improving the world. Wells even had a vision of how it could be done.

Wells's strategist's eyes surveyed the table as Buckhout had set it up, counted the balls and evaluated the angles. It seemed to him that Buckhout had left a very unpromising—even sterile—situation. Before anything could happen, the balls would have to be scattered into a new arrangement. Pool players call this a "break out" shot—a shot that changes the strategic picture on the table, and creates opportunities where there had been none. Wells decided that the eyewitness field needed a break out before a new campaign could be mounted.

———•◦•———

In the fall of 1976 Wells was a newly minted Ph.D. just arrived at the University of Alberta in Edmonton. In fact, Wells was the very picture of a newly minted Ph.D. Blonde, pipe-smoking, invariably wearing tweed jacket and jeans, he looked as if he had born for—maybe even born on—the campus.

Wells had been working during that summer with a graduate assistant, Rod Lindsay, on a series of experiments designed to evaluate jurors' ability to determine the accuracy of eyewitnesses. The process had been elaborate. Over 100 witnesses were recruited to observe a staged theft, then asked to identify the thief from a 6-photo array. Then these witnesses—both accurate and inaccurate—were cross-examined in front of 200 jurors. The question weighed by the experiment was whether jurors could sort the inaccurate eyewitnesses from the accurate ones.

"At some point during this process," Wells remembered recently, "I realized that even *I* couldn't tell who was right and who was wrong."

Wells knew the scientific literature on eyewitness identification pretty well by then: Munsterberg's early work, Buckhout's demonstrations, Loftus's more controlled experiments, even Roy Malpass' pioneering studies[2] on cross-racial identifications. He believed that Buckhout was certainly right in saying that the experiments raised warning flags: It was pretty clear that the eye was not a camera, and that the mind was not a videotape. But that didn't help anyone to decide which witness was right and which wrong. *All* of the eyewitnesses weren't wrong. Wells didn't see any solution to the problem in the literature.

So Wells started thinking. Then he started writing. He would pause over a passage now and then to tease out details, or to clarify or support particular points, but he remembers the writing flowing. He sat up late nights, with a young kid in the apartment, typing away, feeling "jazzed up." He was 26 years old at the time.

"I just feel really lucky," he says now, "to have seen something important so early in my career and to be able to stick with it."

When he was finished he gave his essay a title—"Applied Eyewitness Testimony Research: System Variables and Estimator Variables"—and he mailed it to the *Journal of Personality and Social Psychology*.

For boldness this was the equivalent of a high school English student sending a short story off to *The New Yorker*. The *Journal of Personality and Social Psychology* was one of the blue-ribbon scholarly vehicles in the field. It was immensely prestigious and famously picky: its editors jealously guarded its pages. Psychologists spoke of it in hushed tones of awe.

But the boldness Wells showed in submitting his article was nothing compared to the boldness of the article's content.

The editors of the *Journal of Personality and Social Psychology* loved Wells's manuscript immediately, and even an outsider can see why. Wells's "System Variables" article has the peculiar force and clarity of the few documents you run into now and then that are drafted only after long and intensive thought about fundamental things. The fledgling author means to change the world of eyewitness research, but there is nothing showy or histrionic about the piece; it has a stripped-down-to-essentials feel to it. In fact, the "System Variables" article as it unfolds evokes nothing so much as the icy confidence of a master pool shark, silently stalking around the table, and draining every shot.

The first thing that Buckhout's prospective recruit had to say was that Buckhout had it wrong. Wells's initial shot was aimed to purge the eyewitness field of the lefty-activist tang associated with Buckhout. Wells's opening footnote announces:

> This article will assume that convicting an innocent defendant (false alarm) is no more of an injustice than is releasing a guilty defendant (miss). While this may seem to contradict the views of many social-action groups concerned with criminal justice, any differential weighting of these two types of error might restrict researchers' focus on the broader issues and/or inappropriately affect how researchers operationalize eyewitness variables. On the other hand, differential weighting might be defended by the often-overlooked fact that for "false alarms," the falsely accused suffers and the true criminal is still at large. . . .[3]

According to Wells, the legal system's hostile posture toward psychological expertise was perfectly understandable in light of Buckhout's approach. Since the criminal justice system was obviously not going to eliminate eyewitness testimony altogether, Buckhout's "blanket discountings of eyewitness testimony, even if they are correct, are bound to be greeted with negative reaction by the criminal justice system."[4]

Wells's dismissal of Buckhout's approach couldn't have been more final. Wells was not simply tinkering with a "politically correct" vocabulary in order to market the science in a more palatable form to criminal justice officials. Wells's critique of the course that Buckhout and Loftus had steered so far was far more fundamental, and its criterion was not political; it was scientific.

Buckhout was never surprised when he provoked dissent within psychology. He seemed positively to enjoy jousting with McCloskey and Egeth, and besides, from the very beginning Buckhout's hero, Munsterberg, had faced attacks from academic scientists who argued that Munsterberg's obsession with finding applications for the science had debased the science and created a sideshow. Munsterberg and William James managed to shrug these complaints off as the whining of "brass instrument" psychologists. In the hierarchy of academic prestige, "basic" science ranked above "applied" science, and the "basic" professors were anxious that their applied science cousins should never forget it. Buckhout had dismissed McCloskey and Egeth by consigning them to the nervous camp of prissy academics.

But Wells could not be dismissed as another incarnation of the cramped and laboratory-bound fraternity of mandarins who had sniffed at Munsterberg; Wells was attacking Buckhout's project *as an application*—his claim was that Buckhout provided no basis for making use of psychology's findings in the real world. There is good science, and there is useful science, and if you want to claim that you are "doing" applied psychology, your science must be both good and useful.

Applied social psychology can be very useful, Wells agreed. In fact, for science to be good applied social psychology, the science is *required* to be useful. That was exactly the test that Buckhout and his followers were failing. To be useful, Wells argued, even an applied field cannot live without theory. Of course, Beth Loftus had frankly admitted that her field needed more study and research, but that, Wells calmly announced, was not the problem. The real problem, according to Wells, was not just that the researchers needed to do more studies, but that they couldn't articulate coherently what they were studying or why they were studying it:

> . . . the field of applied eyewitness testimony research needs more than a review; it needs criticism and a collimated line of focus. Researchers of basic theory have maintained direction and focus by precisely demonstrating how their operations apply to a *theory*. Applied eyewitness testimony researchers,

however, have generally been somewhat unclear as to how their operations apply to criminal justice. Although it is the responsibility of individual researchers to make this link, it might prove fruitful to have a general category system that relates eyewitness variables to criminal justice concepts.[5]

That "general category system" was what Wells supplied.

It was the first concrete step on the road that brought Wells—and his science—to the attention of the attorney general of the United States.

———•·◆·•———

Look at the existing body of eyewitness research, Wells said, and you see researchers—including the scientifically scrupulous researchers like Loftus and Malpass—testing two very different kinds of variables which are elements in the process of eyewitness identification.

The first set of variables really can damage eyewitness reliability, but they are not under the direct control of the criminal justice system. For example, the race of the criminal and the race of the witness were genuinely influential variables, and easy to isolate for empirically sound scientific inquiry, but the criminal justice system never chooses the race of the criminal or the race of the witness. The system has to take its crimes and its witnesses as it finds them. The same is true of the severity or stress of the crime incident. The impact of the severity of the crime was there; you could examine it, but you couldn't change it in an actual case. The criminal justice system, Wells pointed out, "Cannot directly control the severity of crimes so as to produce less fallible eyewitness accounts." That didn't mean the study of these factors was pointless; you might learn things from your studies that would help the court system in a retrospective analysis, looking back to consider whether a particular eyewitness was right or wrong. Understanding factors that the criminal justice system could never control is useful in helping the police and the courts to *estimate* the reliability of eyewitnesses after the fact. But it was important to recognize and admit that it was estimation of a very rough kind that you were doing: in Wells's new general system, these event factors—e.g., the race of the criminal, the lighting at the crime scene, the duration of the criminal episode—were called "*Estimator* Variables."

Wells insisted that the important thing that Buckhout had ignored was that when you looked critically at the research you could also see other factors at work which *were* under the control of the criminal justice system. How soon after the crime were the witnesses questioned? Did that have an impact? The "forgetting curve" research suggested that sooner was much better than later, and the system did have control over when the police interviews occurred. The system could apply the laboratory findings to managing the scheduling of interviews. How were the interview questions worded? The Loftus "Yield Sign/Stop Sign" and "collided/bumped/hit" experiments indicated that the wording of questions does matter: the wording can modify the witness's memory. Since the criminal justice system's own agents are asking the questions, the criminal justice system could apply the lessons of the research in designing its procedures for witness interviews, and in training and supervising its officials in those procedures. Does the casual use of mugshots before in-person lineups degrade the reliability of eyewitnesses later? The research indicated that when the lineup was held witnesses who browsed through mugshots were twice as likely to identify an innocent person whose mugshot had been displayed to them as to identify a totally new face. The police could consider and apply the research findings to their use of mugshots in investigations. These factors which were under the direct control of the criminal justice system Wells called "*System* Variables."[6]

Wells' categories could overlap. Even a "system variable" such as the timing of the interview or the composition of a lineup could be useful as an "estimator" variable when the case came to trial. For example, it might help a juror to know that the three-person lineup that generated the identification in the case was less reliable than an eight-person lineup would have been. But how *much* could it help? Wells didn't think estimator variables would turn out to help very much.

Wells argued that Buckhout and Loftus were too optimistic about the expert witnesses' contribution. Expert testimony was no silver bullet for vanquishing trial errors. Wells did not question the scientific validity of the individual studies; he thought the prosecutors were wrong to call them "bullshit." Research really *had* produced results indicating that cross-racial identifications were more difficult, that crime severity mattered, that longer viewing periods were better. But Wells made a part of the prosecutors' argument better than they had made it themselves.

The difficulty was that simply listing factors could not get you to a specific diagnosis of accuracy in individual cases, because there was no way to determine how the factors on your checklist had interacted with each other during a given crime. Take the studies of the effect of witness gender, for example, Wells wrote:

Can it be assumed that these factors only combine as main effects? Of course not. A witness's sex would surely not maintain its effect over long exposure times. Using only the research reviewed thus far, one would have to look at a 19th-order interaction![7]

In other words, while race, specifically whether the witness and criminal are of the same or different races, matters in recognizing people, it matters much more when the encounter is brief than when it is sustained. Race matters a lot less after a two-hour encounter than it does after a two-second one. By Wells' calculation, in a routine eyewitness criminal case in which you could identify 20 "estimator variables"—time, lighting, stress, race, age, and so on—you would have to choose between 1,048,576 potential interactions of the factors even if you arbitrarily limited each factor to only two possible levels of influence! You might be able to show that you had a biased lineup in a case, but maybe viewing conditions were so favorable that the probability of accuracy was 0.95 without the biased lineup, and still 0.92 even *with* the biased lineup.

Besides, Wells continued, "to make a statement about the fallibility of eyewitness testimony on the basis of estimator-variable research, the expert would supposedly rely on an average level of accuracy, a typical accuracy rate, or an average accuracy rate of a 'typical' study." Wells didn't buy it. To begin with, he wrote, "the literature is replete with potential biases." The existing crop of researchers, Wells speculated, might actually *prefer* low accuracy rates:

> [They] may perceive it as infinitely more interesting, more publishable, and more socially important to show low eyewitness accuracy than to show high accuracy. A high accuracy rate is an implicit null hypothesis that is to be rejected, and the stronger the rejection the better.

The Buckhouts of the world, Wells noted, "sometimes feel a greater need to dismiss high accuracy, but not low accuracy, as a research fluke."[8]

"In undertaking an applied project," he wrote, "it is incumbent on the researcher to demonstrate the applied utility of an eyewitness study." System variables research answered this challenge when it changed radically the angle from which the research impacted the criminal justice system. It no longer suggested a blanket skepticism concerning eyewitness testimony; it suggested the potential for improving eyewitness evidence collection and handling techniques to improve reliability.

Estimating whether a mistake had happened in the past was the wrong place to focus your efforts, because there was a much more productive target. Wells argued that system variable research could be crucial in helping the criminal justice system reduce mistakes in the future. System variable research would uncover the criminal justice system's role in *creating* eyewitness mistakes through its own interviewing and lineup techniques. If researchers devoted their time to studying system variables, maybe they could prevent mistakes before they happened.

When you knew that eight of ten eyewitnesses who saw a one-person, show-up identification later identified the wrong person, you still didn't know whether *this* eyewitness in *this* case was like one of the eight mistaken eyewitnesses or one of the two correct eyewitnesses. That had been Wigmore's argument, and it had been one of McCloskey and Egeth's arguments, too.

But Wells managed to leap-frog those objections by arguing that even if the 8:2 ratio is all you know, you still have an excellent argument for eliminating one-person identification procedures from your toolbox—an argument for changing the system. And because the procedures were a "system variable," you have the capacity to do just that.

Wells's "system variables" article defined a watershed. For the first time, the inherently probabilistic and statistical nature of the research knowledge was removed as a barrier to productive collaborations between psychology and the criminal justice system. Wells had articulated a "public health" approach to eyewitness error. Research could cut the number of mistakes before they happened even if it couldn't yet diagnosis them after they had occurred.

———————————

Typically, articles in psychology's scholarly journals are cited once or twice by other academics, then forgotten. Wells's "system variables" article has been cited hundreds of times. The term has now, like "xerox" or "Kleenex," passed out of the realm of proper nouns dressed in capital letters and into the everyday language of the field. It is not uncommon to see the term system variable used with no reference to its origins. It is as though it had always been there.

An inevitable byproduct of this eminence is a certain degree of angst within academic Psychology about Wells's status. "The reason that system variable article is cited so many times," one psychologist noted sourly, "is that Gary Wells is always citing it."

Perhaps it is natural enough that Wells's pervasive role in marshaling research behind the system variables approach would lead some colleagues—and many prosecutors—to suspect him of messianic tendencies. After all, it is not unheard of for the jeans and tweed jacket of a mild-mannered Midwestern professor to cloak megalomaniac secrets.

Talking to Wells about the eyewitness field in which he has become an acknowledged leader leaves a different impression. To begin with, Wells has retained a sense of humor about his misadventures in an uncomprehending legal world.[9] Besides, the thing to remember is that Wells saw the far-reaching implications of the system variable idea with startling clarity right at the very beginning. Although the field sometimes grew at a pace and in directions that Wells did not anticipate, he was remarkably prescient in sensing the reach of his idea. It may be because the system variable idea sprang virtually full-blown from the brow of Wells right at the start, that when Wells describes his long battle to bring it into actual application in the criminal justice system now, he speaks as if he had been *defending* an existing idea—against misunderstanding, distortion, neglect—rather than aggressively promoting a new one. Acts that Wells's more grudging admirers attribute to ambition and academic careerism Wells speaks of as unavoidable consequences of the fact that when the system variable concept needed defending, he was usually the best and sometimes the only willing advocate for the idea within psychology.

It wasn't that Wells had anything against the idea of a career; he wanted a career. He had kids, and he knew what it was like to grow up with no money. When he began to have graduate assistants of his own he always preached practical career management to them: He would warn them that they always had to have one article just out, one "in press," and one more study out for funding. But the career Wells wanted was a career pursuing the study of the psychology of eyewitness testimony, and more specifically, of developing his system variable idea.

Wells was the system variable idea's best advocate almost by default. Others—Roy Malpass, or Beth Loftus, for example—also did brilliant research. But the clarity of Wells's comprehensive vision combined with his temperament, strategic bent, and somewhat unusual focus (for a social psychologist) on experimental cognitive psychology combined to make him unique. Besides, the system variable formulation was Wells's baby, and he did not want to risk someone dropping the baby. As the baby grew, he fought to find it room to grow, but even those efforts were essentially protective.

That is not to say that Wells ignored the maxim that sometimes the best defense is a good offense.

By 1980 Wells had gathered funds from the Canadian government to host a conference on eyewitness evidence at the University of Alberta. He selected the presenters for the conference, and he edited a symposium[10] issue of *Law and Human Behavior*, which published their contributions. It was the first time many of these researchers had met, but their names would be linked over the next 20 years in an accumulating pile of research. One study would spark another, or two others. Roy Malpass would cite Gary Wells's study; Michael

Lieppe would cite Jack Brigham's; Rod Lindsay—who was still a graduate student at that point—would cite Steve Penrod. Dan Yarmey's studies would suggest another study to Ken Deffenbacher. Most of the participants had been press-ganged by defense lawyers from time to time to testify as expert witnesses, and they would report to their colleagues about their adventures. They were all about the same age, and with only occasional detours, they were concerned with "system variables." They wanted to study the things that the criminal justice system could change. It all fell in with Wells's plan.

"I knew right away," he notes, "that the first thing was that it had to be good psychology, respected within the field."

Beth Loftus presented at the Alberta Conference. In her mass market book, *Eyewitness Testimony*, she had conceded that Wells was "right and wrong" in his critique, and she had blazed the trail toward academic respectability that Wells wanted to follow.

But Bob Buckhout was not invited. Within a year or two of the conference, Wells regretted that omission. He recognized that Buckhout was a creative and energetic scientist; he saw his importance to the field. But Wells believed that for the field to attain the credibility it deserved, Buckhout had to be left behind, and everyone in the field would have to *know* that Buckhout had been left behind.

There was no pitched Oedipal battle about this; the Alberta Conference simply came and went, and *Law and Human Behavior* published its proceedings, and for the first time in the recent history of the eyewitness issue, Buckhout was nowhere to be found.

"Bob never complained to me about this," Wells remembers, "and I never really explained it to him. But I was very focused on getting us recognized as good science."

————◦•◦•◦————

Once the system variable idea was loose in the world, researchers saw that the most routine investigatory tasks provide fertile ground for experimentation. Before the results of these experiments began to roll in even lawyers who were worried about eyewitness accuracy felt a certain fatalism about the problem of eyewitness testimony: You can't live with eyewitnesses, they seemed to say, but you can't live without them. You would just have to live with some mistakes. The new wave of psychologists challenged that quietism. If you choose to live with eyewitnesses, they argued, you should improve their performance where you could.

One of the first responses of the "system variable" researchers to Loftus's insights into the fragility of eyewitness memory was provided by Edward Geiselman of UCLA and Ronald Fisher of Florida International University. "Research on eyewitness memory retrieval has produced few positive suggestions for law enforcement personnel," they wrote, and then they set about describing and testing just such a positive suggestion.[11]

The line of memory experiments that had included the Loftus "stop sign/yield sign" study raised serious concerns about hypnosis as a memory retrieval technique. You did seem to get more information from hypnotized witnesses, but you couldn't be sure it was the eyewitnesses' uncontaminated memory you were retrieving; you might be retrieving "facts" inadvertently planted by the interviewer's questions, or memories modified by "post-event" information. Geiselman and Fisher proposed a technique for the first "system variable" likely to have an impact on the eyewitness—the police interview. They would try to get the same benefits as hypnosis without incurring its risks. Geiselman and Fisher developed, then tested a package of techniques which they called the "cognitive interview." It could increase the quantity of information generated by interviews of eyewitnesses, but still protect the information's uncontaminated quality.

The cognitive interview drew on a number of general principles of memory theory. The research had shown, for example, that the effectiveness of a memory retrieval strategy depended in part on the overlap between the features of the retrieval efforts and the features of the "encoded" event—in this context, the crime. The research also showed pretty conclusively that there can be more than one retrieval path for each encoded event.

In the cognitive interview the police could try to increase the "overlap" of the event and the witnesses's efforts to retrieve the encoded memory of the event by encouraging the witness to report everything he or she remembered without editing or ordering the reports according to what was "important" or not. If there was more detail, there would be more overlap. The witness should just let everything flow. One way to do this was to avoid asking "leading questions" (e.g., "Did you see the green car?") and using an "open-ended" style of questioning instead (e.g., "What did you see?"). This approach also helped to avoid the insertion of the questioner's own "post-event" information into the witnesses' account. If you were trying to pry facts loose from a "clammed up" suspect, you *needed* leading questions. But you *didn't* need them for cooperative witnesses, and the "leading" style of questions used in interrogating hostile suspects carried more information from the questioner to the witness than open-ended, who/what/why/when/how questions. Leading questions came with a cost in decreased quantity and quality of information when you were talking to a cooperative witness. By using the cognitive interview the police could also enhance "overlap" by encouraging witnesses to reinstate the whole context of the event as it occurred.

Another cognitive interview technique would mobilize the research insight that there is more than one path to the same memory. The police might try encouraging witnesses to remember the events in a variety of chronological orders. The police could ask the witness to tell the story once from the beginning, then try to tell it again in reverse, from the conclusion back to the initiation. The police could also suggest that witnesses try to remember events from a variety of perspectives: from the point of view of a bystander, if the witness was the victim; from the point of view of the victim, if the witness was a bystander.

The two researchers tested the cognitive interview technique, first by instructing one group of students in cognitive interview memory retrieval techniques, while simply telling a control group of students to "keep trying to remember more information." The trained group gathered substantially more correct information than the untrained group. Even better, unlike hypnosis, the cognitive interview training did *not* lead to the generation of more *in*correct information, or to inflated witness confidence in incorrect information.

Still, those laboratory tests didn't look much like a real-life police interview, and by 1985 Fisher and Geiselman were ready to publish their account of a second study, which addressed that criticism.

They borrowed four realistic training films of staged crimes which the Los Angeles Police used to train officers in life-threatening situations. Subjects saw the films, and about 48 hours later they were interviewed about what they had seen. Three interview techniques were used: one group was interviewed using standard police techniques, one group was interviewed under hypnosis, and the final group was interviewed using the cognitive interview. This last group was told to reinstate the context of the event, to report everything without gauging its importance, to recall the event in different orders, and to recall the event from different perspectives.

The data showed that the cognitive interview was as effective as hypnosis in generating a larger quantity of information during eyewitness interviews, and that the cognitive interview accomplished that result without the contaminating side-effects that made the legal system so nervous about hypnosis.

Buckhout found this system variable approach completely unsympathetic. Who *cared* about teaching the cops this kind of thing? Buckhout once told Fisher that as far as he was concerned, the whole cognitive interview idea was "a gimmick."

But the system variable researchers had left Buckhout behind. Geiselman and Fisher had tested their idea, and they knew it was no gimmick.

Geiselman and Fisher had designed their experiments to test a system variable which could be easily *applied*. Their cognitive interviews did not require elaborate training. The "cognitive" interviewers in Geiselman's and Fisher's experiment had achieved their improvements after reading a two-page description of the technique and taking part in a fifteen minute discussion.

Here, if anyone in the criminal justice system could be persuaded to heed it, was a significant "positive suggestion" for changing the system's handling of eyewitness evidence to prevent mistakes before they happened. Fisher and Geisleman showed that the prevailing habit of simply transplanting your hostile interrogation techniques into the interviewing of cooperative eyewitnesses was the equivalent of pouring your coffee onto the trace evidence at the crime scene. Using the four simple steps discussed earlier, which Geiselman and Fisher had developed, the cognitive interview gave you more information from eyewitness memory—and better information at that.

———————————

The police reflex once a suspect is uncovered through the interviewing and investigation process is to show the eyewitness a photo array or a lineup. Looked at critically, the moment was a "system variable." In fact, the moment contained a whole bundle of potential system variables. What photos did Mike Gauldin show Jennifer Thompson? In what order? What did he tell her about them? These were all choices, and each of these choices had a potential impact on the eyewitness's memory.

In 1981, Roy Malpass was teaching at the State University of New York in Plattsburg when he decided to investigate an element of the lineup event—an element of the police "by-the-book" approach to eyewitness identifications. Police talk to witnesses before lineups. Does it matter what the police tell eyewitnesses they were doing when they conducted a lineup or a photographic array?

Malpass designed an elegant experiment to explore that question.[12] After seeing the same crime enacted, Malpass's witnesses were divided into two groups. Both groups viewed a lineup in which the real culprit was not present. One group was told that the police thought that their culprit was in the group displayed in the lineup. This was not as artificial as it might sound. The police may not always tell the witness that they think the right guy is in the lineup, but the witness—if he or she has any brains—will still know that this is what the police believe. Why else would the police have brought the witness in?

The second group was told that the culprit "may or may not" be present in the lineup.

The results of this single elementary change in the "book" were startling. The proportion of false identifications was radically reduced—from 78 percent to 33 percent—simply by giving the "may or may not" instruction to the witnesses. Even more surprising, this decrease could not have been caused just by increased caution. If the only result of the "may or may not" instruction was that it instilled more caution in witnesses, then when the real culprit *was* present, you would expect the number of correct identifications to decrease, too. The newly cautious group of witnesses would simply make fewer picks.

But when Malpass ran a version of the experiment with the real culprit present, the "may or may not" instruction did *not* decrease the number of correct identifications. After the "may or may not" instructions the witnesses were less likely to pick the wrong guy, but they were still just as likely to pick the right one as they had been before the instruction. Malpass had added another simple, free, no-harm way to cut the number of "false hits" without raising the number of "false misses."

Malpass had discovered and tested, in other words, a one-sentence amendment to the police "book" that could prevent a substantial number of eyewitness mistakes before they happened.

———•◆•———

But giving witnesses new instructions didn't seem to solve the problem all by itself. In Malpass's study, one-third of the witnesses still chose an innocent person from the lineup even *after* the "may or may not" instruction.

Maybe it wasn't the instructions; maybe it was the lineup itself. Maybe, for example, it depended on how you constructed your lineup and who you put in it. In another early experiment, Wells and Lindsay had found that eyewitnesses were more than twice as likely to chose an innocent lineup member when the real culprit was not present in the lineup if the five "fillers" in the lineup did not resemble the real culprit. They were far less likely to make the same mistake when the fillers did resemble the culprit.[13]

So, as it turned out, cops who were bending over backwards trying to be fair by picking "fillers" to resemble suspects were making it harder for witnesses to pick the right guy, but they were *not* making it less likely that the witnesses would pick the wrong guy.

Here was another simple potential change in the "book." For unusual cases where the suspect had a unique feature—a very visible scar or tattoo, for example—you might have to make special arrangements. But for a run of the mill lineup or photo array, match your "fillers" to the description of the real culprit given by the witness, and you would radically cut the number of false identifications of innocent people when—as in Ronald Cotton's case, or Kirk Bloodsworth's—everyone in your lineup was innocent. Was Gary Graham innocent too? No one knows. But we do know that of the people in the photographic array which was shown to Bernadine Skillern, Graham was the only one who fit the description of the shooter from the night of the crime.

----·•·----

Another possibility was that the rate of mistakes could be changed by *how* you showed the lineup members to witnesses.

When Jennifer Thompson first identified Ronald Cotton she did it from a "six pack" of photographs all displayed simultaneously. Kirk Bloodsworth stood in a lineup with a number of fillers, all at the same time. This "simultaneous" display of suspects among "fillers" was the uniform practice among American law enforcement agencies. This format was a "system variable": it could be changed. But why would you want to change it?

Roy Malpass had pointed out that an eyewitness's decision to choose a particular member of a lineup had two elements. First, a Jennifer Thompson or a Bernadine Skillern had to decide *to choose*. Only then was the accuracy of their choice implicated.

There was research bearing on this issue, examining the "decision criterion" the witness used. It showed that the criterion could be influenced by, for example, wanting to appear intelligent, wanting to please the police, or wanting to be good witnesses.

But deciding whether to choose can be thought of as *independent* of the quality of the eyewitness's recollection of the offender's face, or the eyewitness' ability to distinguish the real culprit from the "fillers" in the lineup. A very high rate of choosing might create a lot of mistakes, and Malpass's experiments showed that by giving a good "may or may not be there" instruction you could cut the rate of choosing. Even so, choosing and accuracy were still two distinct things: There was still the question of the accuracy of those people who had decided to make a pick.

Did the system do anything that degraded the accuracy of the choosers? Gary Wells started to work on that question in his laboratory in the early 1980s.

He started with the "who decides to choose?" question that Malpass had investigated. Wells staged experiments with "blank" lineups: exposing eyewitnesses to lineups from which the culprit was absent. He found that by running eyewitnesses through a "blank" lineup procedure first, you might be able to screen out eyewitnesses who were overly prone because of some combination of social forces to choose *somebody* when presented with *any* lineup. Running a preliminary "blank" lineup would enhance the accuracy rates in the second lineups you were really interested in.

This was a solid system-variable discovery, but not one that would ever be applied in real life. Wells could see that "blank" lineups would be extremely unattractive to the police.[14] What cop wanted to run *two* lineups? Who wanted to deal with witnesses who would feel that you were playing games with them? How many *good* witnesses, who would ultimately have made the correct choice in the second lineup, would you have "screened out" in your "blank" lineup? There were perfectly good police objections to blank lineups, to which Wells realized he had no answer.

So Wells tried a different tack: He shifted his attention from the eyewitness's "Do I choose?" question to focus directly on the eyewitness's "Which one do I choose?" decision. Once the eyewitness made a decision to choose, what determined which individual the eyewitness picked from a photo array or lineup? Were there any system variables involved that might be improved?

Wells thought that the improvements that Malpass achieved by adding the "may or may not" instructions might be explained by a tendency for eyewitnesses to choose someone from a lineup by using a process of "relative judgment." They might pick someone from a lineup even when the real culprit was not there because he "looked most like" the culprit. Could that have been what happened to Jennifer Thompson, for example?

If you recognize someone—your brother or sister, for example—you don't have to compare your brother or sister to the other people in the lineup. You "recognize" them in a true/false choice. Relative judgment, on the other hand, was what you got from a multiple choice test when "none of the above" wasn't on the list. This alternative process wouldn't be a problem if the real culprit was actually in the lineup. No one looks "more like" the real rapist, Bobby Poole, than Bobby Poole himself, and if Poole had been in the first lineup Jennifer Thompson had been shown she might have picked Poole. But since Poole wasn't there, maybe Jennifer compared the remaining members of the lineup and chose an innocent person as the "most like" option.

Wells staged the same crime 200 times for 200 eyewitnesses.[15] The witnesses were then separated into two groups, asked to view a lineup, and carefully warned with the Malpass instruction that the real culprit "may or may not be present." Then, half of the witnesses viewed a six-person lineup in which the actual perpetrator was present. Of these first 100 witnesses, 54 picked the right man; 21 made no choice; 13 picked the wrong man.

What happened when the real culprit was removed?

What *should* have happened was that the 54 percent of the witnesses who chose the real culprit would simply migrate to the "no choice" column when the real culprit was removed. There should have been a "no choice" total of 75 percent.

But that did *not* happen. Instead, the "no choice" column, which should have grown by 54 (to 75 percent) rose only by 11 (to 32 percent). Even with the real culprit absent, and even with the Malpass "may or may not be present" instruction, 68 percent of all of the witnesses still chose someone. More disturbingly, 38 percent of the witnesses chose the *same* lineup member: the jeopardy of the "looks most like" innocent person was almost *three times* higher when the actual culprit was removed than it had been when the real culprit was present.

So Wells, working again with Rod Lindsay, his former graduate assistant, staged another experiment.[16] What would happen, they asked, if instead of laying the photographs out on the table all at once, or displaying the lineup members simultaneously, you displayed them one at a time—displayed them "sequentially?"

If the witnesses saw six separate true/false tests of memory, would the results be different from the multiple choice format which the typical "six pack" of photographs suggested? After all, if you showed witnesses pictures or people one at a time, there would be no one to compare them with. No eyewitness could ever be sure that the next picture would not look *more* like the real culprit than the picture they were studying. That might inhibit guessing. And besides, the eyewitness would have to compare each individual photograph with his or her own memory of the real culprit.

This simple experiment had amazing concrete results. There was a strong reduction in the number of false identifications. Even better, this reduction in false identifications did not result in an increase in false "misses"; if the real culprit was in a "sequential" photo array, the eyewitness was just as likely to choose him from a "sequential" as from a "simultaneous" array.

Wells had uncovered not only an individual practice that could be reformed, but a theory—"relative judgment"—which explained why other new practices seemed to work. Relative judgment could explain the effectiveness of Malpass's instructions, for example. The Malpass "may or may not" instruction could have made eyewitnesses more aware of the dangers of relative judgments. Wells' own experimental results, which showed improvements by choosing "fillers" to match descriptions, could be explained by "relative judgment," too. Perhaps the similarity of the "fillers" spread the risk of relative judgment misidentifications across a greater number of innocents, and so the rate of misidentifications of innocents would be statistically less frequent. The success of the blank lineups might be another result of muting the consequences of the "relative judgment" process. Showing witnesses an initial blank lineup might screen out the witnesses most likely to rely on relative judgments.

Finally, the "sequential" presentations of photographs might be working so well because it virtually denies the eyewitness the *opportunity* to rely on relative judgments. If you are a witness asked to look at mug shots, the "sequential" method forces you to make an "absolute" choice: that's him or it isn't; I recognize him or I don't. It leaves no room for comparison.

True, you will eliminate guesses, even some "educated" guesses, and it certainly seemed reasonable to believe that, over the long run, some of those guesses you've eliminated would have been correct guesses. Still, you don't really gain information from a guess. The researchers believed that you weren't losing much.

———◦•◦———

Wells and his colleagues pursued the avenues which the system variable approach opened up for twenty years. Examples of how much you could learn once you conceded that memory was not videotape continued to mount. By the time of Saul Kassin's second survey of the psychological experts, systems variable findings had become the center of gravity of the field. And as examples mounted, and the videotape analogy faded, a new analogy began to take its place.

The researchers began to test the possibility that the right way to think about eyewitness memory evidence was as "trace evidence"—to think of memory not as a photograph but as material like blood, semen, drug, or other biological evidence which you might discover and recover from a crime scene. Like these substances—the focus of traditional forensic crime-scene evidence technicians—eyewitness memory trace evidence could be contaminated. If the researchers' hypothesis was right, eyewitness memory evidence had to be handled very, very, carefully. The ways in which eyewitness evidence was handled were "system variables" choices.

One particular aspect of the eyewitness' testimony stood out above all others in the courtroom: the eyewitness' confidence in his or her own memory. The jurors who heard Jennifer Thompson identify Ronald Cotton and

Bernadine Skillern identify Gary Graham were persuaded by their confidence more than any other factor. In allowing themselves to be persuaded by confidence the jurors were in exalted company. The Supreme Court of the United States also thought that witness confidence showed the reliability of an identification. The perception that confidence was *not* a sure sign of accuracy goes back at least to Munsterberg, but by the time of Kassin's second survey the issue had been the subject of intensive study in parallel lines of research. One body of research showed that confidence and accuracy were very weakly related, when they were related at all. The second indicated that jurors really did rely most heavily on witness confidence in making their decisions. Combine the two, and you have a disaster in the making.

But was witness confidence a "system variable"? Was confidence something that the criminal justice system had any influence over? Or was it just a given, which we have to live with?

Gary Wells and Amy Bradfield attacked that question in 1998.[17] They staged a crime and had witnesses attempt to identify the culprit from a lineup. The witnesses didn't know it, but the culprit was not there: everyone who was making an identification was choosing the wrong man.

These mistaken eyewitnesses were divided into three groups. The first group was given no feedback at all. A second group was told, "Actually, you're wrong, the suspect was Number 'X'." A third group was told, "Good, you identified the suspect."

The third group, in other words, was put in the same position as Jennifer Thompson. Remember, Jennifer, who was anxious to know how she had done when she chose Ronald Cotton at the lineup, had asked Mike Gauldin about it. Gauldin told her she had chosen the suspect, and that Cotton had done "that kind of thing" before. There have been cases in which when a suspect was chosen from a lineup the police applauded, but nothing so dramatic usually happens. Still, it is difficult or impossible for a cop, asked "How did I do?" by a witness—particularly a victim—to answer, "None of your business." Some feedback, explicit or implied, is built into the encounter. There is nothing sinister about these moments; it's just ordinary good manners.

But in the Wells and Bradfield experiment this courtesy had a startling result. The mistaken eyewitnesses who had received the confirming "Good, you identified the suspect" feedback reported drastically inflated recollections of their confidence compared to the mistaken eyewitnesses who had received no feedback at all.

On this basis alone, Justice Blackmun's *Manson v. Braithwaite* opinion, which had enshrined eyewitness confidence as a key indicator of reliability, was called into question. The eyewitnesses in the Wells and Bradfield experiment were *all* wrong; the only thing distinguishing them from each other was that some of them had received feedback and others hadn't. The confident ones were as mistaken as the more tentative ones. Blackmun, in other words, should have listened to Munsterberg.

But there was even more information in the Wells and Bradfield results. Not only had the trivial positive feedback drastically inflated one of Blackmun's criteria, it had apparently distorted the *substance* of the eyewitnesses's memories of the crime. After the positive feedback, the witnesses reported that they had paid more attention to the criminal, that they had a better view, that they could make out details of the culprit's face better, and that it had been easier for them to make an identification.

Wells and Bradfield offered empirical proof, in other words, that if you wanted to pass Justice Blackmun's "reliability" test, one very good way to do it was to give your witness some minor confirming (even if mistaken) feedback. Positive feedback created totally unjustified "improvements" not only in eyewitnesses' confidence in their identifications but in their narrative accounts of both the crime event and their performance at the lineup test.

Whether officials give a witness feedback is a "system variable," because the criminal justice system has the power to instruct its officials to avoid giving feedback. Of course, there are avenues of informal and indirect feedback open even after the system embargoes that level of explicitness. If, for example, every time the witness comes back to court for pretrial proceedings he sees the same guy, the reappearance will tell the witness something about the "rightness" of his or her prior choice. In a later experiment, Wells showed that even if you delayed the feedback for 48 hours it had the same distorting effect. But the criminal justice system can manage the impact even of the informal feedback if officials ask the witness about his or her level of confidence at the moment of the identification, before informal confirmation can intervene.

The Wells and Bradfield "feedback" experiment provided more proof that eyewitness confidence and other aspects of the eyewitness's testimony are "trace evidence," which can be contaminated by feedback. Jennifer Thompson had started with a "looks like" identification of Ronald Cotton, and Bernadine Skillern had started with a "looks like" identification of Gary Graham, but by the time the system's witness processing routines were finished, the confidence of both witnesses had been boosted to certainty. Beyond that, it showed that if you could edit your system to protect against feedback's contaminating impact, you would really accomplish something: something that would both prevent contamination and improve the legal system's after-the-fact evaluation of eyewitness identifications. If you designed procedures to find the trace evidence—as in the cognitive interview—you would have more evidence. Design procedures to protect the trace evidence, and you would have better evidence.

This account may have made the whole research enterprise seem to be a bureaucratic effort, unfolding with agonizing slowness over nearly a quarter of a century. That is not the way it felt for the researchers. There were dead spots of course: experiments that went nowhere, theories that didn't pan out. And there was a lot of boring labor—putting an experiment together takes a lot of people and a lot of work, and collating and analyzing the results can leave you bleary-eyed. But for the psychological researchers, watching the pieces of the system variables puzzle fall into place wasn't just a day's work; it was exciting. The field was just the right size: you could know everyone in it, follow everyone's studies, and benefit from a burgeoning cascade of intriguing results. There was good work being done all over, and it was all tending toward concrete proposals. The researchers were "giving psychology away," and in a way that counted.

They believed that they could cut the rate of eyewitness identification error in half.

***

It is a tribute to Gary Wells's pool-champion's vision that he was in the room with the attorney general of the United States at all. That was something that Buckhout, even Loftus, could never have achieved. By the time Janet Reno asked what he had to say, Wells was the acknowledged leader of Psychology's effort to impress its findings on the legal system. This was a matter of specialization, not of hierarchy. Wells was certainly a leading researcher, but there were other researchers who did brilliant studies, other researchers who testified in court more often.

It was because of Wells' strategic grasp that he could answer Reno not just as Gary Wells, an Iowa State professor with an idea, but as the spokesman for a consensus of the membership of the American Psychology-Law Society. When psychology engaged the legal system this time, the science would not appear in the person of an inspired prophet, like Munsterberg, or a lone-wolf activist, like Buckhout, who had prodded Wells himself into action 20 years earlier. This time psychology would present a consensus built on 20 years of careful peer-reviewed research.

It was a body of work Wigmore himself would have applauded.

And this time, psychology would not appear, as it had during Elizabeth Loftus's witness-stand adventures, on behalf of an individual defendant, straining to use its statistical information to look into the past and to make a clinical, diagnostic decision about whether *this* eyewitness was right *this* time. Now, psychology would be offering tools to cut future eyewitness errors—tools that would not only protect the innocent, but also assist in the apprehension and prosecution of the guilty.

The American Psychology-Law Society had a dormant procedure for publishing "scientific review papers," which stated consensus findings in Psychology to inform the legal system. It had never been used. Wells proposed that the psychology of lineups was an appropriate subject. In 1997, a working group assembled by Wells to fit the parameters set by Richard Weiner, who directed the APLS' scientific review paper project, reviewed, endorsed, and published an authoritative "white paper" setting out a series of system variable reforms—preventive medicine against eyewitness mistakes.

The "white paper" on lineup proposals was co-authored by the veterans of the field.[18] Wells and Roy Malpass had been among the first to publish their experiments. Rod Lindsay and Steven Penrod had been involved since the Alberta Conference. Penrod's book with Brian Cutler had provided the most comprehensive overview of the field, and Penrod himself had earned a reputation for acute research and balanced, judicious commentary on the issues. Lindsay, both with Wells and independently, had done a number of turning-point experiments. Sol Fulero was also trained as a lawyer; he had been a student of Buckhout, had written Buckhout's memorial notice in *Law and Human Behavior*, and had worked tirelessly on the issue ever since.

The "white paper" the group produced was a scientific survey, and underwent stringent scientific peer review, but it was also a careful political document, which by design offered the criminal justice system a menu limited to four simple, concrete "best practices," supported by a substantial body of system variable research.

First, make sure that the lineup or photo array was conducted "double-blind": the cop or official who supervised the lineup or array should not know who the police suspect was. By using this routine—familiar to all scientists, who do all of their testing this way—you would prevent the giving of cues, or confirming feedback either intentionally or inadvertently through body language or facial expressions, and protect the integrity of the memory evidence from disastrous contamination.

Second, utilize Roy Malpass' findings and instruct witnesses that the real culprit "may or may not" be in the lineup. This instruction would lower the number of "false hits" by muting the "relative judgment" effect. It would put "none of the above" on the witnesses's list of choices.

Third, select lineup "fillers" to match the witness's verbal description of the culprit, not to resemble the suspect. The research showed that the conventional "match-to-suspect" approach made identifications more difficult for the witness, but it did not make them more accurate.

Fourth, and finally, take an immediate statement of confidence from the witness before any post-identification feedback can affect the witnesses' sense of confidence. In other words, take an uncontaminated sample of the "trace evidence."

There were other steps to take: use cognitive interview techniques; employ "sequential," one-at-a-time display of suspects and fillers in lineups and photo arrays; videotape all lineups. These opportunities for improvement were mentioned, but not included in the "four rules." The white paper was designed with utility in mind, and its authors thought that, in appealing to the criminal justice system, less would be more. And when, by a happy coincidence, the "Green Book" of DNA exoneration cases was published and it revealed the verified extent of the problem of misidentification, Wells arranged to have an analysis of those cases included in the psychologists' paper.

And if the field was ready, Wells personally was ready, too. He was not enthusiastic about expert testimony; he thought there was too much of it, and he thought that much of it was too weak. In fact, Wells was becoming more and more convinced that the defense lawyers and their obsessive, uncomprehending focus on expert testimony were muffling his more important system-variable reform message. Still, Wells had given a lot of lectures to lawyers over the years. In fact, as Beth Loftus devoted more and more of her energies to the controversies over the existence of "recovered memories" of early childhood sex abuse, Wells had gradually taken Loftus's place as the lawyers' favorite on the Continuing Legal Education circuit. In these talks to lawyers Wells honed his "trace evidence" message to a very fine edge: his clunky slide show had been transformed into a humming PowerPoint presentation. He had noticed the parts of the story that the lawyers didn't get, and he had noticed the parts that motivated them. He made the adjustments.

Even so, when Janet Reno spoke up from the back row of Jeremy Travis's meeting to say, "I want to hear what Gary Wells has to say about eyewitness identification and why so many of these DNA cases involve eyewitness identifications," Wells's heart was in his throat.

Here was 20 years' work—his work, and his whole field's work—on the line. Wells had gotten the ear of the Attorney General of the United States, and now he would have to deliver.

Wells took a deep breath, and then started in on his "trace evidence" speech. It was a perfect subject for Travis's Future of DNA group—"Everyone was already on the trace-evidence page regarding DNA and the issues clearly were focused on problems with how trace evidence was collected," he remembers. Wells thought that he talked for about four minutes, but other people in the room remember him delivering a seamless, spellbinding 20-minute sermon; 20 years of research crammed into 20 minutes.

But Reno had seen enough. At a break she grabbed Wells and Jeremy Travis and questioned Wells closely. Wells couldn't believe his ears. He remembers that:

> She asked about blind testing, about pre-lineup instructions, selection of fillers, the use of composites, leading questions, and the use of live versus photo identification procedures. Incredibly, she never once asked about any estimator variables. She got it!

Wells was stunned. "It was an amazing moment for me. Here I was, a guy who had trouble getting past the PR people in local police stations to talk with a mere detective, now being sought after for advice from the U.S. Attorney General."

The path, which had started with Munsterberg 70 years earlier, had found its way to the pinnacle of the criminal justice system. Janet Reno had heard enough to get the United States Department of Justice started.

Jeremy Travis was told that the National Institute of Justice would investigate the "system variables" that law enforcement could control in eyewitness cases. The attorney general was personally interested, and this attorney general did not let things drop. Within the Department of Justice, Janet Reno's enthusiasms were legend. The word was that when the attorney general got a bee in her bonnet, it buzzed there with great fury.

But there was still no reason to think that this buzzing would produce anything real. The Attorney General of the United States is just one lawyer. Unlike the British Home Secretary, the Attorney General of the United States has no control over the 13,000 state and local police and sheriff's departments who actually investigate eyewitness cases. Law enforcement couldn't be ordered to change the American system of handling eyewitness memory evidence; it would have to be persuaded.

One of the pillars of the law enforcement system—the police—had never heard about the psychology of eyewitness identification; they were busy complying with *United States v. Wade*, the Supreme Court opinion that had mandated the presence of defense counsel at "live" lineups.

For the other pillar of American law enforcement—the state and local prosecutors who tried the cases—the phrase eyewitness psychology called up nothing except acid memories of Buckhout and Loftus. For the prosecutors, the psychology of eyewitness identification was anathema.

The National District Attorney's Association—and Linda Fairstein—thought that the psychologists' road had gone far enough. The prosecutors knew where the levers of power were, and they were perfectly willing to push the levers.

The psychologists' road had covered an enormous distance to get to the office of the Attorney General of the United States. But the road could come to a dead end right there.

CHAPTER ELEVEN

A TECHNICAL WORKING GROUP

The Police Craft a New Book

NINETEENTH-CENTURY ARMIES STATIONED their cavalry just behind the front lines where the cavalry's sabers could persuade infantry deserters tempted to make a run for it that it was safer to return to the battle.

Captain Don Mauro, commander of the Los Angeles County Sheriff's Homicide Unit, was playing a similar role from his position outside the conference room of Washington's Madison Hotel, where the National Institute of Justice's "Technical Working Group On Eyewitness Evidence" was meeting. Mauro was silver-haired and handsome; he beamed benign alertness from behind his rimless glasses, and he had a ton of experience. Lately, a good portion of that experience had been gathered in meetings generating just the kind of pointless conflict that was going on inside the conference room at that moment, and Mauro's growing distaste for that sort of thing was one of the factors that he was weighing as he contemplated possible retirement. On the other hand, Mauro's status as a whole-skinned survivor of bureaucratic minefields and cop traps in meetings just like this one cemented his role as the acknowledged leader of the 18 police and sheriff's representatives who comprised the majority on the Technical Working Group, which Jeremy Travis and his staff had drafted into the service of Janet Reno's determination to see something done about eyewitness error. All of the cops in the group had plenty of street experience—over 200 years in total, in crowded alleys in Chicago and on isolated two-lane blacktop in Montana—but in their view, meeting experience was entitled to special respect. For the time being, Mauro was content to wait in the hallway and see what happened.

Mauro could bide his time because he knew that he had a counterpart inside the conference room, a recently retired Chicago Police detective sergeant, Paul Carroll, who was pursuing the opposite approach—an approach that was perfectly in harmony with Carroll's own ebullient temperament. Paul Carroll had been a Chicago cop for 30 years, starting on the day when, just for the hell of it, he had accompanied a friend who was taking the police exam (the friend failed) and took the exam himself because he was bored. Boredom was Carroll's chronic enemy. Inside the Technical Working Group, Carroll was shaking things up.

Carroll and Mauro had been the two law enforcement members of the Planning Panel which had put the Technical Working Group together. Gary Wells had represented the researchers on that panel along with Ron Fisher, who had done the basic cognitive interview work. There had been NIJ staffers, two prosecutors, even a token defense lawyer (the current author) around that table too.

But Mauro and Carroll were convinced that this topic, whatever the lawyers and researchers thought, was about cop business, and they refused to see it handed over to the professors or the lawyers.

Carroll and Mauro knew that the first challenge would be to get their cops to open their mouths. Place the average cop in the unfamiliar environment of a conference room and he will fold his arms, put his head down, and stare at the table until it is all over. Put the cops in a room filled with lawyers, and the cops' nonparticipation wouldn't even be noticed: the lawyers would cheerfully yak away at each other until someone turned out the lights, and would never notice that the cops were dozing. So when the full panel began to meet, Carroll put his training experience, his streetsmarts, his educational creativity, and a profane, humorous persona—something like the Thinking Cop's John Belushi—to work on seeing to it that no problem would go unventilated. Paul Carroll might have been sent from Central Casting to see that nobody dozed while *he* was in the room.

Inside the conference room he teased the researchers; he goaded the lawyers; he *exploded* over misconceptions of life on the street. Roughly one-third of Carrol's sentences began with, "Come *on*, are you *kidding* me? Do you really think that we. . . ." He would violently defend one proposition, then turn around and violently attack it. He would accuse researchers or lawyers of taking outlandish positions which in fact they had never even considered. There was a highly intelligent method to this madness, but after a brief interval of shock, it was madness that it created: Pretty soon everyone was yelling.

One of the people who got into the fighting spirit was Ken Patenaude, a Lieutenant on the Northampton, Massachusetts, police force. Patenaude had not been a member of the Planning Group, and had come to the first meeting of Reno's Technical Working Group not knowing quite what to expect. Once he was there he found everyone doing unexpected things—everyone including himself. Ordinarily gentlemanly and under control, he enmeshed himself in a screaming match with a female defense lawyer who seemed to be arguing that everyone knew that police rigged lineups as a matter of policy. He tried several times to explain to the researchers that the cops had actually read the materials and understood them, but had some questions and suggestions. No one listened; they were too busy arguing with each other.

It was just after this that Don Mauro intercepted Patenaude on his way to the elevator.

"Where are you going?" Mauro asked politely.

"To tell you the truth," Patenaude said, "I'm going to see if I can change my flights and get out of here."

He recounted for Mauro the incident that had just occurred. He was still annoyed at his own loss of control. Mauro was completely sympathetic.

"Yeah," he said, "there's no reason to put up with that. Unbelievable. Maybe you can change your flight."

They stood for a moment while Mauro shook his head in grief over the irritation to which Patenaude had been subject.

Then, almost as if speaking to himself, Mauro added, "Of course, if guys like you go, they'll just go ahead and decide this stuff without us."

He said this in the kindliest tones imaginable. Patenaude turned around and went back into the conference room.

———————

Dr. Richard Rau did not hear this exchange, but it would not have surprised him. In fact, it would have fulfilled his hopes. Dick Rau was the veteran National Institute of Justice official to whom Jeremy Travis entrusted the job of ramrodding some kind of something about the eyewitness reform through the mixed lot of cops, researchers, prosecutors, and lawyers. Rau had overseen the production of the "Green Book" and had a sense of the territory. Rau had placed his bet on the cops. He felt that if anything got done—and Miss Reno certainly wanted something done—it would be because the cops bought the program. With this in mind, Rau had recruited Mauro and Carroll, whom he knew from earlier projects which had produced a series of *Guides* to *Death Investigations* and *Crime Scenes*, with just this sort of scene in mind.

A mathematician by training, Rau is a small, immensely spruce man, with a neat moustache and thick wire-rimmed glasses, given to blazers and bow ties. Rau had something of the look of a high school principal in a Broadway musical comedy—the sort of bright-eyed principal who frustrates the schemes of his rascally students for the first three acts, but during the finale turns out to have been secretly on the side of the romantic leads all along—and, incidentally, a pretty good hoofer, too. But Rau's natty exterior concealed a will of iron and a riverboat gambler's nerve. He would need both, because his charges were becoming extremely unruly.

"Bring everyone to the table" was Janet Reno's creed at the Justice Department, but they weren't used to being at tables together, and once you got them to the table you didn't know how they would behave. That was Rau's challenge. To produce anything Rau needed a consensus of the criminal justice system's representatives, and it didn't look as if those representatives were going to provide one. They weren't mixing well. With the small Planning Panel Group, Rau had managed to park them in hotel conference rooms, handcuff them to the table, and forge a consensus around three uncontroversial principles. The goals of the group, the Planning Panel eventually agreed, would be to gather more evidence from eyewitnesses, to get a higher quality of evidence from eyewitnesses, and to enhance the system's ability to evaluate eyewitnesses. So far, so good. Who could disagree with that? But now, in the larger group, which was supposed to achieve these goals, although Carroll and Mauro could be counted on to hold the cops together, all of the other fragments were flying off in different directions. In part this was due to misconceptions about each other, which the protagonists brought to the party.

Gary Wells, for example, was there leading a group of researchers.[1] They were cautiously optimistic that their research was finally going to be put to use—after all, they were there at the invitation of the Attorney General of the United States, who plainly understood Wells's system variable formulation. All the same, they were nervous. All the researchers knew about Munsterberg, and they realized that the *next* invitation from an Attorney General would be 100 years away. The researchers believed that the big threat would come from the cops, whom the researchers saw as inherently suspicious and resistant to change. Fortunately—or so it seemed to the researchers, the prosecutors would be there, too. The prosecutors were all college-educated; they would understand the data; and, even more important, if the system variable reforms the researchers advocated—"blind" lineups, sequential photo arrays, immediate confidence measurements, lineup instructions, careful selection of "fillers"—were enacted, the prosecutors would be the prime beneficiaries. In the bright new, post-reform world, the prosecutors would have only invincible, "pristine" cases to try. The defense would be left with nothing to say. Could the defense argue that the cops had fingered the suspect? Not if the lineup was conducted "blind" by a cop who didn't even know who the suspect was, it couldn't. Wells and the other researchers saw the prosecutors as their allies, even their beneficiaries.

This illusion lasted until the third minute of the first meeting of the Planning Panel, which was setting the ground rules for the larger Technical Working Group, when Wells was introduced to Melissa Mourges, an assistant district attorney from Linda Fairstein's Sex Crimes Unit in New York. Mourges is a slender, attractive woman who is hilariously witty in private conversation but whose public manner for Technical Working Group purposes could be better characterized as "no prisoners" than as "all business."

"I think that you are the devil incarnate," she said to Wells.

Wells was pretty sure that this must be a joke, although Mourges didn't seem to be laughing.

He became less sure as things wore on. The researchers were not going to get a warm welcome from this prosecutor. Mourges didn't like anything about the proceedings: in fact, she thought it was a bag job. Wells may have thought that he was offering the prosecutors "pristine" procedures that would trump defense attacks, but what the prosecutors thought he was doing was handing defense lawyers a new weapon with which to beat cops over the head.

Mourges could just see wild-eyed Barry Scheck types sneering at well-meaning cops in feigned amazement: "You mean you didn't do a blind lineup as recommended by the United States Department of *Justice?!!*" This proposed set of Wellsian "guidelines," or whatever they were, promised only courtroom disaster from the prosecutors' point of view. That's why the title mattered: The prosecutors felt that the term "guideline" meant that anyone who did not follow them was out of bounds. And why was this federal task force overreaching this way? To deal with an unproven non-problem with a set of laboratory procedures developed by a group of self-proclaimed wizards who had never even *met* a rape victim.

Besides, Mourges had a sense that the train had already left the station—that Rau and Reno were so enamored of their *Crime Scene* and *Death Investigation* guidelines that they were going to get eyewitness guidelines no matter what. She also believed—rightly—that Wells had been allowed to hand-pick the researchers involved in the discussions. The prosecutors' suspicions were confirmed when Mark Larson, the First Assistant District Attorney in Seattle, suggested that maybe some pilot projects or field testing might be in order as a more cautious first step, and that suggestion had been brushed aside as a nonstarter.

The researchers brushed the suggestion aside because they were reasonably satisfied with the data, and they knew that "field testing" a procedure was more easily said then done. "Field tests" can quickly degenerate into uninformative, uncontrolled jumbles of mismatched facts and near-facts. The researchers believed that controlled experiments were *better* than field tests. It was a reprise of the old conflict between the lawyers' preference for "realistic" over "scientific." From the researchers' point of view, it was ridiculous to assume that human memory worked one way in a laboratory and some completely different way in other settings; memory was memory. Besides, the researchers didn't believe that the prosecutors' objections were being made in good faith; all of the researchers had endured bruising experiences with jeering prosecutors over the years. They saw the prosecutors' objections as the equivalent, as Beth Loftus once remarked, of saying, "OK, you've proved that if you are shot in the head you'll be killed, but you haven't proved that if you are shot in the head *in a bowling alley* you'll be killed."

If the prosecutors were so worried about field tests, the researchers wondered, why hadn't they noticed that the procedures that were currently in use were nothing better than an ad lib effort to deal with the Supreme Court's *Wade* decision and that the existing procedures had never been field tested *or* laboratory tested. If you were looking for "tests," the only "tests" of the current procedures were the DNA exoneration results. The researchers thought the prosecutors' "field test" idea was a stall. There wouldn't be another Attorney General like Reno for 100 years after the "field tests" were done. Larson, who was mildly intrigued by the researchers' ideas, and took a more conciliatory stance than Mourges, was driven to exasperation by the Data-Is-Truth (meaning *Our* Data Is Truth) mindset of the researchers.

All sorts of things that the researchers expected would be obvious to prosecutors, the prosecutors regarded as near-fantasy.

At one particular low point, Gary Wells, trying to show that knowledge about the psychological findings was getting around, pointed out that his web page was getting 1,500 "hits" each month.

"So does "ElvisIsAnAlien.Com," Larson exploded, "That doesn't make it *true!*"

———•◦•———

The prosecutors brought their own misconceptions to the process. Among these was the idea that the law enforcement side of the table was a homogenized team and the prosecutors the unanimously designated voice of the team.

It was easy to see how that impression took hold. The cops—with the exception, of course, of Paul Carroll—spent the first few sessions with their arms folded, drinking coffee, and staring at the little pads the hotels provided. Ron Fisher's materials about cognitive interviews weren't controversial: everyone could see that if you could discipline yourself and avoid asking leading questions in eyewitness interviews you had a better chance of getting more information from the witness. But the rest of the stuff—the Wells and Malpass lineup procedure techniques—sounded to the prosecutors exactly like the nonsense the defense lawyers had been peddling in court since Buckhout revived the issue. So the prosecutors, who had grown used to defending the police against this sort of thing in the courtroom, naturally assumed that leaping to their defense in the meetings was the thing to do. The prosecutors' reflex was to launch an immediate adversary attack on the researchers on the assumption that the attack was: (a) the right thing to do, and (b) what the police wanted and expected.

The second assumption was mistaken in a number of ways.

Although the police were certainly accustomed to having the prosecutors speak for them, that did not mean that the police always enjoyed the experience. Prosecutors have a tendency to assume that they know the law enforcement side of every issue *plus* the legal implications that the cops don't grasp. The police, on the other hand, see the prosecutors as essentially just another bunch of lawyers: in general they may be more sympathetic than defense lawyers or divorce lawyers, but they are still lawyers. Veteran cops with 20 years' experience have had plenty of frustrating encounters with tyro prosecutors who had 6 *months'* experience and felt fully authorized to boss the cops around. From the police point of view, there were plenty of things about police work that prosecutors didn't understand.

To begin with, the police actually see lots of misidentifications. Witnesses—20 to 25 percent in one survey—are always identifying fillers in photo arrays or lineups. These confident but mistaken witnesses never make it to the prosecutors because their cases are screened out, but they are a regular feature of an investigator's life. The prosecutors, by contrast, seldom see a case unless the police had a solid identification and something to corroborate it.

Besides, the two roles created fundamentally different perspectives on eyewitness issues. The police encounter eyewitnesses early in the process, and they saw better screening procedures as a way to get on with their work and to get the right guy without wasting time on the wrong one. The prosecutors, generally speaking, usually encountered the eyewitness when it is already too late to do anything about the choice: The choice has been made by the time the prosecutor gets the case and the witness is very confident. The only road open to the prosecutors is to make the original identification stick. The police were engaged in a process of looking forward to find the right guy; the prosecutors were engaged in a process of looking back, arguing that the right guy had in fact been found. The police didn't like wrongful acquittals any more than the prosecutors did, but because of their point of contact with the problem it was easier for the police to see that every wrongful conviction was *also* a wrongful acquittal—the right guy got away with it whenever you convicted the wrong one.

From the prosecutors' vantage point, anything resembling standardized procedures represents a potential danger. The prosecutors were morbidly conscious of the fact that the defense lawyers were lying in wait, eager to pounce on any deviation from the new "standard" procedures. That didn't bother the police; the police accepted the fact that the defense lawyers were going to find something to yell at them about, no matter what they did.

And—here is a second fundamental difference between the police and the prosecutors—the police actually like to have regularized, standard procedures, while the prosecutors tend to see procedures principally, in the words of one cop, as "something that the police fuck up." Following routine procedures is a fundamental part of police culture. It has even been said that investigative routine is the moral foundation of police work: You put a procedure in place, and you follow it wherever it leads, without bias or favoritism. Prosecutors, on the other hand, are allergic to procedural constraints. They want to be free to exercise independent judgment in pursuit of justice in any situation that may arise. Prosecutors hate procedural constraints on themselves, and they usually feel the impact of police procedures only when somebody embarrasses them in the courtroom with some "routine" procedure that the police should have followed but forgot—leaving the defense lawyer free to shout about sloppiness or conspiracy. "Look!" the defense lawyers would say, "Here's what they're *supposed* to do, right here in their own General Orders!"

The police not only liked procedures: they had confidence in their ability to follow them. Of course, real life includes messy situations where someone screws up, but that didn't mean that the police in general operated on the Keystone Kops level that the prosecutors seemed to be worried about. As a matter of fact, the more the prosecutors talked about the dangers that new standard procedures created, the more irritated the police became. The prosecutors seemed not only to be talking for them but talking *about* them in ways that suggested they were morons.

As the meetings ground on, the prosecutors exacerbated these tensions. Reacting to their feeling that Gary Wells had stacked the deck by choosing a cabal of researchers who agreed with him, the prosecutors called in Dr. Ebbe

Ebbesen, a psychologist from the University of San Diego, who had been fighting the antiexpert testimony fight since the earliest days of Bob Buckhout's reawakening of the issue, and he had become the prosecution's go-to guy whenever the issue was raised.[2] Ebbesen delivered a lecture to the full Technical Working Group which attacked the Wellsian approach. The lecture was not particularly well-designed for a novice audience; Ebbesen employed at least six different colored pens in drawing an increasingly elaborate diagram and a heady mixture of technical jargon in explaining his points. Still, although most of the police thought the Ebbesen talk was gibberish, they at least took away from it the feeling that there was some disagreement within the psychological community.

The difficulty for the prosecutors arose just after the Ebbesen lecture. The prosecutors had noticed early in the process that the important role of the prosecutor was not scheduled to be addressed, and decided that they would withdraw and write the prosecution sections, taking Ebbesen with them as their scientific consultant. The cops were left to battle with the researchers over the drafting of guidelines for interviewers. Finally, after a grueling afternoon, the cops and researchers produced a draft.

When the prosecutors emerged from their cloistered conference at the close of the day, they announced two things. First, it was impossible to draft any guidelines for prosecutors, because prosecutors needed complete discretion to make case-by-case judgments as the need arose. Second, they were now ready to rewrite everything the police had done in their absence.

In other words, they lived down to the cops' expectations. The prosecutors weren't going to submit to any guidelines, the cops thought, because the prosecutors thought that guidelines are only for cops. Even worse, several of the cops were confirmed in their suspicions that, as one of them put it later, "All the prosecutors care about is convictions, and they don't care if the guy is guilty or innocent. They just want the scalp on the wall."

The prosecutors did not succeed in driving the cops into an alliance with the researchers because the researchers didn't understand the cops any better than the prosecutors did.

In the world of science, "double-blind" testing—for example, tests of drug effectiveness in which neither the experimenter nor the subject knows which is the real drug and which is the placebo—is a matter of routine. It isn't done because of fear of corruption; it is done because of an enormous body of studies proving that researchers can *un*consciously influence the outcome of studies, even when they are making strenuous efforts to avoid that. The researchers thought that it would be perfectly reasonable to suggest to the cops that they apply those lessons to the process of identification. If you are going to show photographs to an eyewitness, you simply have to go to the next cubicle, find a detective who doesn't know which photograph is your suspect's, and have him administer the photo array. That way, unconscious influence is impossible. Even better, the new technique came with a carrot: after a "blind" array, the police could *prove* that they hadn't fingered anyone, because the cop who ran the array did not know whom to finger.

For the police on the panel, like Grand Rapids Detective Sgt. Ed Rusticus, this blind testing idea was nothing more or less than a violent assault on the integrity of every one who wore the badge. Rusticus was a bright guy who was willing to learn something new, but when he heard this "blind testing" idea he couldn't believe his ears. "Do they really think we have *time* to rig these lineups?" he asked himself, "I mean, *come on.*" The initial police reaction to the "blind testing" idea was immediate, and it was angry.

The prosecutors around the table brightened at these signs of police opposition to the researchers, and did what they could to fan the flames. The researchers seemed to dig themselves in deeper and deeper. There was, for example, the issue of post-identification feedback. One advantage of "blind" administration was that it was unlikely that the witness would take a confidence boost from the reaction—the smile, or the body language—of a cop who did not know who the suspect was. One curious police representative asked the researchers what they should do if a witness wanted to know how they did on the photo array or lineup "test." The answer from a researcher— "Tell them that it's not their business"—confirmed the police suspicion that the researchers were from another planet. For the police the whole business of investigation was a *social* challenge: it involved handling people. A good investigator had to sustain a relationship with his or her witnesses, calm their fears, keep their interest, make sure they stayed cooperative for the months between an arrest and the trial. "Tell them it's none of their business!" That response made it sound to the police as if the researchers thought that the cops spent their time among lab rats. You couldn't treat people that way and put a case together.

Someone suggested that the group move on for the time being from the contentious "blind" lineup issue to the more interesting proposed reform of doing lineups and arrays "sequentially"—showing people or pictures one at a time, not in a group all at once. The police had been intrigued by this idea. It didn't cost any money, it didn't question their integrity: it was worth a look. But at the moment that the discussion started to move in that direction, one of the researchers helpfully noted that a photo array that was "sequential" but not "blind" might be *more* dangerous than the current practice because it was easier for the cops' preconceptions to leak into the "sequential" presentation. That sent everyone back to a ferocious review of the "blind" lineup argument. By the time it was over, there wasn't a cop in the room who was ready to go back to his colleagues and advocate for "blind" lineup administration.

A pretty quick consensus had been reached about Ron Fisher's cognitive interview reforms, and draft advice to police about how to use those techniques had been prepared. But it looked as if that might be the high-water mark for this century's interaction between psychology and the justice system. Wait another 100 years and try again.

Outside the meeting rooms things weren't going too well either. Melissa Mourges had been reporting her doubts to Linda Fairstein in New York. It looked to both of them as if this was all moving in the wrong direction—a direction that could have been predicted from the first "Green Book" list of 28 mistaken victims—all sex crime victims, *their* victims. This was a trendy, knee-jerk resort to junk science run amok, all fomented by Barry Scheck. It was going to result in delighted defense lawyers, baffled jurors, and freed rapists. Fairstein did not believe in turning the other cheek in these situations; she decided to open a second front. She got on the telephone to like-minded prosecutors in the National District Attorney's Association, and she got on the telephone to Jeremy Travis.

Within the National District Attorney's Association (NDAA), Fairstein, and then Lynn Abrams, the veteran Philadelphia district attorney, got things buzzing. Lots of conference calls ensued, and dire threats were issued. People were really becoming quite worked up. The more they talked to each other, the angrier they became. The National District Attorney's Association's professional staff in Alexandria did lots of business with the Department of Justice and was not immediately alert to this problem, but now respected and well-known members of the association were beating the war drums about the eyewitness issue. The NDAA let Attorney General Reno know that it was opposed to this whole project of subjecting state and local law enforcement to the meddling "guidelines" promulgated by an all-knowing federal government. Reno was a former elected state prosecutor herself; she ought to see this point. Reno's response was laconic. She simply turned to Jeremy Travis at a staff meeting, and said, "Fix this."

Travis became the target of a series of increasingly angry telephone calls from the prosecutors. The calls became increasingly angry because Travis, who after all was supposed to be working for the chief federal prosecutor, seemed unimpressed by the prosecutors' arguments. The police couldn't follow these procedures? Don't be silly, Travis said, following procedures is what the police do all day; I used to be a Deputy Commissioner in New York; the cops *like* procedures. The police won't see the reasons for these procedures? They won't care about the reason, Travis answered—the most used sentence in police life is, "There *is* no reason; it's Department policy."

The one argument that Travis seemed willing to listen to was the argument that this whole effort to draft federal "Guidelines" was disrespectful. State and local governments don't need the guidance of the feds. To this charge Travis replied mildly that the National Institute of Justice didn't speak in that kind of voice. It didn't issue *Miranda*-style commands to the system at large. The prosecutors sensed a little give on this point, and they began to focus their energy and their righteous indignation on this horrible federal overreaching. In fact, Travis was privately skeptical about this line of attack. He thought that the prosecutors' solicitude for the poor overburdened police and the sacred rights of the states was actually a cover for the prosecutors' own allergic reaction to any constraint from any source on their own absolutely untrammeled discretion to do whatever they thought was right in any situation. Travis had reports from Richard Rau inside the meeting rooms which indicated that the prosecutors in the Technical Working Group were fighting a scorched-earth campaign over every trivial point. Still, Travis was content to have the conversation moving in this direction. He endured a week's worth of harangues on the subject, until the prosecutors made it clear that they were not obstructionists or uncooperative; they were prepared to consider this eyewitness issue in good faith. But this "guidelines" issue was a matter of principle. The prosecutors would walk out and call down anathema on the whole thing. When the organized resistance had climbed sufficiently out on the limb which that matter of principle provided, Travis sawed off the limb.

"You really object to calling all these things 'guidelines'?" he asked.

Ten minutes of fervid advocacy followed.

"O.K.," Travis said, "We won't call them 'guidelines.'"

He was as good as his word: the National Institute of Justice's Research Reports were all changed from "guidelines" to "guides." The matter of principle was resolved, and Travis blandly sent everyone back to the conference room with the air of a man who had made a tremendous concession.

Asked several years later whether the prosecutors could have torpedoed the whole effort by following through on their threat to walk out, Janet Reno thinks for just a moment and answers simply, "No." But no one knew that at the time, and it was plainly better for Reno's purposes that the prosecutors stay at the table.

And the prosecutors did stay at the table. Travis' "concession" had left them with no matter of principle to walk out on. When it came to lesser matters, walking out and leaving the field to the researchers—not to mention the previously marginal defense lawyers who would be left alone to speak to, and maybe for, the NIJ—was a dangerous move. There was damage control to be done.

———————◦•◦•◦———————

Back inside the meeting room, Rod Lindsay, the researcher who had been Wells's graduate assistant back in the days of the Alberta Conference 20 years earlier, proposed that there was probably some simple way to do photo arrays that were both "blind" and "sequential." What if, instead of using the traditional "six pack" approach of showing six mug shots all at once, you put each mug shot in a separate envelope and handed them to the witness? Then no one would know. The witness could write his or her identification on the outside of the envelope, and hand it back, with no police interference, or even the possibility of police interference.

The prosecutors had a good deal of fun with this brainstorm. They started to talk about it as "the envelope trick" and they invented hilarious slapstick performances of the "envelope trick" in action. The police didn't like the "envelope trick" either.

But the police reaction was, in a quiet way, fundamentally different from that of the prosecutors. The "envelope trick" actually intrigued the police. They played with it. At least one went home between meetings and tried to work it out. Experienced investigators like Ken Patenaude who had thought the whole enterprise was growing increasingly sterile made serious efforts to think through how you could make a technique out of these ideas. They got into it, and they started to work over the details with Lindsay. What if this happens, or that? Who puts the envelopes together? What do you do if the suspect is in the first envelope? What do you write after the choice? Who writes it?

The "envelope trick" actually provided one of several moments in the Technical Working Group where the police found their balance and realized that they could move forward in the direction that Mauro and Carroll were urging.

The police had silently watched the battle between the prosecutors and the researchers and they concluded that they did not agree with either side. The prosecutors kept predicting apocalypse if *anything* was done, and the police did not buy that. The researchers kept predicting a Dark Age unless *everything* was done, and the police did not buy that either. The prosecutors were dominated by criteria of legality. The researchers were dominated by criteria of science. But the police had their own criteria.

The primary police criterion was not legality or science; it was workmanship, professionalism. The police did not believe that this package of eyewitness research was a Big Thing, good *or* bad. They believed that it was a small but real adjustment in their practice, which could help them catch the guilty instead of the innocent.

But, paradoxically, these small improvements in their workmanship are A Big Thing to the police. In fact, there is nothing more important. To refuse to make a small but real improvement in standard investigative technique would be to repudiate your professional identity. If someone showed you that wearing rubber gloves on a crime scene preserved important evidence, then you wore your goddamned gloves at the crime scene. If you didn't, then it wasn't bad because it was illegal or unscientific, it was bad because it made *you a bad, sloppy, second rate cop!* Don Mauro's view, for example, was that law enforcement simply could not afford to walk away from anything that made daily practice more accurate.

For investigators like Ken Patenaude, the process of rejecting the envelope trick technique was a reminder that they might be able to take the researchers' data and build new techniques on their own. Mauro's and Carroll's preaching that the police had to take charge began to resonate. Carroll had been saying all along that this was about training and professionalism. Patenaude, who had once been ready to walk away from the whole thing, joined Mauro and Carroll as a leader in the movement to discover police-generated techniques that could make this whole thing work.

Patenaude was calm, he was respectful, he had good questions, and he started to ask them. He was a new voice in the room. The researchers started to listen to his questions and to try to answer them. It became a conversation about police-centered details, not about big legal and scientific principles.

The police knew by that point that Don Mauro had tried to suggest to Lynn Abrams and other NDAA activists that the prosecutors could gain credit in heaven if they proposed procedures of their own, and that the suggestion had been met without interest. The police were now ready to take the lead. Patenaude kept asking good questions, and now he insisted on answers. All the cops began insisting on answers—and from everyone.

————•◦•————

But the researchers' frustration had *them* considering whether *they* shouldn't walk out. They had made some progress. The police had agreed with the cognitive interview recommendations and they were in the draft product (now, thanks to Jeremy Travis's maneuver, called *A Guide For Law Enforcement,* not a set of "guidelines"). Roy Malpass, who was one of the researchers in the Technical Working Group, had convinced the Group that his prelineup instruction that the real perpetrator "may or may not be present" was a step worth taking. Some departments had already done it on their own. The Technical Working Group also saw Gary Wells's "match-to-description" test for "fillers" in lineups as something that helped their witnesses and their investigations. In a half dozen meetings over the course of 18 months the Group was also been convinced that it was important to have only one suspect in each lineup or photo array.

Still, the issue of "blind" testing was terrifically important to the researchers. It had been one of their four recommendations in the original "white paper," and there was nothing they thought was more worth fighting for. The "blind" lineup was a kind of keystone. Without it, the legitimacy of the whole process was called into question. Besides, the nature of the legal system's reaction to the idea—which bordered on contempt—made them wonder whether any of these people they were talking with understood what science was, still less respected it.

Don Mauro, in his quiet way, came to the rescue of the process with the researchers. He sidled up to Gary Wells at a break, and politely suggested that the researchers would just have to let go of the "blind testing" issue. Look, Mauro said, I understand now why this is so important to you. But I didn't understand it at the beginning. You have to realize that you've had 18 cops locked in rooms listening to you about this for a total of close to 20 hours and you've only convinced maybe about one third of us of us. But that third is only going to have about five minutes to convince their departments when they get back home. Even the guys you've convinced are not going to do it; they know their audience. They know that this is going to sound like an attack on their ethics. People will howl. It's a non-starter. It can take the whole thing down. You've made progress: let people get used to your ideas. Move on, come back again.

The best that Wells could say was that the researchers would hang in for a while and see what happened.

What happened was a punishing period of drafting, line by line, the text of the recommendations that the Technical Working Group would publish for the general law enforcement community—if it published anything at all. Dr. Rau kept his troops at it in a series of airless hotel meeting rooms. Members of the Technical Working Group suspected Rau of running a subtle behavior modification program. When he thought they were doing well, he would reward them with a meeting in San Francisco; when they disappointed him he would threaten a meeting in Newark. But wherever the meeting was held, Rau saw to it that a very effective group of NIJ staff had a role.

The most involved of the staff was Lisa Kaas, who had worked for Rau on other projects. Kaas was extremely bright—she would start law school during the next year—unfailingly tolerant, and completely uncomplaining. It also didn't hurt that the police found her to be extremely good-looking, a fact that put them on her side from the beginning. Technically, her formal role in the actual meetings was to type for computer display the text of the *Guide's* provisions and edit them onscreen as the debate swirled around the room. Everyone knew that Kaas had also mastered all the material and did a great deal of work in the background, too, and when a visiting consultant told her to "shut up and type" when she offered a rare suggestion, he turned every member of the entire Group against him in chivalrous outrage in an instant.

But Kaas's role as scribe in the typing/editing project turned out to be very influential.

The best example of Kaas's impact might be one from a final drafting session in San Francisco. The subject matter was the researchers' recommendation that as soon as a witness makes an identification, the police should ask for an *immediate* statement of eyewitness confidence. It was a crucial point for the researchers. If the witness' confidence could be sampled before any feedback could come from the police that would inflate the witness' confidence, then that would be some mitigation of the loss of the "blind" procedures standard. Without the immediate confidence measurement the failure to recommend "blind" procedures threatened the whole project.

Debate over the wording of the sentence ground on for an entire morning. No progress was made. The researchers would put something in, and Kaas would put it on the screen. The lawyers kept shouting apparently out of sheer love of argument. The prosecutors would demand that it be taken out, and Kaas took it out and put the prosecutors' new version on the screen. The researchers objected: blood was shed over semicolons. The police would add their version, and Kaas put that up on the screen. The whole thing turned into a wearisome slugging match between equally matched adversaries. No progress was made.

Dr. Rau called a break.

When everyone returned to the room, there was a new formulation on the screen: "If an identification is made, avoid reporting to the witness any information regarding the individual he/she has selected prior to obtaining the witness' statement of certainty." The author of that formulation was Lisa Kaas. The exhausted antagonists looked it over suspiciously; Rau called for a vote. Kaas' language was accepted, and it was in the *Guide*. It was a tribute to her judgment that she knew when and how to intervene, and a tribute to the credibility she had built up that the group acquiesced.

By this sort of piece by piece, *ad hoc* process, *Eyewitness Evidence: A Guide For Law Enforcement*, took form. Dr. Rau kept them at the table, and finally, late in the day in San Francisco, the thing was finished.

The prosecutors didn't walk out; the researchers didn't walk out. In part this was because each side felt that a walkout was exactly what their adversaries were hoping for. Gary Wells, for example, thought for a while that the prosecutors had an explicit strategy of trying to raise the frustration level so that the researchers would drop the whole thing. But people stuck with the process for another reason—a reason they had been given at the beginning of the first meeting in Chicago.

———————

The first meeting of the full Technical Working Group on Eyewitness Evidence had opened with a screening of Ben Loeterman's *Frontline* documentary, "What Jennifer Saw." Police officers from all over the country, prosecutors, researchers, and defenders sat together in a darkened room and watched the story of Jennifer Thompson and Ronald Cotton. They saw the destruction of Ronald Cotton's life. They saw Det. Mike Gauldin's anguish at the disastrous results of following the existing "book" of identification procedures to its tragic destination. They saw Jennifer Thompson's agony. They saw the smirking face of Bobby Poole. They didn't see, but they couldn't help imagining, the faces of Poole's other victims, the victims whom Poole had brutalized while Ronald Cotton served Poole's sentence.

And by the time the meetings got underway, the members of the Technical Working Group knew about a final act in the drama.

The broadcast of "What Jennifer Saw," which made Jennifer Thompson a hero for so many people, had crystallized Jennifer Thompson's own dissatisfaction with herself—called her attention to the fact that she had un-finished business. She made a call to Mike Gauldin, who knew her pretty well by then, and guessed immediately why she was calling.

"You want to see Ronald Cotton," Gauldin said.

That was true. Jennifer wanted to see Ronald Cotton and apologize.

A private meeting was arranged in a church not far from the scene of the rape and the scene of the trial. Jennifer did not know what to expect—rage, or insult both seemed within the potential range. She wouldn't have blamed Cot-ton if he spat on her. She just knew that she wanted to see Cotton and apolo-gize. She knew in fact that she *had* to see Ronald Cotton and apologize.

They met in the pastor's study. Jennifer steeled herself, and apologized. She knew, she said, that no apology could be adequate, but she had to apologize.

"I never blamed you," Cotton said. "I forgive you. I want you to have a good life."

The story of the Thompson and Cotton encounter was told often during the course of the Technical Working Group process. When, for example, someone argued that there was no such thing as a "pure" eyewitness case, that no one would bring a prosecution based on an eyewitness without corrobora-tion, Rod Lindsay pointed out that Mike Gauldin had corroboration too, and that ended the discussion. But the Thompson/Cotton story came up outside the meeting rooms, too—over drinks, or on walks around the city. At least for some of the group's members, it made a crucial difference. Thompson's brav-ery was impressive enough; Cotton's large-spirited forgiveness was transcen-dent. It transformed Cotton from a victim into a hero, and it amounted to a call to duty.

"I mean," Dave Niblack, the senior defense lawyer on the group, said, "If she can ask him for forgiveness in that situation, and he can *give* it, who the hell in our group can walk away from this stuff?"

And, in the end, no one did walk away, although there were 100 moments when that could have happened. Like Waterloo, the Technical Working Group was "a damned close-run thing." When an impasse arose in the de-bates, someone stepped forward with a suggestion. When someone seemed to be sulking, someone else would make an effort to bring them back. Some-one—not always the same someone—stepped up.

A consensus was reached on *Eyewitness Evidence: A Guide for Law Enforce-ment.*[3] No one got everything he or she wanted. "Sequential" lineups were in-cluded, but there was no preference for them stated. "Blind" lineups were omitted from the text, but singled out in an introduction as a prospect for fur-ther study.

Still, the *Guide* did call for cognitive interview techniques, for pre-lineup instructions to witnesses, for immediate measure of eyewitness confidence. It called, in the end, for perhaps three-quarters of what the psychologists would have wanted, and it acknowledged that the psychological studies had something fundamental to offer legal practitioners. The prosecutors had to settle for warnings that these procedures were only recommendations, but they did settle for them, and they did not jump ship.

The *Guide* was published, with a message from the attorney general of the United States, hailing it as an "important tool," in October 1999. It was the first concrete product of a collaboration between the legal system and the psychologists who study eyewitness memory.

It was nearly 80 years since Wigmore had first argued for a "friendly and energetic alliance." Although there were friendships formed during the process, it would be going too far to call the Technical Working Group "friendly." It would be hard to argue that the Technical Working Group, at least until its very last moment, was an "alliance." But it was something.

Maybe, in light of the role that *Frontline*, Jennifer Thompson, Ronald Cotton, and Mike Gauldin played in the minds of the participants the Technical Working Group was a form of bearing witness.

CHAPTER 12

A ROAD AHEAD

The Continuing Study of Wrongful Convictions

THE PUBLICATION OF THE *GUIDE* WAS A SYMBOLIC MILESTONE, but it had no immediate practical effect. The *Guide's* insights weren't self-executing. There was a nice blue pamphlet, but nothing had changed on the ground.

Dr. Rau kept the core of his Working Group together, and they drafted a manual for police training programs. For some reason once the *Guide* itself was issued, the process was less contentious. The police did not need to be urged to participate this time; they knew all about police training, and they dug into the nuts and bolts aspects with enthusiasm. The Working Group was divided into two teams: Paul Carroll and Ron Fisher led a team that concentrated on the interviewing sections; Ken Patenaude and Gary Wells led a team which concentrated on the identification procedures. Several of the more vehement members of the Working Group drifted away from the process, and those who remained had developed a proprietary feel about the *Guide's* lessons. Mark Larson stayed on to represent the prosecutors on the interviewing team, and Michael Barrasse who had retired as the Lackwanna County District Attorney to become a judge, represented the prosecutors on the identification procedures team, and they set a helpful—if cautious—tone. In fact, the process of drafting the training manual was so harmonious that when it was over the members unanimously decided to dedicate the product to the memory of a *defense* lawyer, Dave Niblack, who had died during the drafting process.

A draft was completed, tracking the *Guide's* suggestions. It was a sophisticated training tool, including detailed lesson plans, illustrative slides, and a CD-ROM designed to ease the local police trainer's work. It also contained an introduction that contained a brief summary of the psychological findings on the nature of memory. The police members of the group felt something along these lines was necessary to orient the trainers to the "trace evidence" aspects of eyewitness evidence, and within the group the Introduction was not controversial. The draft training manual was circulated for comment, and as soon as the response from the National District Attorney's Association arrived, it was clear that any declarations of victory which Gary Wells and his researchers might have been inclined to make were premature.

———————•◦•———————

The NDAA may have lost a battle, but it did not concede the war. In fact, it wasn't clear that the NDAA was prepared to concede that the original battle was quite over.

By this time Janet Reno and Jeremy Travis were out; John Ashcroft was the new Attorney General, and Sarah Hart was the new Director of the National Institute of Justice. The NDAA, through its President, Kevin Meehan, a Wyoming District Attorney, went back to the old battlefield in a letter to Hart.[1]

Apparently still smarting over the effect of Jeremy Travis's trap, NDAA complained about the title of the original document. NDAA admitted that the final title, *Eyewitness Evidence—A Guide for Law Enforcement* ameliorated the concept of a national standard that was endorsed by the United States Department of Justice, it argued that the distinction was usually lost in the context of the entire report. The publication was being routinely referred to as a "guide" rather then as a "research report."

Still, that objection was made in passing. The problem was more fundamental. The NDAA's real target was not Jeremy Travis' new title; it was not even Gary Wells and his newfangled identification procedures.

The NDAA's attack was actually focused on Munsterberg and the modern psychological conception of memory. Followed to its logical conclusion the NDAA's claim was that there was really nothing to be learned about human memory. The NDAA believed that the whole issue should be off the table, that what a witness sees and experiences during any event, especially during a crime, is highly variable and does not lend itself to a standardized approach.

In other words, you knew an accurate eyewitness when you saw one—or at least your District Attorney did—and there is no legitimate general science of memory that can be brought to bear in any meaningful way. The NDAA complained that memory was set out in the manual as having the same characteristics for all circumstances, all persons, and all purposes. The NDAA's position seemed to be that unless that was true, then no use could be made of the memory research, and it was *not* true—or at least not proved true.

Nor, the NDAA argued, was any help from psychology *needed*. Eyewitnesses were being unfairly criticized in this process, which ignored the cases in which eyewitness identifications are corroborated by confession, DNA testing, fingerprint evidence, or the recovery of property. The DNA "exonerations" were not really "exonerations" at all; they were "failures of DNA corroboration." The DNA may not have proved that five eyewitnesses were *right* about Kirk Bloodsworth, this argument went, but it certainly didn't prove that they were *wrong*.

The striking thing about the NDAA response is that every complaint in it could have been aimed at the expert witness trial testimony controversy without reference to the "system variable" approach which the *Guide* embodied.

NDAA was determined to ignore the radical difference between its unhappy history with psychologists used by defense lawyers in the process of looking *back* at trial to ask whether an error had occurred and the Working Group's efforts to prevent errors *before* they happened. The NDAA's strategy was to treat the two issues, prevention and adjudication, as if they were identical—and the science identically useless in resolving both.

If an embargo on psychology is your goal the benefits of this strategy are pretty evident. No psychologist, not even Munsterberg or Buckhout, had ever claimed that any "general rule" could be sufficient to resolve every individual case; but the second, preventative, issue could not even be discussed unless you believed that the memories of individual humans had *something* in common. To suggest that you apply the same "general rule" to the retrospective evaluation each individual eyewitness identification after it is made certainly made very little sense.

The NDAA submission depended on the even less plausible claim that you might as well use an individualized, customized, interview or lineup procedure for each individual witness before an identification was attempted. The NDAA was fighting to deny Psychology any place in the criminal justice system.

The NDAA had drawn a line: there was nothing to be learned from psychology about eyewitness memory. To give even the appearance of credence to any of the lessons of experimental psychology threatened the credibility of all eyewitnesses, in every case.

And the NDAA was not dealing with Janet Reno and Jeremy Travis any longer. Sarah Hart, the New Director of the National Institute of Justice, delayed publication of the Trainer's Manual to think things over. A peculiar situation had been created: Every defense lawyer in the country knew about *Eyewitness Testimony: A Guide for Law Enforcement;* virtually no cop outside the original Working Group had ever heard of it.

The *Training Manual* was not released for two years. When it was released, the material on the nature of memory had been deleted.

—————◆◆◆◆—————

The NDAA is the institutional voice of the elected District Attorneys, and carries enormous potential leverage in the political process. But here and there individual prosecutors—abetted by individual police officers—branched off cautiously from the main line.

The individual prosecutors who were willing to break step were generally those who had for one reason or another been exposed at length (and in depth) to the scientists' materials outside the context of the adversary courtroom battle. One working group alumnus, Seattle prosecutor Mark Larson, for example, co-authored with two defense lawyer members of the Working Group (Caterina Ditraglia and current author) an article for the American Bar Association's *Criminal Justice* magazine which pointed out the enormous persuasive power that the new techniques would give prosecution eyewitnesses in court.[2] Larson began to give talks to prosecutors and judges suggesting that these new techniques were worth at least a guarded, skeptical look.

And there were other individual prosecutors who had reasons of their own for taking an immediate look at identification procedures. In at least two jurisdictions, New Jersey and Illinois, eyewitness identification reform found a place on lists of things to do in a crisis situation.

The crisis in New Jersey was the result of a disastrous series of studies revealing pervasive race discrimination in the state's criminal justice system. The studies, which crystallized around a protracted and widely publicized debate over the "racial profiling" practices of the state police. One episode in this drama was a punishing campaign of litigation in a case that resulted in the New Jersey Supreme Court's issuing a turning point opinion[3] requiring New Jersey courts to instruct juries about the dangers inherent in cross-racial eyewitness identifications.

The New Jersey situation had become so bad that the credibility of the criminal justice system in general seemed to be jeopardized, and John Farmer,

the New Jersey Attorney General, was more than open to some concrete reform which would indicate that someone in law enforcement was trying to do
something about this crisis.

A deputy of Farmer's, Debra Stone, had come across Gary Wells' articles
while studying the cross-racial issue, and she had Wells invited in for a talk. For
Wells, the opportunity to address prosecutors outside the adversarial riptides of
the courtroom was rare, and welcome. He was particularly intrigued by the idea
of speaking to the New Jersey prosecutors when he learned that the attorney
general in New Jersey occupies a unique status. Like the British Home Secretary—and unlike American attorneys general—John Farmer presided over a
centralized criminal justice system. He controlled all of the prosecutors in all of
the counties: he genuinely was the chief law enforcement officer.

Wells cranked up his Power Point show for Farmer's deputies, and eventually for Farmer himself. The N.I.J. Guide gave the process some legitimacy, but
Farmer decided to go well beyond the Technical Working Group's product. In
fact, Farmer agreed to the whole package: to everything the psychologists had
wanted from the N.I.J. report but failed to get. Farmer was prepared to order
that all New Jersey jurisdictions use "blind" and "sequential" identification procedures. His staff drafted a series of guidelines which might have been drafted
by Wells himself. Farmer had only one proviso, "We're going to go ahead with
this," he said, "But I'm not going to ram it down people's throats."

So, Wells started to spend lots of time in New Jersey: not as a defense witness, but as a teacher, speaking to audiences of cops and prosecutors. No one
in the audience swooned with delight at his findings, but no one reacted toxi-
cally either. Stone, and then another Deputy Attorney General, Lori Linskey,
ran diplomatic interference for Wells, while politely making it clear that the
Attorney General was firmly behind this initiative. Finally, in October 2000,
Farmer issued his guidelines to New Jersey law enforcement.

The psychologists' research was now functioning in the real world. If
nothing else, New Jersey would provide the field-test laboratory that skeptics
had been demanding. It was a diverse state, where local police departments
faced a variety of challenges. As the early reports came in, it turned out that
the local police and prosecutors actually liked the new way of doing things.
They got slightly fewer "hits," but the "hits" they got—and the court cases
that followed—were much stronger.

Meanwhile, in Illinois, there was a different crisis brewing. Northwestern
journalism students, working with lawyers from the clinic at Dean Wigmore's
old law school, had uncovered an astonishing list of wrongful convictions in
the Illinois criminal justice system. The *Chicago Tribune* adopted the story and

ran a brilliant exposé that showed—among other appalling things—that the list of exonerated, wrongly convicted Illinois death row prisoners just outnumbered the prisoners actually executed. Confidence in criminal justice in Illinois plummeted.

Illinois governor George Ryan convened a Commission to investigate systemic problems. As before, eyewitness identification cases screamed for attention, and Gary Wells was on the road again. The Illinois Governor's Commission was, like Janet Reno's Technical Working Group, a mixed group: everyone was at the table. But this group was considerably more prestigious: it included a eminent judges, a former United States Senator, a number of past and present prosecutors. One of the prosecutors, Scott Turow, was also a celebrity: a best-selling novelist.

Wells succeeded again: the Illinois Governor's Commission recommended to the legislature a menu of changes in eyewitness identification procedures.[4]

The media had not lost interest in eyewitness issues, and the new reforms were met with amazing enthusiasm. It just seemed to be one of those issues that reporters and editors liked. The *New York Times*[5] ran an approving story on the New Jersey guidelines on the front page. Scott Turow included a reference to eyewitness reform in a *New Yorker* article[6] describing his Governor's Commission experience. *USA Today* splashed its own story on the front page. *The Wall Street Journal* weighed in favorably; so did the *Atlantic Monthly*. National Public Radio's "All Things Considered" ran a lengthy segment featuring Wells, Ken Patenaude, and other Technical Working Group members.[7]

Wells and the psychology of "system variable" reform were having a media run unequaled since Munsterberg's amazing string of articles in 1907. The *New Yorker* published an admiring profile of Wells himself.[8] The "sequential" lineup was selected by the *Sunday New York Times Magazine* as an "Idea of the Year" for 2001.

Still, as gratifying as all of this was to Wells, there was a question of whether the media, for all of its friendliness, wasn't running in the wrong direction. Lurking in the coverage was a feature which he had not anticipated. For some reason, of all of the findings and reforms that the system variable approach had generated the media loved the "sequential" lineup best. Wells thought that on balance the sequential lineup was still an excellent policy change, but he thought that the focus on it was disproportionate. Other elements of the reforms—

pre-lineup instructions, immediate confidence statements, "blind" administration of identification procedures, "match-to-description" selection of fillers—seemed to him to be at least equally important.

Besides, "sequential" lineups were not the first ground Wells would have chosen to defend; although Wells thought the science supporting the sequential technique was strong, he recognized that it could have been stronger, and psychologists he respected, like Roy Malpass, were still extremely hesitant about mandating the sequential approach.

Among the dangers that the media fascination with the "sequential" approach created for Wells was that media fascination would lead to defense lawyer frenzy. The defense lawyers, in their combative way would forfeit the "bring everyone to the table approach" which had worked for Wells in New Jersey and Illinois, by employing their own traditional "wack the prosecutor over the head" approach in courtrooms. The defense lawyers were used to seeing eyewitness psychology as their property, and now that it was getting all of this praise, they were likely to use it as a sword, not a shield.

In a number of places that was just what happened, and the results were true to form. In Philadelphia and New York, defenders immediately began to seek judicial orders that police conduct only "blind" and "sequential" lineups. The prosecutors, once they saw that the defense was in favor of these things, knew that they must be opposed at all costs. It didn't help that these first two battlegrounds were the homes of Lynn Abrams and Linda Fairstein, who had been vehemently opposed to the whole project from the beginning and had spread the news that this new unholy defense-psychology threat was looming. Bronx public defender David Feige picked up the banner, filing motions for reformed procedures, and announcing that the psychologists had discovered "a silver bullet" for the problem of wrongful convictions.[9]

To this, the prosecution answered, "Like hell they have."[10] Maybe this "sequential" lineup thing did cut down on the number of eyewitness guesses, but some of those eyewitnesses guessed *right*, and the prosecutors felt that they could figure out which ones. One thing was certain, cutting out guesses would inevitably decrease the absolute number of convictions, and for the prosecutors, that was the ultimate criterion. In Massachusetts, when identification reform legislation was introduced by—and regarded as the baby of—the defenders, the prosecutors' first reflex was to dig in their heels.

The judges, for better or worse, ducked the whole issue. One or two expressed doubts about the science, others adopted it, but most simply declined on institutional grounds to interfere in police identification procedures before they had occurred. The judges would deal with the problems in court, let the cops run their own procedures.

One potential shortcut was shut down. Wells could comfort himself with the thought that, given the history of the issue in the adversary process, the litigation route might have been a shortcut to disaster.

Still, with litigation proving fruitless, you had to wonder whether only states confronting seismic upheavals like those in Illinois and New Jersey would be willing to look at this issue at all, no matter how delighted the media seemed with the psychologists' ideas.

———————•◦•———————

Judges could see that there was a problem with eyewitness evidence: they had seen that all along. They didn't necessarily see it as *their* problem. They thought the cops should be careful with it; they hoped that the jurors would sort it out. There were institutional reasons—or at least dignified rationalizations—for leaving the issue to the cops and the jurors.

North Carolina's Chief Justice, I. Beverly Lake, Jr. is a solidly conservative Republican jurist, and not a knee-jerk liberal. But Chief Justice Lake took seriously his position at the pinnacle of North Carolina's justice system, and besides, he had as his former law clerk a dynamo named Christine Mumma.

In Lake's view responsible officials of the criminal justice system could not ignore the steady drum beat of DNA exoneration cases. The tragic results of the individual cases were bad enough. And there was a less obvious, perhaps more insidious impact too. It wasn't just that the prosecutors had won cases which they should not have won; it was also that the exposure of these tainted victories would result in the prosecutors losing cases they should win as public cynicism grew.

He saw no reason to wait for a New Jersey–style cataclysm before doing something, and with Chris Mumma's tireless and diplomatic staff work, he brought into being the North Carolina "Actual Innocence Commission."[11]

Like Janet Reno, Chief Justice Lake brought everyone to the table. Only Lake's enormous prestige *could* have brought everyone to the table. The North Carolina justice system was divided by fault lines of every kind. Besides the prosecution-defense divide, there was a Republican-Democratic divide and a death penalty–anti-death penalty divide. Each of these individual wars was ferocious. Still, no one was prepared to ignore Chief Justice Lake, and everyone showed up: police, prosecutors, defenders. Lake told them to park their death penalty and party political disputes outside the door, and brought them all into the room.

Once they were there, Lake, in a quiet and courtly manner, in the words of one participant, "knocked their heads together pretty good." In doing that he had some help from the topic which he and Mumma thought would be a good one to start with: eyewitness identification. Reno's Technical Working Group, the New Jersey attorney general and the Illinois Governor's Commission had already blazed a trail. Brian Cutler, who had been a long time leader in the field and a co-author of the original American Psychology–Law Society "White Paper" was teaching in North Carolina and agreed to serve. Everyone in North Carolina knew the story of the Jennifer Thompson/Ronald Cotton case, and North Carolina had experienced a number of exonerations in eyewitness cases since then.

And no one on Chief Justice Lake's Actual Innocence Commission was going to forget those experiences, because Richard Rosen who had represented Ronald Cotton was on the Commission. So were Jennifer Thompson herself and Mike Gauldin. Gauldin still remembered how the "book" he had followed all of those years ago had led to the conviction of an innocent man, and to the temporary freedom of Bobby Poole, who had used the time to commit several rapes while Cotton served his sentence.

Chris Mumma saw to it that Lori Linskey was brought in from New Jersey to describe the favorable reaction of New Jersey police and prosecutors to their "field test" of the reforms. Gary Wells was brought in for a lengthy session too. He thought it went well, but what really raised his hopes was a statement he overheard.

"I really don't see," Wells heard Mike Gauldin say, "How *any*one can be against these reforms."

And in the end, no one was against them. The Commission recommended a full program of system-variable changes. It was only a recommendation of course, but it was the right thing, done in the right way, and it had the broad support of the criminal justice professionals.[12]

Looking back over the discussions, Rich Rosen said, "It was pretty much a straight line: from the NIJ Technical Working Group, to New Jersey, to North Carolina."

That was true in a sense. But you could argue that the line was actually a circle that had begun in North Carolina with Ben Loeterman's *Frontline* piece on Thompson and Cotton.

Or you could argue that if it was a straight line, it started much earlier: when William James decided to bring Hugo Munsterberg to Harvard.

CHAPTER THIRTEEN

AN ENDGAME

Looking Back on Gary Graham

WHEN KIRK BLOODSWORTH WAS EXONERATED and released, people asked him to agree that, however tragic his situation, and however sad that he had spent all those years in prison, at least the system had worked in the end.

"If that guy had just murdered the little girl, and not raped her," Bloodsworth replied, "the State of Maryland would have killed me by now."[1]

In fact, it took 20 years and a DNA match to the real murderer of Dawn Hamilton before the Baltimore County District Attorney could bring herself to admit that Bloodsworth was innocent all along.[2]

But the murder of Bobby Lambert was a typical shooting in a local market's parking lot, not a sex crime, and there was no DNA to come to Gary Graham's rescue.

———◦◦◦———

Gary Graham promised that he would fight them when they came for him at the end, and he did. It took a five man "extraction team" to overpower him and wrestle him from his cell—to hold him down and to strap him to a gurney, where he was immobilized so that the IV tubes which would carry the poisons designed to paralyze his muscles and stop his heart could be inserted into his veins.

When the blinds obscuring the execution chamber were opened and the witnesses could first see Graham, he was already strapped down. His last speech was a confused mixture, and there was nothing especially eloquent about it. Graham was not an educated man; he had been in prison since he was 18, and eloquence would be too much to expect from anyone under the circumstances. Graham knew that as soon as he stopped speaking, they would kill him. He did better than most people would have done. Along with thanking his supporters, he managed to declare his innocence one last time.

> I would like to say that I did not kill Bobby Lambert. That I'm an innocent black man that is being murdered. This is a lynching that is happening in America tonight. . . . There's overwhelming and compelling evidence of my defenses that was never been heard in any court of America. . . . This is nothing more than pure and simple murder. This is what is happening tonight in America. Nothing more than state sanctioned murders, state sanctioned lynching, right here in America, and right here tonight. . . . They know I'm innocent. But they cannot acknowledge innocence, because to do so would be to publicly admit their guilt. This is something these racist people will never do. We must remember brothers, this is what we're faced with. You must take this endeavor forward. . . . Keep marching black people, black power. Keep marching black people, black power. Keep marching black people. Keep marching black people. They are killing me tonight. They are murdering me tonight.[3]

Graham paused, and the warden gave a signal. The valves on the IV tubes were opened, and the toxic drugs were released into Graham's bloodstream. He was declared dead eight minutes later.

Out on the campaign trail, Governor Bush issued a statement saying that Graham had full access to the courts over a period of many years.[4] As is sometimes the case, it was difficult to tell whether Mr. Bush intended to mislead, misunderstood the meaning of what he was saying, or was simply reading without much attention something that had been prepared for him by others.

It was true that Gary Graham's case had been in the courts for many years, but although various legal aspects of the case had been batted around for a decade, the one question that mattered—whether Bernadine Skillern's eyewitness identification of Gary Graham as the shooter was correct or mistaken—had been reviewed only once, by the jury at Graham's initial trial. No reviewing court had ever looked at it again.

One thing was certainly clear: Jennifer Thompson's account of her own honest and confident mistake, published in the New York Times the day before the execution, made no impression on Governor Bush.[5]

In the absence of DNA evidence we may never know whether the execution of Gary Graham was simply a harsh punishment administered to a guilty man. But perhaps we can all agree right now that it is painfully unfair for the responsibility for Graham's execution to be placed on Bernadine Skillern's eyewitness memory and the jury that evaluated it.

If the wrong man was killed, it shouldn't be blamed on Skillern and the jury.

———•◆•———

To begin with, Gary Graham's trial didn't have to come to down to Skillern's memory. There was a pile of evidence that the jury never heard because of the lethargy of Graham's trial counsel. On the night of the shooting Houston police had identified *five* eyewitnesses who had seen the shooter. Of these five, only Ms. Skillern identified Graham. Two others later affirmatively stated that Graham was *not* the shooter. One of these, a longtime postal service employee and ordained minister who had been working in the store adjacent to the parking lot where the shooting occurred, had seen the shooter twice: once before the shooting, and once fleeing the scene. The second witness, a cashier at the store, saw the shooter from a distance of a few feet for some minutes before the shooting. Both were certain that Graham was not the man who shot Lambert. The jurors never heard from either.

When Graham was arrested, he was carrying a gun, but the gun that was found on Graham did not match the murder weapon. Robbery was supposed to be Graham's motive, but there was money found in Lambert's pockets. Besides, why would Graham, an experienced armed robber, shoot Lambert anyway? He never shot any of his ten other robbery victims; he simply took their money and ran. Graham had no motive to vary this pattern and shoot Lambert if a simple hold-up was what had occurred.[6]

We now know—but the jury didn't—that there were other criminals who *did* have an excellent motive for assassinating Lambert. Lambert, a pilot, had been arrested flying drugs into Oklahoma, and had been forced by federal prosecutors and the DEA to give testimony against the conspirators in his drug smuggling scheme under a grant of immunity. There was a further grand jury subpoena outstanding for Bobby Lambert when he was killed. Lambert's Oklahoma lawyer believed that Lambert was killed by the drug gang for whom he worked in an effort to prevent his testimony. None of these facts had been reviewed by a court.[7]

———•◆•———

Besides, even if the Graham case *did* have to come down to Bernadine Skillern's memory—and many eyewitness cases do, after all, come down to a single witness—the handling of Skillern's memory by the traditional processes used by the Houston investigators raises this question: Did Bernadine Skillern's sincere testimony represent Skillern's own memory of events? Or was it a product of the system's unwitting contamination of her memory?

Before Graham was arrested, Skillern had helped to develop a composite sketch of the parking lot shooter. She had engaged, in other words, in the same process as Jennifer Thompson. The face in the Skillern drawing is markedly thinner than Graham's.

After Graham's arrest, Skillern was shown a "simultaneous" array of five photographs. The photographs in this array had not been chosen to match the description given on the night of the shooting. In this array, only Gary Graham fit the description of a man with a short Afro haircut and no moustache or beard, which is how the culprit was described on the night of the killing.

Even so, Skillern declined to positively identify Graham. She said that his face "looked like" the shooter, but that the shooter's face was thinner and his complexion was darker.

Later, Skillern viewed a live lineup. The members of the lineup were displayed simultaneously, not "sequentially." Skillern was not cautioned that the shooter might not be in the line, and of the people Skillern had seen in the photo array only Graham reappeared in the lineup. This time, Skillern identified Graham.

By the time of Graham's trial, Skillern was certain. By the time of Graham's execution she was unshakeable.

Would Skillern even have noticed Graham if the photo array had contained six men who matched her verbal description of the shooter, rather than just one? Would she have chosen Graham at all if she had been told that the real shooter might not be in the array? Would she have chosen Graham if the photographs, or the lineup members, had been shown one at a time, to inhibit a "looks-most-like" comparative choice based on relative judgment? Would her confidence have progressed from "looks-like-but-with-a-too-wide-face" to "certain" if she had been insulated from post-identification feedback?

Perhaps the answer to all of these questions is yes, and better processes would have led to the same result. Skillern might still have identified Graham; her confidence might have grown just as dramatically; the jury might still have trusted her choice.

But this much is certain: If investigators had used the better processes that psychology has identified, we could be twice as confident in the result. There is "a book" on eyewitness memory based on psychological research that can be twice as likely to avoid eyewitness error as the procedures currently in use.

After the initial thrill of horror at a wrongful conviction has passed away; after the mistake has been exposed, the innocent man released, and the reporters have all gone home, an abiding sense that the world is not quite back in balance remains.

The mistaken eyewitness cases leave the corrosive residue of doubt that John Adams described, when he argued in defense of the British officers charged with manslaughter in the Boston Massacre. "When innocence itself is brought to the bar and condemned, especially to die," Adams warned, "Then, the subject will exclaim, 'Whether I behave well or ill is of no account; for virtue itself is no security.' And if such an idea as that takes hold in the mind of the subject, that would be the end of all security whatsoever."[8] Ultimately, the hope of eliminating that fundamental insecurity is what is at stake.

This story has stretched across almost a century since Hugo Munsterberg first took the lawyers to task and John Henry Wigmore first tried to teach Munsterberg the facts of legal life, but the conclusion of the story can't be provided in this book; the conclusion of the story is still being written, right now, in state and local criminal justice systems all over the country.

We have many Gary Graham cases in our future—many Ronald Cotton cases, many Kirk Bloodsworth cases, too. We will have DNA in a fraction of those cases; in the rest we will have the memory of the witness, nothing more. How those cases will be handled is still an open question.

A growing handful of scattered jurisdictions and departments lucky enough to have individual leaders willing to come forward (even in the absence of an acute crisis) to nurture reform, have addressed their eyewitness identification procedures.[9] Ken Patenaude of the Northampton Police, Mark Larson in Seattle, prosecutor Amy Klobuchar in Minneapolis, and Chief Justice Lake in North Carolina, have all spurred reforms. New Jersey and scattered Minnesota jurisdictions have adopted, and North Carolina and Illinois recommended, comprehensive redesigns of identification procedures. In Boston and surrounding Suffolk County, District Attorney Dan Conley, his first assistant, Joshua Wall, and police superintendent Kathleen O'Toole went to work on the problem. They drafted Gary Wells to serve on their eyewitness task force, added some defense lawyers, and then put Boston police superintendent John Gallagher to work, making sure that their schemes didn't conflict with the gritty big-city realities his detectives faced. Gallagher got the troops on board. A "gold standard" eyewitness memory evidence reform program emerged. The Boston guidelines became the first to include standards for prosecutors evaluating eyewitness cases.[10]

In neighboring Norfolk County, Massachusetts, immediately south of Boston, District Attorney William Keating, convinced that the eyewitness evidence reforms championed by Gary Wells and Janet Reno's Working Group presented a "win-win" opportunity for law enforcement to catch the guilty while protecting the innocent, convened a meeting of all of the police departments in his jurisdiction. Over 200 cops showed up to learn about the new techniques. Ken Patenaude brought his Working Group experience to bear and provided the audience with a training program, cop-to-cops.

District Attorney Keating's luncheon speaker was Jennifer Thompson. To ask a speaker to hold the attention of over 200 hungry cops seemed crazy, but by the second minute of Jennifer's account of her experience, every knife and fork had been placed on the table, conversation had died, the waiters and waitresses had stopped serving, and the attention of the whole room was riveted on the petite blonde woman at the microphone. The police left Keating's meeting determined that no future victim would repeat Jennifer's ordeal.

Still, there are roughly 12,500 jurisdictions in which future Cotton cases and Bloodsworth cases and Graham cases could still be handled in the same way as the old ones, and in which some of the results will be the same too: innocent men serving time, guilty men going free to commit more rapes, and executions when we simply aren't as sure as we could be that we are killing a guilty man.

How many of these jurisdictions will by bringing their criminal justice system's actors to the table as North Carolina, Minnesota, Boston, and New Jersey have done, and by confronting those officials with the lessons of the science, produce, in the words Minneapolis, Minnesota, County Attorney Amy Klobuchar, "stronger cases and more justice?"[11] How many will assume that the familiar processes which gave us an incarcerated Ronald Cotton and a free Bobby Poole, are close enough for government work? Or be content to let the prosecutors and defense lawyers slug it out, one case at a time, in the adversary atmosphere that consumed Wigmore and Munsterberg right at the beginning?

It is a tribute to Jennifer Thompson, Ronald Cotton, Kirk Bloodsworth, Elizabeth Loftus, Gary Wells, Don Mauro, Janet Reno, the Scheck and

Neufeld team, and all of the others who have played a role in trying to bring the science of memory and the procedures of the justice system into line with each other that these questions have finally been asked in legislatures and rule-making bodies around the country. Even so, it remains to be seen whether these successes mark the end of a beginning—the arrival of a "tipping point"—or comprise nothing more than a group of dead ends. Things may stop just where they are, and that would be a shame. It would be a shame not because we would forfeit this particular discrete handful of eyewitness identification procedures, but because we would abandon a new tradition of learning from the criminal justice system's mistakes.

There is more for the parties to talk about.

The science will not stay frozen. Will further research prove that sequential lineups really are no better than simultaneous ones?[12] Can anything be learned about the problem of cross-racial identification error? Police identification techniques are not permanent, either. What will be the impact of digital technology, and *portable* digital technology, on police eyewitness identification techniques? Will future photo arrays be conducted at the crime scene on a laptop or a Palm Pilot? How will those procedures be designed?

And what about other areas revealed by the DNA cases? What about the cases where false confessions were obtained?[13] Or where jailhouse informants were misused? What about cases where the demonstrated miscarriage of justice is not a wrongful conviction, but a guilty man wrongly acquitted? Are we prepared to study those?

This story—and the stories of Ronald Cotton, and Jennifer Thompson, and Kirk Bloodsworth within this story—argue for bringing everyone to the table, for creating forums where Wigmore's "alliance in the noble cause of justice" might take root and grow.

True, the alliance that Dean Wigmore saw as "friendly and energetic" turns out, 100 years later, to be "elusive and fragile" instead. Even so, we should make the effort. Shrugging and walking away will leave a legacy of wrecked lives. If we can summon the discipline to confront our own mistakes, we can make a difference.

NOTES

PREFACE

1. Adams' argument for the defense, *Rex v. Wemms*, in L. Wroth and H. Zobel, eds., *The Legal Papers of John Adams*, vol. 3 (Cambridge, Mass.: Harvard University Press, 1965), 242.

CHAPTER ONE

1. Frank Bruni and Jim Yardley, "With Bush Absent, Inmate Is Executed," *The New York Times*, June 23, 2000, p. A1.
2. *State v. Cotton*, 99 N.C. 615, 617, 394 S.E.2d 456, 458 (1990).
3. The transcripts that follow are from the Public Broadcasting System's *Frontline* documentary series production "What Jennifer Saw," posted at "http://www.pbs.org/wgbh/pages/frontline/shows/dna/." They are used by permission of PBS.
4. Barry Scheck, Peter Neufeld, and Jim Dwyer, *Actual Innocence* (New York: Doubleday, 2000), Appendix B, 255.
5. Brian L. Cutler and Steven D. Penrod, *Mistaken Identification: The Eyewitness, Psychology, and the Law* (Cambridge: Cambridge University Press, 1995) provides one responsible attempt to estimate the recurrence of eyewitness cases in law enforcement practice.
6. Oliver Wendell Holmes, *The Common Law* (Boston: Little, Brown & Co., 1881), 1.

CHAPTER TWO

1. The comment "scathing" is from J. Brigham, "What Is Forensic Psychology Anyway?" *Law and Human Behavior* 23 (1999), 273, at 276; "Miserable failure," is from D. N. Bershoff, et al, "Training In Law And Psychology: Models from the Villanova Conference," *American Psychologist* 52 (1997), 1302; "Irreparable damage," is found in D. N. Bershoff, "Preparing for Two Cultures: Education in Law and Psychology," in R. Roesch and S. D. Hart, eds., *Psychology and Law: The State of the Discipline* (New York: Plenum, 1993).
2. T. Kinlen and T. B. Henley, "Hugo Munsterberg and modern forensic psychology," *History of Psychology Newsletter* 4 (1997), 70.
3. The story of the painting is from Matthew Hale's extraordinarily acute study of Munsterberg, *Human Science and Social Order: Hugo Munsterberg and the Origins of Applied Psychology* (Philadelphia: Temple University Press, 1980). Variants appear

in Abraham Roback, *History of American Psychology* (New York: Library Publishing, 1952) and "Munsterberg Was Painted Out," *Harvard Alumni Bulletin*, February 18, 1956, 384. The painting is reproduced, without comment, in Margaret Munsterberg, *Hugo Munsterberg: His Life and Works* (New York: D. Appleton & Co. 1922). There is a photograph in existence from which the painting was evidently copied. In the photograph Munsterberg occupies a central position in the group, and whatever the reason for his disappearance, it seems certain that he was at one time at least present.

4. The basic biographical materials on Munsterberg are found in *Hale*, and in Margaret Munsterberg, *Hugo Munsterberg: His Life and Work* (New York: Appleton and Co., 1922) (hereinafter, *Margaret Munsterberg*).

5. Rollo W. Brown, *Harvard Yard in the Golden Age* (New York: Current Books, 1948) 49.

6. *Margaret Munsterberg*, 45–56.

7. *Margaret Munsterberg*, 45–54; *Hale*, 45–56.

8. William James to H. Munsterberg, Feb. 21, 1892, James papers cited in *Hale*, at 45.

9. Louis Menard, *The Metaphysical Club* (New York: Farrar, Straus & Giroux, 2001), 325.

10. William James to Hugo Munsterberg, Feb. 21, 1892, James papers, quoted in *Margaret Munsterberg*, 32.

11. William James to Henry James, *Letters of William James*, vol. 2 (Boston: Atlantic Monthly Press, 1920), 318.

12. These misadventures are catalogued in *Margaret Munsterberg*, 143–147.

13. Professor Edward Bradford Titchener, quoted in *Hale*, 6.

14. Hugo Munsterberg, *The Photoplay: A Psychological Study* (New York: D. Appleton & Co. 1916).

15. Elizabeth Sprigge, *Gertrude Stein: Her Life and Work* (New York: Harper & Bros., 1957), 24–25. Munsterberg wrote to Stein saying she embodied many of the features of his "ideal student."

16. Lawrence Thompson, *Robert Frost: The Early Years, 1874–1966* (New York: Holt, Rinehart & Winston, 1966), 239.

17. George F. Moore, "Foreword" in *Margaret Munsterberg*, at *x*.

18. Hugo Munsterberg, *Eternal Values* (New York: Doubleday, 1908).

19. R. Kargon, "Expert testimony in historical perspective," *Law and Human Behavior* 10 (1986) 15, 23.

20. William James to Hugo Munsterberg, June 28, 1906; Hugo Munsterberg to William James, July 1, 1906. The exchange is recounted in *Hale*, at 6–7.

21. *Margaret Munsterberg*, 146–48.

22. *Ibid.*, at 145–50. The Heywood trial is also discussed by *Hale*, 116–18.

23. *Ibid.*

24. *Hale*, ix.

25. The citations here are to the book version, *On The Witness Stand* (New York: McClure, 1908) (cited hereafter as *OTWS*).

26. *Ibid.*, at 40–41.

27. *Ibid.*, at 43.

28. *Ibid.*, at 61.

29. *Ibid.* at 55.

30. *Ibid.* at 50–51.

31. *Ibid.* at 27.
32. *Ibid.*, at 48.
33. *Ibid.*, at 55.
34. *Ibid.*, at 56.
35. *Ibid.*, at. 47.
36. *Ibid.*, at 60.
37. *Ibid.*, at 45.
38. *Ibid.*, at 46.
39. *Ibid.*, at 10.
40. Robert Gault, "Memories," in box 17, folder 11, series 17/20, Wigmore papers, Northwestern University Library, Evanston, Illinois. Gault, interestingly enough in this context, was a psychologist. Wigmore's correspondence indicates that he was attempting to secure copies of all of Munsterberg's published works on the topic in 1907. See, for example, John Henry Wigmore to Times Magazine Company, November 7, 1907, in Wigmore papers.
41. An extensive collection of facts and anecdotes about Wigmore's life is provided in William R. Roalfe, *John Henry Wigmore: Scholar and Reformer* (Evanston, Ill.: Northwestern University Press, 1977).
42. Robert Gault, note 40.
43. John Henry Wigmore, *A Treatise On The System of Evidence in Trials at Common Law, Including the Statutes and Judicial Decisions of All Jurisdictions of the United States* (1904), hereafter cited as *Treatise.*
44. Edmund M. Morgan, "Book Review," *Boston University Law Review* 20 (1940), 776, 778.
45. Joseph H. Beale, Book Review, *Harvard Law Review* 18 (1905), 478, 479.
46. Felix Frankfurter, Book Review, *Northwestern University Law Review* 58 (1963), 443.
47. *Roalfe*, at 125–130.
48. *Ibid.*, at 109, quoting Manley O. Hudson, "Recollections," Wigmore papers, box 17, folder 11, series 17/20, Northwestern University Library, Evanston, Illinois.
49. John Henry Wigmore, book review, *Journal of Criminal Law and Criminology* 23 (1932), 320; John Henry Wigmore, "The Public Defender in our Cities," *Illinois Law Review* 25 (1931), 687.
50. John Henry Wigmore, 40 *American Bar Association Reports* 40 (1915), 736.
51. *Roalfe*, at 109, quoting Manley O. Hopkins, "Recollections," Wigmore papers, box 17, folder 11, series 17/20, Northwestern University Library, Evanston, Illinois.
52. *Roalfe*, at 143.
53. *Ibid.*, at 56.
54. Hugo Munsterberg to John Henry Wigmore, August 20, 1907, Wigmore papers, box 92, folder 16, series 17/20, Northwestern University Library, Evanston, Illinois.
55. *Ibid.*, at 85. See also, Gault, note 40.
56. *Illinois Law Review* 3 (1909), 399, cited hereafter as Wigmore.
57. Ibid., 406.
58. Ibid., 417–419.
59. *Roalfe*, at 148, quoting, James F. Oates, "Wigmore the Lawyer and Business," Wigmore papers, note 47.

60. Wigmore, 412.
61. Ibid., 415.
62. Ibid., 434.
63. *Margaret Munsterberg*, 332.
64. William James to Josiah Royce, June 22, 1892, quoted in Robert Perry, *The Thought and Character of William James, Volume II, Philosophy and Psychology*, (Boston: Little, Brown, & Co., 1935), 141.
65. John Henry Wigmore to Hugo Munsterberg, January 3, 1913, Wigmore papers, box 92, folder 16, series 17/20, Northwestern University Library, Evanston, Illinois.
66. See, Gault, note 40.
67. John Henry Wigmore, *The Science of Judicial Proof*, 3rd ed. (Boston: Little, Brown & Co., 1937).
68. Robert Buckhout, "Eyewitness Testimony," *Scientific American* 231, 6 (December,1974), 23, 30.

CHAPTER THREE

1. B. W. Behrman, and S. L. Davey, "Eyewitness Identification in Actual Criminal Cases: an Archival Analysis," *Law and Human Behavior* 25 (1991), 475; D. B. Wright, and A. T. McDaid, "Comparing System and Estimator Variables Using Data from Real Lineups," *Applied Cognitive Psychology* 10 (1996), 75.
2. Jamie Talan, "Eyewitness Testimony Study: Stress Limits Memory's Ability," *Newsday*, June 4, 2004, A34, reporting research by Dr. Charles Morgan, III, of the Yale University School of Medicine.
3. C. R. Huff, "Wrongful Conviction: Societal Tolerance of Injustice," *Research in Social Problems and Public Policy* 4 (1987), 99, 103.
4. Steven Penrod, "Eyewitness Evidence: How Well are Witnesses and Police Performing?" *Criminal Justice* 18 (Spring, 2003), 36. See also, Brian Cutler and Steven Penrod, *Mistaken Identification: The Eyewitness, Psychology, and the Law* (Cambridge: Cambridge University Press, 1995) at 3–14, hereafter cited as Cutler and Penrod.
5. Barry Scheck, Peter Neufeld and Jim Dwyer, *Actual Innocence* (New York: Doubleday, 2000), Appendix B, 255.
6. *United States v. Smith*, 122 F.3d 1355 (11th Cir. 1997).
7. The excerpts from the account of the Cotton trials are taken from the PBS *Frontline* transcripts, posted at http://www.pbs.org/wgbh/pages/frontline/shows/dna. They are used with the permission.
8. *Goodwin v. Balkcom*, 684 F.2d 794, 805 n.13 (11th Cir. 1982).
9. E. F. Loftus, "Reconstructive Memory: The Incredible Eyewitness," *Psychology Today* 8, 116 (1974).
10. Ibid., 116–119.
11. N. Brewer and A. Burke, "Effects of Testimonial Inconsistencies and Eyewitness Confidence on Mock-Juror Judgments," *Law and Human Behavior* 26 (2002), 353; G. L. Wells, R. C. L. Lindsay, and T. J. Ferguson, "Accuracy, Confidence, and Juror Perceptions in Eyewitness Identification," *Journal Applied Psychology* 64 (1979), 440.
12. Ibid.

13. R. C. L. Lindsay, G. L. Wells, and F. J. O'Connor, "Mock Juror Belief of Accurate and Inaccurate Eyewitnesses: a Replication and Extension," *Law and Human Behavior* 13 (1989), 333.

14. Hugo Munsterberg, *On The Witness Stand* (New York: McClure, 1908), 56.

15. R. C. L. Lindsay, G. L. Wells, G. and C. M. Rumpel, "Can People Detect Eyewitness Identification Accuracy Within and Across Situations?" *Journal of Applied Psychology* 66 (1981), 77.

16. Connors, Lundegran, Miller & McEwan, *Convicted By Juries, Exonerated By Science: Case Studies in the Use of DNA Evidence To Establish Innocence* (Alexandria, Va.: National Institute of Justice, 1996). See also, Barry Scheck, Peter Neufeld, and Jim Dwyer, *Actual Innocence* (New York: Doubleday, 2000), Appendix B, 255.

17. *Frontline*, "What Jennifer Saw," note 7.

18. Ibid.

CHAPTER FOUR

1. *State v. Bloodsworth*, 307 Md. 164, 512 A.2d 1056 (Md. 1986).

2. Ibid.

3. R. Buckhout, "Through a Bag Darkly," *American Psychologist* 23 (1976), 41.

4. Reginald Major, *Justice In The Round* (New York: The Third Press, 1973), p. 200. (Cited hereafter as Major.)

5. Major, 24, quoting San Quentin's Associate Warden, James Park.

6. Ibid., 41.

7. Ibid., 44.

8. Mary Timothy, *Jury Woman: The Story of the Trial of Angela Davis* (Berkeley: Volcano Press, 1976), 184. (Cited hereafter as Timothy).

9. Timothy, 220–221.

10. Major, 199.

11. Ibid., 200.

12. Ibid., 192.

13. R. Buckhout, "Nobody Likes A Smartass," *Social Action and The Law* 6 (1976), 41.

14. Ibid.

15. R. Buckhout, "Eyewitness Testimony," *Scientific American* 231 (1974), 23.

16. R. Buckhout, "Nearly 2000 Witnesses Can Be Wrong," *Social Action and the Law* 2 (1975), 7.

17. M. McCloskey, H. Egeth, and J. McKenna, "The Experimental Psychologist in Court: The Ethics of Expert Testimony," *Law and Human Behavior* 10 (1986), 1.

18. R. Buckhout, "Personal Values and Expert Testimony" *Law and Human Behavior* 10 (1986), 127.

19. Ibid.

20. M. McCloskey and H. Egeth, "Eyewitness Identification, What Can a Psychologist Tell a Jury?" *American Psychologist* 38 (1983), 550.

21. M. McCloskey, J. McKenna, and H. Egeth, "The Experimental Psychologist in court: The Ethics of Expert Testimony," *Law and Human Behavior* 10, (1986), 1, 8.

22. Ibid.

23. *State v. Bloodsworth*, 307 Md. 164, 512 A.2d 1056 (Md. 1986).

24. R. Pachella, "Personal Values and the Value of Expert Testimony," *Law and Human Behavior* 10 (1986), 145.

25. M. McCloskey and H. Egeth, note 20; V. J. Koneci and E. B. Ebbesen, "External Validity of Research in Legal Psychology," *Law and Human Behavior* 3 (1978), 39.

26. M. McClosey and H. Egeth, note 20, at 552.

27. V. J. Konenci and E. B. Ebbesen, "Courtroom Testimony by Psychologists on Eyewitness Identification Issues: Critical Notes and Reflections," *Law and Human Behavior* 10, 117 (1986), 120 .

28. Ibid.

29. Robert Buckhout, "Nobody Likes A Smartass," *Social Action and the Law* 4 (1976), 50.

30. Michael Saks, "Law Does Not Live By Eyewitness Testimony Alone," *Law and Human Behavior* 10 (1986), 678.

31. Brian Cutler and Steven Penrod, *Mistaken Identification: The Eyewitness, Psychology and the Law* (New York: Cambridge University Press, 1995), 41.

CHAPTER FIVE

1. *United States v. Wade*, 388 US 218, 235 (1967).

2. *Miranda v. Arizona*, 384 U.S. 436 (1966).

3. Patrick Wall, *Eyewitness Identification In Criminal Cases* (Springfield, Ill.: Charles Thomas, 1965).

4. *United States v. Wade*, 388 US 218, 235 (1967).

5. Ibid., at 221, citing John Henry Wigmore, *The Science of Judicial Proof* (Boston: Little, Brown & Co., 1937).

6. *Manson v. Braithwaite*, 432 U.S. 98 (1977).

7. *Neil v. Biggers*, 409 U.S. 188 (1972).

8. F. Levine and J. Tapp, "The Psychology of Criminal Identification: the Gap from *Wade* to *Kirby*," *University of Pennsylvania Law Review* 121 (1973), 1079.

9. J. Doyle, "Applying Lawyers' Expertise to Scientific Experts: Some Thoughts About Trial Court Analysis of the Prejudicial Effects of Admitting and Excluding Expert Scientific Testimony," *William and Mary Law Review* 25 (1984), 619.

CHAPTER SIX

1. The account of the Chambers murder case is drawn from Elizabeth Loftus and Katherine Ketcham, *Witness For The Defense, The Accused, The Eyewitness, And the Expert Who Puts Memory On Trial* (New York: St. Martin's Press, 1991). (Hereafter cited as *Witness*.)

2. *Witness*, 166–175.

3. J. Neimark, "The Diva of Disclosure," *Psychology Today*, Jan. 1996, 48.

4. Ibid.

5. Elizabeth Loftus, "Reconstructing Memory: The Incredible Eyewitness" *Psychology Today*, December, 1974, 112.

6. E. Loftus, E. "Ten Years in the Life of an Expert Witness," *Law and Human Behavior* 10 (1986), 241. (Hereafter cited as "Ten Years.")

7. Ibid., 242.

8. Elizabeth Loftus, *Eyewitness Testimony* (Cambridge, Mass.: Harvard Univ. Press, 1976).
9. E. Loftus, "Silence Is Not Golden," *American Psychologist* 65 (1983), 9.
10. Daniel Schacter, *Searching for Memory* (New York: Basic Books, 1996) 115.
11. E. Loftus and J. Palmer, "Reconstruction of an Automobile Destruction: an Example of the Interaction Between Language and Memory," *Journal of Verbal Learning and Verbal Behavior* 13 (1974), 585.
12. Elizabeth Loftus, *Eyewitness Testimony*, note 8, reporting Loftus, E., et al, "Effect of Post-Event Information," *Journal of Experimental Psychology: Human Learning and Memory* 4 (1978), 19.
13. Elizabeth Loftus and James M. Doyle, *Eyewitness Testimony: Civil and Criminal* (Charlottesville, Va.: Lexis Law Books, 3d ed. 1997) 57.
14. *Frye v. United States*, 293 F.2d 2013 (D.C.Cir. 1923).
15. M. McCloskey and M. Zagora, "Misleading Post-event Information and Memory for Events: Arguments and Evidence Against Memory Impairment Hypothesis," *Journal of Experimental Psychology, General*, 114 (1985), 1.
16. F. Woocher, "Did Your Eyes Deceive You?" *Stanford Law Review* 29, 969 (1997).
17. S. D. Penrod and B. L. Cutler "Assessing the Competency of Juries," in I. Weiner and A. Hess, eds., *The Handbook of Forensic Psychology* (New York: Wiley, 1987); R.C.L. Lindsay, G.L. Wells and C.M. Prinpel, "Can People Detect Eyewitness Identification Accuracy Within and Across Situations?" *Journal of Applied Psychology* 66 (1981), 79.
18. *State v. Chapple*, 135 Ariz. 281, 660 P.2d 290 (1983).

CHAPTER SEVEN

1. M. McCloskey and H. Egeth, "Eyewitness Identification: What Can A Psychologist Tell a Jury?" *American Psychologist* 38 (1983), 550.
2. S. M. Kassin, P. C. Ellsworth, and V. L. Smith, "The 'General Acceptance' of Psychological Research on Eyewitness Testimony: a Survey of Experts," *American Psychologist* 44 (1989), 1098; S. M. Kassin, and K.A. Barndollar, "On the Psychology of Eyewitness' Testimony: a Comparison of Experts and Prospective Jurors," *Journal of Applied Psychology*, 22 (1992), 1241; S. M. Kassin, V. A. Tubb, H. M. Hosch, H. M. and A. Memon, A., *American Psychologist* 56 (2001), 405.
3. R. S. Malpass, "Racial Bias In Eyewitness Identification?" *Personality and Social Psychology Bulletin* 1 (1974), 42; J. C. Brigham, and R. S. Malpass, "The Role of Experience and Contact In the Recognition of Faces of Own and Other-Race Persons," *Journal of Social Issues* 41 (1985), 139.
4. Brian Cutler and Steven Penrod, *Mistaken Identification: The Eyewitness, Psychology and the Law* (New York: Cambridge University Press, 1995).

CHAPTER EIGHT

1. The statement of facts is borrowed from the prosecution's submission in *People v. Felipe Soler*, Supreme Court, New York County. The case was resolved by a guilty plea.
2. H. Packer, "Two Models of Criminal Process," *University of Pennsylvania Law Review* 113 (1964), 1, is the more succinct version of Packer's argument on this point.

3. J. Griffiths, "Ideology In Criminal Procedure or a Third 'Model' of the Criminal Process," *Yale Law Journal* 79 (1970), 359.
4. Ibid.
5. Erik Erikson, *Identity, Youth and Crisis* (New York: Random House, 1968).
6. Linda Fairstein, *Sexual Violence* (New York: William Morrow, 1993).
7. Tom Wolfe, *Bonfire of the Vanities* (New York: Scribners, 1987), 67.
8. Rivka Gewirtz Little, "Ashe Blonde Ambition," *Village Voice*, Nov. 20, 2002, 12, is an example of a hostile sketch of Fairstein, focusing, like many others, on her participation in the Central Park Jogger case.
9. *Cosmopolitan Magazine*, uncredited brief article, "How to Dig What You Do; Contentment in One's Professional Life," *Cosmopolitan*, September 1, 2001, 102.
10. Interview, Linda Fairstein.
11. An affectionate portrait of Jane Wood Reno is provided in George Hurchalla, ed., *To Hell With Politics: The Life and Writings of Jane Wood Reno* (Atlanta: Peachtree Publishers, 1994).
12. Paul Anderson, *Janet Reno: Doing The Right Thing* (New York: John Wiley & Sons, 1994). (Hereafter cited as *Janet Reno*).
13. Ibid., 22.
14. Ibid., 13.
15. *Janet Reno*, at 126–127.
16. *To Hell With Politics*, note 11, at 164, 177.
17. *Janet Reno*, at 203.
18. Jerry Seper, "Lady Law," *Washington Times*, Feb. 22, 1993, D1.
19. Ibid.
20. *Janet Reno*, 19.
21. Ibid., 26.
22. Ibid.
23. John Ellement, "Man Imprisoned on Rape Charges Freed DNA Evidence Clears," *Boston Globe*, April 4, 2003, B4.
24. Interview, J. W. Carney, Esq.

CHAPTER NINE

1. Susan Levine, "Md. Man's Exoneration Didn't End Nightmare," *Washington Post*, February 24, 2003, A1.
2. Interviews with numerous sources.
3. Interview, Janet Reno.
4. Edward Connors, Thomas Lundregan, Neil Miller, and Tom McEwen, *Convicted by Juries, Exonerated by Science* (Alexandria, Va.: NIJ 1998).
5. Jim Dwyer, Peter Neufeld, and Barry Scheck, *Actual Innocence: Five Days To Execution and Other Dispatches From the Wrongly Convicted* (New York: Doubleday 2000).
6. Ibid.
7. Ibid., 67.
8. Ben Loeterman to Jennifer Thompson, July 18, 1996. Unpublished letter used by permission of Ben Loeterman/Loeterman Productions.
9. This and the following *Frontline* excerpts are from "What Jennifer Saw," posted at "http://www.pbs.org/wgbh/pages/frontline/shows/dna/."
10. Ibid.
11. Ibid.

CHAPTER TEN

1. Interview, Gary Wells.
2. R. Malpass, and J. Kravitz, "Recognition of Faces of Own and Other Race," *Journal of Personality and Social Psychology* 13 (1969), 330.
3. Gary Wells, "Applied Eyewitness-Testimony Research: System Variables and Estimator Variables," *Journal of Personality and Social Psychology* 30 (1978) 1546, 1547. (Hereafter cited as "Systems.")
4. Ibid.
5. Ibid., 1548.
6. Ibid., 1551.
7. Ibid., 1552.
8. Ibid.
9. A. Gawande, "Under Suspicion: The Fugitive Science of Criminal Investigation," *The New Yorker*, Jan. 8, 2001, 50.
10. Gary Wells, "Eyewitness Behavior: The Alberta Conference," *Law and Human Behavior* 4 (1980), 237.
11. R. Fisher, R. E. Geiselman, and M. Amador, "Field Test of the Cognitive Interview: Enhancing the Recollection of Actual Victims and Witnesses of Crime," *Journal of Applied Psychology* 4, 722 (1989); R. E. Geiselman, R. Fisher, E. MacKinnon, and H. Holland, "Eyewitness Memory Enhancement in the Police Interview: Cognitive Retrieval Mnemonics Versus Hypnosis," *Journal of Applied Psychology* 70 (1985), 401.
12. R. Malpass, and P. Devine, "Eyewitness Identification: Lineup Instructions and the Absence of the Offender," *Journal of Applied Psychology*, 66, 482 (1981).
13. Gary Wells, "Police Lineups: Data, Theory, and Policy," *Psychology Public Policy and Law* 7 (2001), 791.
14. Gary Wells, "The Psychology of Lineup Identifications," *Journal of Applied Social Psychology* 14 (1984), 89.
15. Ibid.
16. R. C. L. Linday and Gary Wells, "Improving Eyewitness Identifications from Lineups: Simultaneous v. Sequential Presentation, *Journal of Applied Psychology* 70 (1985), 365.
17. Gary Wells and Amy Bradfield, "'Good, You Identified the Suspect.' Feedback to Eyewitnesses Distorts Their Reports of the Witnessing Experience," *Journal of Applied Psychology* 83 (1999), 688.
18. G. L. Wells, L. Small, S. Penrod, R. Malpass, S. Fulero, and C. Brimacombe, "Eyewitness Identification Procedures: Recommendations for Linueps and Photospreads," *Law and Human Behavior* 22 (1998), 603.

CHAPTER ELEVEN

1. Gary Wells, et al., "From the Lab to the Police Station: A Successful Application of Eyewitness Research," *American Psychologist*, June 2000, 581.
2. V. J. Konenci and E. B. Ebbesen, "Courtroom Testimony by Psychologists on Eyewitness Identification Issues: Critical Notes and Reflections," *Law and Human Behavior* 10 (1986), 117, 120. Dr. Ebbesen's unpublished paper focusing on the systems variable issues, E. Ebbesen and H. Flowe, "Simultaneous v. Sequential Lineups: What Do We Really Know?" is posted at http://www.pscy.ucsd.edu/~eebbesen/SimSeq.htm.

3. Technical Working Group on Eyewitness Evidence, *Research Report: Eyewitness Evidence: A Guide For Law Enforcement* (Alexandria, Va.: National Institute of Justice, 1999).

CHAPTER TWELVE

1. Kevin P. Meenan, President, National District Attorneys Association, to Sarah I. Hart, March 18, 2002. (On file with author.)
2. J. Doyle, M. Larson, and C. DiTraglia, "The Eyes Have It, Or Do They?" *Criminal Justice*, Fall 2001, p. 13.
3. *State v. Cromedy*, 158 N.J. 112, 727 A.2d 457 (1999).
4. Report of the Governor's Commission on Capital Punishment
5. Gina Kolata and Iver Peterson, "New Way to Insure Eyewitness Can ID the Right Bad Guy," *New York Times*, July 21, 2001, p. A1.
6. S. Turow, "To Kill Or Not To Kill," *The New Yorker*, Jan. 6, 2003, at 40.
7. M. Talbot, "The Year In Ideas: A to Z; False Identification Prevention, *New York Times*, Dec. 9, 2001, (Magazine Section) at 52; S. Begley, "Inertia, Hope, Morality Score TKOs in Bouts With 'Solid Science'," *Wall Street Journal*, June 6, 2003, at p. B1.
8. A. Gwande, "Under Suspicion," *The New Yorker*, Jan. 8, 2001, at 52.
9. Feige, David, "I'll Never Forget That Face: The Science and Law of the Double-Blind, Sequential Lineup, 26 *Champion* 28 (2002).
10. Seth Liebman, "Sequential Lineups: A Closer Look Gives Reason To Pause," *New York Law Journal*, Dec. 3, 2003, p. 4.
11. *North Carolina Political Review*, August, 2003, "A Conversation With Christine Mumma," http://www.ncpoliticalreview.com/0803/print/mumma.
12. Matthew Eiseley, "Better ID Sought in Criminal Inquiries, *News and Observer* (Charlotte, N.C.) Sept. 13, 2003, B1.

CHAPTER THIRTEEN

1. Bloodsworth's story is told most fully in Timothy Junkin, *Bloodsworth: The True Story of The First Death Row Inmate Exonerated By DNA*, (Chapel Hill: Algonquin, 2004).
2. Stephanie Hanes, "New Peace, New Purpose," *Baltimore Sun*, Oct. 24, 2003, p. 1A.
3. The Texas Department of Corrections maintains a website on which it posts the final words of executed prisoners.
4. Frank Bruni and Jim Yardley, "With Bush Absent, Inmate Is Executed," *The New York Times*, June 23, 2000, p. A1.
5. Jennifer Thompson, "I Was Certain, And I Was Wrong," *New York Times*, June 18, 2000, p. A15.
6. The summary of exculpatory facts is from Graham's "Petition For A Recommendation Of A Reprieve of Execution and Pardon, Or Alternatively, a Conditional Pardon or Commutation of Death Sentence," submitted to the Texas Board of Pardon and Paroles, one the eve of the execution. *In Re: Gary Graham*.
7. Ibid.

8. Rex v. Wemms, in L. Wroth and H. Zobel, eds., *Legal Papers of John Adams* vol. 3, (Cambridge, Mass.: Harvard University Press 1965), 242.

9. Daniel F. Conley, "Our Duty to Free The Wrongly Convicted," *Boston Globe*, March 19, 2004, p. A14; Maggie Mulvihill, "A Big Push For Justice: City Makes Sweeping Moves to Stop Wrongful Suspect IDs," *Boston Herald*, July 20, 2004, 2.

10. Suzanne Smalley, "Police Update Evidence Gathering," *Boston Globe*, July 20, 2004, B2.

11. Jim Adams, "Minneapolis, Suburbs Test Witness ID System," *Star Tribune*, (Minneapolis), Nov. 4, 2003, B3.

12. Seth Lieberman, "Sequential Lineups: A Closer Look Gives Reasons To Pause," *New York Law Journal*, Dec. 3, 2003, 4.

13. Adam Liptak, "Taping Interrogations Is Praised by Police," *The New York Times*, June 13, 2004, A23.

CURRENT EVENTS

A Brief Bibliographical Note

The issue of the reform of eyewitness evidence collection is very much in doubt in individual jurisdictions across the United States and Canada. Readers can expect to see the issues debated in their daily newspapers. Readers interested in following law and psychology as they continue their investigations of eyewitness performance have a number of resources available.

The most current of these resources are web pages maintained by protagonists in the story of science's efforts to penetrate the legal system.

Several of the leading psychological researchers have banded together to form The Eyewitness Consortium, which posts a variety of helpful materials at: "http://eyewitnessconsortium.utep.edu/ecmembers.html."

Many of the researchers also maintain individual web pages. For example, Professor Roy Malpass, who broke new ground in the field, maintains an eyewitness page at his headquarters in the Psychology Department of the University of Texas at El Paso: "http://eyewitness.utep.edu/." Professor Ebbe Ebbesen, who has been a leading skeptic concerning the claims of the reformers and a frequent prosecution expert in courtroom battles, posts his critiques, along with links to others, at "http://www.pscy.ucsd.edu/~ebbesen/.html." Professor Steven Penrod, of the John Jay College of Criminal Justice, who has long been one of the most judicious and insightful of the commentators on the issue posts materials at: "http://web.jjay.cuny.edu/~spenrod/penrod/." Professor Gary Wells's page, "http://www.psychology.iastate.edu/faculty/gwells/homepage.htm" is perhaps the most frequently updated. Professor Wells's page, which is almost certainly the best "one-stop" source of current information, also offers links to many of the major documents discussed in the text, including the National Institute of Justice's *Eyewitness Evidence: A Guide for Law Enforcement*, and its *Training Manual*.

On the legal side, Barry Scheck and Peter Neufeld's pioneering Innocence Project posts the results of its efforts, with useful commentary, at: "http://www.innocenceproject.org/". Kirk Bloodsworth, the Maryland Marine sentenced to death on the testimony of five mistaken eyewitnesses, continues to work on the issue of wrongful convictions at the Criminal Justice Reform Education Fund, which maintains a website at "http://cjreform.org/." A biography, Timothy Junkin, *Bloodsworth: The True Story Of The First Death Row Inmate Exonerated by DNA* (Chapel Hill, N.C.: Algonquin, 2004) tells Bloodsworth's story in compelling detail. John Henry Wigmore's heirs at the Northwestern University School of Law and the Northwestern University Medill School of Journalism operate an energetic and effective Center on Wrongful Convictions which tracks individual cases and national trends at "http://www.law.northwestern.edu/wrongfulconvictions/."

Two lengthy treatises designed for lawyers are also updated annually. The current author's treatise, co-authored with Elizabeth Loftus, *Eyewitness Testimony: Civil and Criminal* (Charlottesville, Va.: Lexis Law Books, 3d ed. 1997) emphasizes the interaction of law and psychology in litigation strategies and tactics. Nathan R. Sobel's *Eyewitness Identification: Legal and Practical Problems* (New York: Clark Boardman, 2d ed. 1983), which is scrupulously updated annually by Lawrence Vogelman, emphasizes legal authority. An excellent resource on the story of the law/psychology relationship, now, unfortunately, somewhat out of date, is Brian Cutler and Steven Penrod's meticulous and comprehensive *Mistaken Identification: The Eyewitness, Psychology and the Law* (Cambridge: Cambridge University Press, 1995).

INDEX

National District Attorney's Association
(NDAA), 167, 190–192
Neufeld, Peter, 130–135
New Jersey reforms, 192–194
Niblack, David, 186, 189
Nixon, Richard, 61
Northwestern University School of Law,
10–17

Omnibus Crime Control and Safe Streets
Act, 74
O'Toole, Kathleen, 204
"overbelief" by jurors, 64–65

Pachella, Robert, 62, 64
Patenaude, Kenneth, 70–71, 75, 203
Penrod, Steven, 26, 68, 97, 106, 164
photo arrays, 74–76, 105; *see also* lineups
Poole, Bobby, 5–7, 39, 43
police procedures, 69–79, 80–81, 153–160,
175–179, 183–185, 203–205
psychology, applied, 14, 91–95
public health approach, 150

race as a factor, 103–104, 147, 205
Rau, Richard, 140, 171–172, 180,
184–185, 189
Reagan, Ronald, 53
recovered memory, 86
relative judgment, 159–161
Reno, Henry, 123–124
Reno, Jane Wood, 119–121
Reno, Janet, 118–124, 140, 141, 163,
165–167, 203
Richardson, James, 122–123
Rosen, Richard, 135, 197
Royce, Josiah, 32
Rusticus, Ed, 178–179
Ryan, George, 194

Schacter, Daniel, 90
Scheck, Barry, 130–135
"sequential" method of lineup
presentation, 159–160, 165,
181–182, 194–195

Simpson, O. J., 130
"simultaneous" method of lineup
presentation, 69–71, 159–161
Skillern, Bernadine, 1–2, 199–202
Social Action and the Laws, 58
State v. Chapple, 97–98
Stein, Steve, 84
Stein, Gertrude, 14
"system variables," 148–163

Technical Working Group on
Eyewitness Evidence, 166–187,
189–192
Thompson, Donald, 105
Thompson, Jennifer, 2–7, 34, 42–47, 70,
76, 111, 136–139, 157, 185–187,
200, 204–205
trace evidence, 98–99, 160–161
Travis, Jeremy, 78, 128–130, 140, 166,
179–183
Turow, Scott, 194

United States v. Wade, 72–79

verdicts, reliability of, 30, 36, 106–107
videotape conception of memory, 21–22,
42–43, 91–92

Wall, Patrick, 72
"Warren Court," 71–74
Wells, Gary, 67, 68, 140–167, 189–190,
201, 203–204
What Jennifer Saw (documentary film),
136–139, 185–187
"White Paper" of the American
Psychology-Law Society,
163–165
Wigmore, John Henry, 9, 10, 23–34, 75,
107, 203, 204–205
Woocher, Frederick, 96
wrongful convictions, 127–129,
133–134.
Wundt, Wilhem, 31

Zagel, James, 75